VOICES *of* SIAM

ILLUMINATING THE BUDDHIST PATH
TO NATURAL REALITY

Compiled and translated by

BRUCE EVANS

SHAMBHALA

Shambhala Publications, Inc.
2129 13th Street
Boulder, Colorado 80302
www.shambhala.com

© 2025 by Bruce Evans

Cover photograph: Nikko Odiseos
Cover design: Daniel Urban-Brown
Interior design: Lora Zorian

All rights reserved. No part of this book may be reproduced
in any form or by any means, electronic or mechanical, including
photocopying, recording, or by any information storage and
retrieval system, without permission in writing from the publisher.

9 8 7 6 5 4 3 2 1

First Edition
Printed in the United States of America

Shambhala Publications makes every effort to print
on acid-free, recycled paper.
Shambhala Publications is distributed worldwide
by Penguin Random House, Inc., and its subsidiaries.

ISBN 978-1-64547-307-7
LC record available at https://lccn.loc.gov/2024060822

The authorized representative in the EU for product safety
and compliance is eucomply OÜ, Pärnu mnt 139b-14, 11317
Tallinn, Estonia, hello@eucompliancepartner.com.

CONTENTS

ACKNOWLEDGMENTS

My thanks go out to the following:

Phra Khru Kittikhunsathon (Mun) of Wat Borom Niwat in Bangkok for background information on the *Girimānanda Sutta* and the publications of Chao Khun Upāli. Also David Wharton in Vientiane, Laos, for further information on the palm-leaf scripture.

Khun Karunphol Phanid, Khun Pairot Singbun, and Khun Supavadee Teeraditthanan from the Buddhadasa Indapañño Archives in Bangkok for permission to include the translation of Ajahn Buddhadāsa and background information for his biography. Also to Professor Peter Skilling in Bangkok for putting me in touch with the Buddhadasa Indapañño Foundation.

Venerable P. A. Payutto (Somdet Phra Buddhaghosācāriya) for gracious permission to include in this collection the talk "Helping Yourself to Help Others" (an earlier translation of mine has been published for free distribution in Thailand).

Khun Mae Chee Sunantha, Abbess of Khao Suan Luang Dhamma Centre, for permission to translate and publish the talk by Upāsikā Kee Nanayon.

Venerable Ajahn Pramote (Pāmojjo) for his gracious permission to include the translations of his talks. Thanks also to Khun Chompoo, Khun Faa, and Khun Hataitip at Luangpu Pramote Pamojjo's Teaching Media Foundation for their assistance.

Venerable Ajahn Paisan (Visālo) for his gracious permission to include the translations of his teachings and for assistance in putting together his biography.

ACKNOWLEDGMENTS

Venerable Hasapañño Bhikkhu, abbot of Vimokkharam Forest Hermitage in Kallista, Melbourne, for feedback on the translation of some tricky Pali and Thai terms.

A NOTE ON TITLES

When a man becomes a bhikkhu in the Theravada tradition, he is given a new name in Pali, called a *chaiya* in Thai. The name is usually aspirational, such as Santacitto ("He with a peaceful mind"). Western bhikkhus who took ordination in Thailand would often use these *chaiya* as their preferred names of reference. Thai bhikkhus, while also receiving a *chaiya*, would usually retain their Thai names, with the *chaiya* in parentheses afterward, e.g., Venerable Boonmee (Santacitto). For female renunciants, there is a much less established pathway. Traditionally, laywomen who live for a while in monastic settings and keep the eight precepts are called *upāsikā*. If a laywoman wants to dedicate herself more completely to the practice, she can shave her head, wear white robes, and keep the eight precepts as a *mae chee* (nun). However, this is sometimes regarded as an "unofficial" kind of ordination since, unlike for bhikkhus, there is no registry of mae chee. In more recent years, some women have taken on bhikkhunī ordination from other countries, but the lineage is still so recent that there are few cultural mores for interacting with bhikkhunīs, and they are more often than not simply referred to as "Bhikkunī," as in "Bhikkunī Supaññā."

Bhikkhus are referred to in Thailand as Phra or Tan (Venerable). If a bhikkhu stays in the robes for some length of time, to the point where he takes on teaching duties, he is usually referred to as Ajahn (Teacher) or Tan Ajahn or Phra Ajahn (Venerable Teacher). As a bhikkhu becomes older in years, he may be referred to as Luang Por (Venerable Father); and if even more advanced in years, he could be a Luang Pu (Venerable Grandfather). The system is informal, and there is no fixed age for when these titles apply.

Apart from these traditional forms of address, there are also the monastic titles that are conferred on bhikkhus by the king on a regular basis. The titles are graded and, in rough order, begin at Phra Khru, then to Chao Khun, and finally to Somdet, the highest rank a bhikkhu can obtain, the highest level of which is the Somdet Phra Sangharaja, the ecclesiastical head of the Thai saṅgha. Each of the titles comes with a name, such as Phra Khru Dhammathon or Chao Khun Depmoli. Some of the names also signify ranking, e.g., a Chao Khun with a title beginning with Raj is ranked higher than an "ordinary" Chao Khun. Dep is higher than Raj; Dham is higher than Dep; and Phrom is the highest level of Chao Khun title.

Many of the teachers presented in this book could be known by any number of these combinations of names. For instance, Ajahn Buddhadāsa could also be referred to as Phra Ajahn Ngeuam, Luang Por Buddhadāsa, Luang Pu Buddhadāsa, or by his ecclesiastical title Phra (or Chao Khun) Dhammaghosācāriya. (His case is a little different in that the name Buddhadāsa is one that he adapted himself. It is not his *chaiya*, which was Indapañño.)

For this book I have used the title that has become common in Western publications—Ajahn—which, while not entirely accurate in Thai terms (by which the title should be Phra Ajahn or, preferably, Luang Por), is the term that most Western readers will be familiar with. Exceptions are Chao Khun Upāli, which is the name most often used to refer to him, and Bhikkhu P. A. Payutto, which is the pen name of the Phra Buddhaghosācāriya.

INTRODUCTION

THERE IS A DELIGHTFUL SUTTA in the collection of Middle Length Discourses (Majjhima Nikāya) of the Pali Canon called the *Mahāgosiṅga Sutta*. It relates how a group of the Buddha's great disciples was staying in the sal tree (*gosiṅga*) forest. At that time the sal trees were in full bloom, infusing the forest with their fragrance. Toward evening the bhikkhus[1] all came together from their various secluded places of meditation, and a discussion ensued among them about what kind of bhikkhu would best illuminate the beautiful sal tree forest.

Each of those great disciples answered differently: Venerable Ānanda stated that it would be a bhikkhu who has learned much and teaches the Dhamma; Venerable Revata stated that it would be a bhikkhu who delights in solitude and meditation; Venerable Anuruddha stated that it would be a bhikkhu who has superhuman abilities such as clairvoyance; Venerable Mahā Kassapa said that it would be a bhikkhu who is dedicated to the allowable ascetic practices, such as living at the foot of a tree and wearing rag robes; Venerable Mahā Moggallāna stated that it would be two bhikkhus engaging in conversation about the Dhamma; Venerable Sāriputta stated that it would be a bhikkhu who has mastery over his own mind.

When they had all stated their views, the bhikkhus agreed to go see the Buddha and ask his view. The Buddha praised all the bhikkhus' answers, as they had all responded according to their own personalities and tendencies. Then he added that, for him, the best kind of bhikkhu to illuminate the sal tree forest would be one who sits at the foot of a tree and determines in his mind to not break from his sitting position until he has attained final liberation.[2]

The story is uplifting for a number of reasons. First, it paints a picture of bhikkhu life in the early days of Buddhism: a less structured experience than would be the norm these days, with the bhikkhus engaged during the day in solitary meditation and coming together in the evening to discuss the Dhamma. Second, it features a number of the Buddha's great disciples, many of whom would probably have been *arahants* (fully enlightened beings) at the time of the events recounted in the sutta. Third, as many of the great disciples mentioned in this sutta were likely fully realized, it illustrates that being an arahant does not fit one picture: these arahants retained their personalities and personal preferences.

Similarly, the Dhamma—the Buddhist teachings—while having core tenets and immovable truths, can be presented in various flavors. Thailand, as a country with a long and proud Buddhist heritage and unique tradition of meditation practice, is blessed with a bountiful supply of illustrious teachers. This collection of translations is the result of a long-held dream to bring together some of what Thailand has to offer and showcase the richness of that cultural heritage.

This collection is not intended to be a definitive "best of" Thailand's teachers. While it does in my opinion contain texts from some of the best teachers, this is only a sampling. There are a number of notable omissions from the collection, the most glaring of which is Luang Pu Mun, who is almost universally acknowledged as one of the greatest of the Thai meditation teachers—recognized not only for his own attainments in Dhamma practice but also for almost single-handedly founding an outstanding lineage of forest monks, known as the *kammaṭṭhāna* or Thai forest tradition. He left behind an astonishing number of disciples, many of whom are recognized for their own accomplishments. Within this collection, only Ajahn Chah was directly taught by Luang Pu Mun. Ajahn Chah was my own teacher, and many of my translations of his teachings have already been published. For this volume, I have opted to include a chapter on my experiences of living with the great teacher with the hope that it will help convey something of what it means to live in close proximity with one of Thailand's great "voices." Since Luang Pu Mun passed away in 1949, his teachings were given before the time of portable tape recorders, computers, and YouTube, so there is very little that remains of his teaching.

In addition, such eminent teachers as Ajahn Paññānanda, Ajahn Thien, Ajahn Khamkhian, and Phra Phayom (Kalyāṇo) are not represented here due to space limitations. It is hoped that a second volume may redress these omissions.

While not necessarily in strict chronological order, there is a rough progression to the teachings in this book. The *Girimānanda Sutta*, the first chapter, is by far the oldest text here, while the second chapter contains talks and writings by Venerable Chao Khun Upāli dating to around the early twentieth century. From there the various chapters represent teachers from the late twentieth to early twenty-first century, with only three—Venerable P. A. Payutto, Ajahn Paisal (Visālo), and Ajahn Pramote (Pāmojjo)—still actively teaching at the time of writing.

I have resisted the urge to cherry-pick the highlights of the teachings. Instead I have endeavored to offer the teachings in context. The "cherries" are there, but they are embedded within the context of the leaves and branches. In Thailand, when devout Buddhists go to temples to listen to a teaching, they are not only going for instruction. In many instances, as the listeners hear the familiar themes of Buddhist discourse, the gentle flow of the teaching is like a soothing balm for the heart; listening to a Dhamma teaching becomes a meditation in itself. This is illustrated in the suttas, in which we can find passages describing a person being greeted with the exclamation, "Your features are radiant, friend. Surely you have just been anointed with a teaching from the Blessed One?"

In the same way, these teachings are to be taken not only as instruction, but as a soothing balm. This is perhaps nowhere better exemplified than in the *Girimānanda Sutta*, which may come across as somewhat rambling. It is in no hurry to deliver any knockout blow of revelation: the journey itself is the destination. In this respect, listening to Dhamma teachings is regarded as itself a kind of Dhamma practice, requiring the application of such skillful qualities as clear attention and faith.

It has been my great honor to compile and translate these teachings. If the reader derives at least some measure of the joy I have experienced in putting this collection together, I will consider the project a success.

Voices of Siam

Ajahn Chah (center) with Jāgaro Bhikkhu
(John Cianciosi, left) and Puriso Bhikkhu
(Bruce Evans, right)

LIVING WITH AJAHN CHAH

IN 1975 I WAS TRAVELING through Southern Thailand with my guitar and a mission to find a Dhamma teacher. I had practiced Zen Buddhism for a number of years with friends in Melbourne and had the crazy notion of going to a Zen temple in Japan to develop my meditation, achieve *satori*, and then go out and become an enlightened rock star. On the way I passed through Thailand, a country I had visited before and loved, to use the opportunity to visit some teachers there.

A friend had recommended Ajahn Buddhadāsa's temple in Chaiya. I somehow found my way there and was guided by one of the monks to a *sala* (temple hall) where I could dump my stuff and sleep. Apart from that there was no guidance, and I was left to my own devices.

I remember Suan Mokkh, Ajahn Buddhadāsa's monastery, as a beautiful forest decorated with replica Buddhist sculptures and a Dhamma gallery. But my memories are tainted by a lingering sense of shame. Not only did I take out my guitar and play loudly in the temple hall, but after being told by one of the monks that playing music was not allowed in the temple, the next day I took out my clarinet and gave that a blast. On top of that, when finally given a chance to meet the great teacher, I almost sat right next to him on the bench where he sat—a great cultural blunder—to the shock of his attendant bhikkhus. All in all, the experience was a good demonstration of my oafishness as a Westerner ignorant of Thai language and culture.

I did not stay long at Suan Mokkh and unfortunately wasted my opportunity to hear any teachings from Ajahn Buddhadāsa. At the time I was just too agitated and not ready to receive teaching. However, two good things did come out of my visit; I gave up cigarettes, which was one of the aims of my journey of spiritual discovery, and I came across a couple of small pamphlets: *Fragments of a Teaching and Notes from a Session of Questions and Answers*, translated and compiled by Jack Kornfield, and *A Guide to the Meditation Temples of Thailand*. *Fragments of a Teaching* was probably the first translation of Ajahn Chah ever published, and the simple and direct manner of the teaching touched my heart. In the guide to meditation temples, I read how Wat Nong Pa Pong (or simply Wat Pa Pong), Ajahn Chah's monastery, was a strictly run forest monastery with a schedule of chanting, meditation, and chores within the rustic environs of a Thai forest. A more disciplined environment sounded like exactly what I needed—something to regulate my sloppy nature.

After three days at Suan Mokkh enduring the mental torture of nicotine withdrawal, my restlessness carried me north to Nong Khai, where I visited one of the temples recommended in the guide: Wat Nern Phanao. Unbeknownst to me at the time, this temple had been one of the first that Ajahn Sumedho, Ajahn Chah's senior Western disciple, had stayed at before he made his way to Wat Pa Pong. I knew nothing about it other than it was right on the border of Laos, which I intended to visit, and so it seemed like a convenient place to stay and perhaps further my Dhamma practice.

When I arrived in Nong Khai with my guitar and small suitcase, I was approached by a young Thai man who offered to accompany me to the temple some way out of town. Although I spoke no Thai, I tried to make it clear that I did not require a guide and could make my way on my own. Unfortunately my command of Thai, or perhaps my insistence, was not strong enough to convey this message, and he ended up following me all the way to the temple. The monks assumed that he was my traveling companion, and so they put us up together in a room. When the bell rang for morning chanting the next day at 4 a.m., I awoke to find my wallet, my camera, my guitar, and the young man gone.

Losing the guitar—a beautifully crafted piece I had bought a few years previously in Granada, Spain—was a big shock. I ran out of the monastery and all the way to the local police station, a couple of kilometers away. (I don't think I'd ever run so far before in my life, nor since.) I burst into the station waving my hands around in a gesture of playing a guitar followed by a hands-in-the-air pantomime of losing something. Of course, my performance was met with bewilderment, and I trudged back to the temple feeling devastated.

During those days I had a habit of jotting down little poems inspired by haiku, and the one I wrote at that time summarized my feelings perfectly:

> O the misery
> and the relief
> of at last
> having lost
> my guitar

Wat Nern Phanao turned out to be a meditation monastery. The monks would go into retreat in isolated huts (*kuti*) and there follow a stylized system of very slow movements designed to keep the attention focused. I resolved to stay there for a while and learn the technique. My "teaching," such as it was, consisted of basically practicing to master the slow, almost dance-like movements, but I had no idea what I was supposed to be doing with my mind. As I understood it at the time, the aim was to move only one part of the body at a time, and all movements were extremely slow. Eating the one daily meal, for instance, took three hours.

Apart from the weeklong meditation retreat, two good things came out of my stay at Wat Nern Phanao. One was meeting an old monk who took a shine to me and invited me over to his kuti every day for a few days. He taught me how to say his name—Luang Por Thom Phet—making me repeat it over and over until I got it right. It was here that I learned the cardinal rule of speaking Thai—follow the tones. When I said "Luang" with a downward inflection, he would shake his head and repeat it with rising inflection. After a few dozen times it dawned on me that the inflection was part of the word's pronunciation, so it was "Luang" (rising inflection) "Por" (falling inflection) "Thom" (rising inflection) "Phet" (sustained high tone). This was something of an epiphany for me, and from then on I made relatively rapid progress in speaking Thai and have always found the language to be more a familiar friend than an alien tongue.

The second major thing that came out of my stay at Wat Nern Phanao was something that happened not in that temple but across the river in Vientiane, Laos. The monks were accustomed to crossing the river on a regular basis, and they took me across to a sister monastery where a similar style of meditation was practiced. This was in 1975, just before the Pathet Lao overran the capital and Laos became a communist state. After paying respects to some senior monks at the temple, we walked around the grounds, and it was there that I saw one of the monks in solitary retreat, performing the slow movements of what I have since learned was the Ajahn Thien system of meditation. In just a few seconds of watching him I grasped how the technique was meant to be performed—with an empty mind. This monk had evidently been in retreat for some time, for his body exuded a sense of profound stillness even in movement that I had never seen before. When we returned to Wat Nern Phanao and I entered my seven-day retreat, it was this vision that inspired me in my practice more than any words the teacher had given me. This episode instilled in me the importance of seeing good examples—something that was pivotal later on when I went to Wat Pa Pong.

After leaving Wat Nern Phanao I took a brief detour to Vientiane and then made my way to Wat Pa Pong in the province of Ubon Ratchathani. I had been to a few temples in Thailand before Wat Pa Pong, but I will never forget the impression it made on me the minute I walked through the high concrete walls of the temple into the silent, immaculately kept forested grounds—an impression I continue to receive every time I go there. The central path led through the forest to a plain, concrete sala, which constituted the main building of the temple.[1] This was where the monks gathered in the morning and evening for chanting and meditation, and where on observance days laypeople would join them. Adjoining the sala was a long, narrow extension for the eating hall. Here the monks would gather together after alms round and sit on long benches that ran on either side of the hall behind their alms bowls. The monks assigned to distribute the food would put it directly into the bowls—if they felt kind, they would not put the sweets on top of the curries. At the end of the eating hall was a small room that constituted the *uposatha* hall (*boht* in Thai). It was here that the monks gathered every two weeks to recite the training rules (Pāṭimokkha) and from time to time to conduct ordinations.

Away from the cleared area around the sala, tall trees stretched away in every direction, and squirrels of many different colors—brown, gray, white, and black—scampered around in the branches.

In contrast to the bright yellow or orange robes worn by the monks in city temples, the monks here wore ocher to dark-brown robes, the colors obtained from dyeing and washing the cloth in water boiled with heartwood from the jackfruit tree. The monks went about their business with reserve and composure and seemed oblivious to my presence.

I didn't meet Ajahn Chah that first day but was directed to sleep on the floor in the sala and given a pillow and a cloth to cover the linoleum that served as the only cushioning on the concrete surface. Now many decades after that time, I cannot imagine how I managed to communicate my needs to the people around me, as none of the monks spoke English and at the time I spoke only a few words of Thai. At the ungodly hour of 3 a.m. I was awoken by the mournful peal of the monastery's morning bell and sat on the floor as the monks did the morning chanting in a combination of Pali and Thai. The sound was eerie to my ears. Because the changes of intonation followed the tones of Thai language, the chanting sounded like a song with no fixed tune. Lines would end on an upward tone where my Western ears were expecting a downward inflection and go down where I expected them to go up. It was long, too—droning on for about forty-five minutes. Although it proved a painful experience for me, and indeed continued to be painful for months afterward due to the unfamiliar kneeling with pressure on the toes, the morning and evening chanting became my main vehicles for learning correct Thai pronunciation and so were infinitely useful, not only for finding out the meaning of the chants but for my picking up the language.

For mealtime, the monks all filed out on alms round just after dawn. As an *anagārika* (lay resident), I was assigned to help sweep up and prepare the eating hall. I was given what I took to be a washbasin, from which I would eat my one meal of the day: sticky rice and a combination of whatever the monks had obtained on alms round after they had taken their share.

Later that day I was directed to the kuti of the one Western monk staying at Wat Pa Pong at the time, Venerable Varapañño (Paul Breiter). I found him to be refreshingly down to earth, and I have regarded him as a *sahadhammika* (Dhamma friend) ever since. He explained some of the basics of living at Wat Pa Pong, including the news that if I stayed longer than three days I would have to have my head shaved. He also told me that there were many other Western monks, but most had gone to stay at the nearby branch monastery, Wat Pa Nanachat (International Forest Monastery) near Bung Wai village, which had only just been established a few months earlier.

Wat Pa Pong was an education on many levels. The wildlife, for instance, always kept you on your toes. It was, after all, a dense forest with the associated populations of snakes, ants, scorpions, spiders, and other crawling things. On one of my first days in the temple, as I was walking along one of the forest paths, I suddenly felt a fiery sting on my toe. I looked down to see a shiny black ant latched onto it, injecting some substance into me with its tail—and about a thousand others all swarming around my sandaled feet. I jumped. I had met the notorious *mot din*. My first thought was, "Wow, just one of these critters can inflict so much pain, but there are *thousands* of them!" *Mot din*[2] means "jumping ants," although it's not the ants that jumped but the people who got bitten by them. These ants would mass in the thousands along the swept forest paths, looking for the big fat worms that came out after a rain, but also ready to jump on absolutely anything that got in their way. For years afterward, the telltale flip-flop of a monk's sandals as he did the "mot din hop" over a swarm of the ants was a common sound at Wat Pa Pong.

Other inhabitants of the forest were the snakes—mostly green tree snakes, but cobras were not uncommon—and of course mosquitoes. Snakes were ubiquitous throughout all the forest monasteries, but they never posed a threat to the monks who lived there. As long as you watched where you were walking, you would be all right; the most dangerous snake is the one you don't see. The one creature that instilled a special awe among the monks, however, was the giant centipede. These critters seemed to wriggle and bite quite randomly, and a bite from one of them was said to exceed the pain of even a snakebite. Fortunately, I managed to avoid that experience, although I did manage to sustain * numerous scorpion stings over the years.

Varapañño took me to meet Ajahn Chah ("Luang Por" as he was affectionately referred to). Luang Por's kuti was in the center of the temple grounds. It was a fairly large structure on two levels. The upper level of timber was Luang Por's living quarters. The lower level consisted of an open area with a floor made of colored polished concrete (*terrazzo*). This was the reception area. It was here that Luang Por sat most afternoons in his wicker chair, receiving visitors of all descriptions. The monks would come to sit and listen in on the conversations and attend to Luang Por by fanning him or tending to any chores that needed doing.

I do not have a clear memory of much that was said at that first meeting. Luang Por was a commanding presence. He was portly, and his large face was impassive but would readily break into a smile, revealing unmistakable kindness. Through Varapañño, Luang Por asked a few things about me. When Varapañño relayed to him that I had had my guitar stolen, Luang Por retorted, "The devas stole your guitar so you can concentrate on practicing the Dhamma." I don't know about devas, but the guitar was a huge attachment, and losing it was definitely a boon to my practice.

Luang Por must have noticed my discomfort sitting on the floor of his kuti, with my knees sticking up in the air. He gave me a simple stretching exercise for loosening the hips, one that I still do to this day. What I remember more from that occasion is the impression that I got from seeing Luang Por—an impression that never changed—of someone who is totally there and totally at ease with the present moment. It was an image of what I needed to aim for, much like the image of the monk practicing the meditation technique in Vientiane.

My first stay at Wat Pa Pong did not last long, maybe one or two weeks, during which Varapañño introduced me to the esoteric art of evening coffee (black, lots of sugar)—a ritual whose importance would only be more reinforced the longer I stayed in temples, especially those with Western monks.

Luang Por wanted Varapañño to go and spend the rains retreat at the branch monastery for Westerners, Wat Pa Nanachat, and to take me with him. This must have been around May or June, just before the rains retreat started.[3] We took leave of Luang Por, and Varapañño led the way, walking through the villages, back roads, and rice paddies for about one and a half hours to Nanachat. Along the way he told me about his experiences at the branch monastery he had just returned from. The branch monasteries were usually newly established and quite rustic. Wat Nanachat, in fact, was more rustic than most, having only been established a few months earlier. The main hall was no more than a grass-roofed affair with a slightly raised pounded-earth floor, bamboo rails, and no walls.

This was where Ajahn Sumedho would learn to lead a saṅgha of Western monks. That first year there were twelve monks and one *pakhao*[4] (myself) to spend the rains, and all of us got sick at one time or another. Typhoid and scrub typhus both made an appearance in those first few years. The forest near Bung Wai village was a charnel ground for the surrounding villages and, as such, was thought to be haunted. That is why the forest had escaped the fate of the surrounding land, which had become rice paddies. It was a perfect place for a forest monastery.

Soon after arriving at Wat Nanachat, I gathered that the practice for Luang Por and Ajahn Sumedho was very much one of commitment: to become a bhikkhu. This was not part of my original plan—which was to become a rock star, remember?—so it took some time for me to reach some acceptance. I recall two incidents that helped change my mind. The first was a long talk given to the monks by Ajahn Sumedho about the benefits of the bhikkhu life, at the end of which he said, "I don't think five years is too much to ask, Bruce." The second, after I had asked to postpone my first scheduled ordination as a novice, was Ajahn

Sumedho saying, "Luang Por said tell Bruce he can stay a pa-khao for as long as he likes!" followed by Ajahn Sumedho's inimitable laugh. It made me feel a bit like an idiot.

The shift in attitude for me was seismic. I had never intended on taking on the robes but had always thought of practicing "on my terms" (with the underlying idea that I would practice for a while, get enlightened, then go out and have a good time without feeling guilty about it). The idea of actually giving up some of my dreams had never occurred to me, but the longer I stayed, the more I saw the need to remain and wash off the conceit of my worldly ideas.

One of the catalysts for my change of heart was the chance to see with my own eyes the value of the bhikkhu life at Wat Pa Nanachat. First there was the camaraderie: although all of us staying there had come from different walks of life, and in normal circumstances may not have bothered to talk to each other, we were held together by a common aim and all subjugated our own conceits and arrogance to the bhikkhu discipline (the Vinaya). Second, the chance to live a life that was aimed at something higher than struggling to make a living and establish some kind of name for oneself in the world was a precious and rare opportunity. A corollary of this was the simplicity of not having to worry about one's bank account (bhikkhus at Wat Pa Pong and branch monasteries do not have money or personal funds) and all the busyness of family life and responsibilities. And finally there was the natural environment of the forest temple. Nowadays many forest temples have electricity, but in the 1970s most did not. We used candles and kerosene lanterns for light, and water was hauled from a well. All in all, the simplicity was a great boon to meditation practice.

By the time I had agreed to become a novice I had been a pa-khao for eight months and had spent my first rainy season at Wat Pa Nanachat. After the rains retreat, I traveled to Wat Pa Pong and ordained as a *samanera* (novice) with Luang Por, and then, just before the following rains retreat, I was ordained as a bhikkhu and spent my first rains retreat at Wat Pa Pong.[5]

Wat Pa Pong was spreading its influence, and around that time in 1976, there must have been twenty or thirty branch monasteries, mostly in the northeast of Thailand. In my early years I would often meet Western monks who had just returned from a stint at one of these, usually a few kilos thinner than before and looking somewhat pale. Many of the branch monasteries were in remote and poor locations, and malaria was not uncommon. The diet was notoriously rustic. In my mind the branch monasteries began to take on mythical connotations, and the thought of going to stay at one was daunting.

In that first year at Wat Pa Pong my Thai was developing but still limited, so my interactions with Luang Por consisted of short exchanges. During that rains retreat, Luang Por invited me to accompany him on a group trip to one of these notorious branch monasteries— probably the most notorious of them all—Wat Kheuan (Dam Temple: its official name is Wat Pa Wana Pothiyan). This was a one-thousand-acre forest surrounded on three sides by the waters of the Sirindhorn Dam. It was renowned for its wildlife (deer, wild boar, snakes, and all kinds of birds) and malaria. The only road in then was impassable, a sandy track on which vehicles became bogged down on a regular basis, so the best way to get there was by boat across the dam. The monks had their own boat, a long-tail job powered by an old truck engine.

It was quite an experience. The morning we arrived it was raining up a storm. We waited at the makeshift boat landing as the monks steered the boat up, and then we clambered aboard with Luang Por. I watched as the young monk at the helm, muscles glistening in the rain and looking like some clerical Rambo, navigated the waters of the dam to the temple's boat landing. I don't remember much else about that first visit, except that on the way back, Luang Por turned to me and said, "Burut,[6] do you like it here?" I replied "Yes," not knowing what else to say. Then Luang Por said, "If you came to live here, that would be really good." At the time it was the furthest thing from my mind. The place looked positively terrifying. Little did I know that seven years down the line I would indeed go live there and end up staying as the abbot for nine years and grow to love the place.

For forest monks there is a special affection for these kinds of remote environments, and Wat Kheaun and another temple, Wat Tham

Saeng Phet (Jewel Cave Monastery), were Luang Por's favorites. Indeed, Wat Pa Pong to this day retains some of that sacred, still forest atmosphere sought out by forest monks.

The lifestyle at Wat Pa Pong, the monastic community and communal activities, the cleanliness and orderliness of the grounds, the swept floors of the buildings and the forest paths: all were a reflection of Luang Por's teaching. Living in a community was an important part of the practice. Learning to curb one's pride and desires for outward exuberance was an aspect of the development of mindfulness, and Luang Por gave many teachings to illustrate this. On one occasion, the monks at Wat Nanachat were discussing the thorny issue of cheese. Cheese is somewhat controversial for bhikkhus as it is sometimes interpreted as one of the "allowables" that monks are permitted to consume in the evening (i.e., not regarded as food), due to the obscurity of the meaning of some of the original Pali terms in the monks' discipline. At that time, Wat Nanachat was going through one of its "cheese is not allowable" phases. One of the Western monks, however, had done some thorough research of the English translations of the Vinaya Piṭaka and concluded that it definitely *was* allowable. When Luang Por came to visit Wat Nanachat, the monks presented the case to him. He listened for a while, and rather than try to resolve the question, he said, "Venerable, if all the monks here do not eat cheese, and you are convinced that cheese is OK, are you going to go and eat cheese by yourself?" Rather than prolong the potentially endless discussion, Luang Por had brought it down to a simple matter of practice: what is a skillful way to relate to this?

The first few weeks of the rainy season were suitably inspiring, although difficult. The morning and evening chanting continued to be challenging for me, sitting on my toes for that period of time. But I experienced some moments of clarity. One of them was in relation to music, which had always been a strong attachment for me, to the extent that while I was a layperson I would rarely be sitting still but have one or more fingers tapping out beats to the various tunes of my mental music library. As I became quieter, however, I began to see the burden this attachment created and to appreciate simple quietness. The bliss resulting from meditation practice exceeded any fleeting delight of listening to music. I wrote a few lines expressing my feelings:

> Fine it is
> to hear good music.
> Even finer
> not to hear.

Life at Wat Pa Pong was not all chanting and walking meditation. Work was also an aspect of practice, and it was held that the attitude you brought to work was an indication of the attitude you brought to meditation. And so shortly after the rains retreat finished, Luang Por sprung one of his surprises on us. Wat Pa Pong at the time was in the process of building a new boht. This was an architect-designed structure, and the plan called for it to be situated on a flat-topped mound about two or three meters high. In preparation, truckloads and truckloads of earth had been brought in and dumped in the vicinity of where the boht would go. I guess it should have come as no surprise that we monks and novices were the ones who were going to be moving that earth. There were three main jobs in the process: some of the monks would work with hoes and shovels to heap the earth into little baskets called *bung-gee*. Another group would carry these baskets up to dump them on the mound. A third group would be on the top of the mound, pounding the earth with pounders to pack it tightly. The work would be done at night by lantern light after evening chanting, and sometimes in place of it. All the while we were working, I'd be thinking, "We should be meditating. We should be chanting, and here we are up until ten o'clock, eleven o'clock at night with the lanterns going, working away shoveling all this dirt." I'd be so agitated that I'd be working like a maniac, thinking "Let's get it finished tonight," which of course was not going to happen. One time, Luang Por was doing his rounds, and he saw me working frantically and said, "Oh Burut, you work really well." I had to smile. I was not actually working well, I was working like an idiot, but Luang Por's kind words brought me back to reality.

Over the years my knowledge of Thai developed, and I was able to understand more and more of what Luang Por was saying. On one memorable occasion a few years later, I happened to be staying at Wat Pa Pong when one of Luang Por's younger disciples returned to the temple to pay his respects, after being away on *tudong*[7] for a number of years. This monk had developed a reputation as someone who had reached a high level of realization. Luang Por had been chatting with this monk for some time, and it was on account of this that the bell had been rung and the monks gathered at Luang Por's kuti for a special meeting. Luang Por proceeded to address the monks with a Dhamma talk. I did not take notes at the time, and I don't believe it was recorded. These many years later I cannot remember much detail, but two points stand out in my memory.

The first was *yah pramaht* ("don't be heedless"). Luang Por elaborated to point out the objective of the bhikkhu life, which is realization, and that the aim of the bhikkhu life is to strive for that release from suffering.

The second was *yah prakaht* ("don't make announcements"). The meaning is, even if you do have a realization, there is no need to make any announcements about it. This point is supported by rules in the monk's discipline. If a bhikkhu knowingly lies about having superhuman attainments, such as enlightenment, deep meditation states, or psychic powers, this is a very serious offense, one of the defeat (*pārājika*) offenses, a result of which a bhikkhu automatically ceases to be a bhikkhu. However, even if one does have superhuman attainments, one of the minor rules forbids bhikkhus from sharing this with a layperson. When I reflect on my life with Luang Por, I cannot remember him ever engaging in discussions about attainments or making announcements about his own attainment or that of anyone else. In fact, it seemed that the question was irrelevant. If you know, you know. Why do you need to tell anyone else about it? If one has really experienced something that transcends the world, why would one reduce it to worldly statements?

Looking at it on a social level, I have seen a few instances of monks in Thailand who publicized various so-called attainments and as a result amassed great followings of dedicated supporters. In some cases the announcements were based on a misunderstanding on the monk's part, but some were more clearly fraudulent: spinning tales to take advantage of a gullible population. When those monks were found out, the damage done to their followers was painful to watch and caused loss of faith on a wide scale.

When one thinks about it, a lot of harm comes from obsessing over such matters, and for that reason I am eternally grateful to Luang Por for keeping things simple, keeping things real, and not indulging people's desires to create and attach to spiritual identities. Just do the practice, see it for yourself, and that's enough. If you have the opportunity, help others along the way.

It might be argued that if a teacher has a spiritual attainment, announcing it would be helpful to their followers as a means of instilling faith and fervor in the practice, but even here the benefits are dubious: First, there is the obvious fact that followers are in no position to verify whether the announcement is true or not. They may end up following a teacher into further delusion. Second, it is arguable that having the kind of faith that focuses too much on the teacher is not so healthy. Real faith is the faith that comes from inside: seeing suffering and striving for a way out. This is what keeps us on the true path. If you find a teacher who helps to increase your self-awareness rather than attachment to the teacher, that teacher is worth staying with, and no announcements are required.

By the time I became fully fluent in Thai, Luang Por was much less available for conversations. He traveled overseas twice, and not long after returning from his second trip, he began to feel the symptoms of the illness that would eventually render him paralyzed. At this time, I would have loved to have had more in-depth discussions with him, but it was not to be. At the time a little stanza arose in my mind:

> When the Master was teaching
> I had no questions.
> Now that I'm asking,
> the Master is silent.
> Truly,
> in this world
> there are no favors.

My most intimate interaction with Luang Por's teaching came in the form of translation. In my fourth rains as a bhikkhu I went to stay at the branch monastery run by Ajahn Khun in Ban Na Pho, Ubon Ratchathani.

Wat Pa Na Pho was a wonderful experience: while it lacked spectacular forest (being regenerated farmland), it was a small community, and had decent food, a nice, not-too-damp climate, simple lodgings (the sala, such as it was, consisted of a concrete floor, corrugated iron roof, and walls made of bamboo latticework over which was placed the paper bags from the cement used for the floor), and an impressive teacher. Ajahn Khun was soft-spoken but loved to chat, and the legacies of my staying with him for almost a year were multiple. He liked to experiment and instituted a regime of having all of us read from a Thai text that he had selected for us after the evening chanting. There were only four of us staying the rains that year: Ajahn Khun; Luang Ta,[8] an elderly monk who had taken the robes later in life; myself; and a novice, Nen Thavee. Luang Ta read from the *Girimānanda Sutta*, I read from *Advice on Looking Inwards* by Upāsikā Kee Nanayon,[9] and the young Nen Thavee read from another text, the title of which eludes me these many years later.[10]

Ajahn Khun also had a supply of old tapes of Dhamma talks by Ajahn Chah on three-inch reels and a reel-to-reel tape recorder on which to play them. The sum of all this was that not only did my knowledge of written and spoken Thai and the Isan dialect develop significantly, but I also gained access to a body of Ajahn Chah's teaching that I began translating and later published as a small booklet entitled *A Taste of Freedom*.

I found my meditation becoming very peaceful too. At one stage it felt that my mind was verging on stillness, but hadn't quite gotten there. I asked Ajahn Khun what I could do to make it absolutely still. He reminded me of one of Luang Por's teachings, which I later found among the tapes that I translated: "The objective is not to make the mind absolutely still, i.e., without thoughts. Thoughts are just thoughts; the mind is the mind. The two are different things. The thoughts of our mind are like a busy road. You can't go charging onto the road waving your arms around to try and stop the cars, shouting 'Stop! Don't come this way.' You'll only get run over! So what do you do? You get off the road. In the same way, when thoughts arise, don't go picking a fight with them. Just note them and leave them be. Focus on your awareness." It was a teaching that sank in and allowed to me move forward in the practice.

In later years, while translating Luang Por's teaching "Still, Flowing Water," I realized he had been saying this in different ways on many occasions over the years.

While I did eventually leave the bhikkhu life, there are a number of key teachings from Luang Por that will always be with me. The first is his emphasis on right view. It is a subtle theme, one that can be interpreted in many ways, but to me it is a view that keeps one grounded. One does not practice to gain anything but to see what is around us more clearly. As Luang Por often said, "Everything is Dhamma, if our mind is Dhamma." This is supported by the standard scriptural definition of right view, which is to see the four noble truths. It is learning to see what is there in front of us with clarity rather than attaining some projection of what we want to be there. Luang Por succinctly summarized this beautifully with his comparison of the ordinary unenlightened mind as "wanting a duck to be a chicken and a chicken to be a duck."

Simple and *direct* are the two words that come to mind when describing Luang Por's teaching. A good example of this simplicity is one of his discussions of the profound Buddhist teaching of dependent origination (*paṭiccasamuppāda*). It is a complex and exciting teaching, and many books have been written about it, but Luang Por, in his characteristic simplicity, said, "When you fall from a tree, you don't go counting the branches you pass on your way down. You just fall and then 'ouch!' The teaching of dependent origination is the teaching that things arise because of causes. You don't necessarily have to see each cause for every effect: the key is having an insight into the principle at work."

While simple, this does not mean his teaching was shallow. Some of his simple teachings can be taken on many levels—some of them quite profound. For instance, he once likened the state of enlightenment to a man walking down the street who gets abused by a random stranger. Every time he walks down that street, the stranger abuses him. He feels very uncomfortable about it, and every time he remembers the words of abuse, he feels piqued. But then one day another person tells him, "Oh, that guy? He's crazy. Has been for years. He abuses everyone like that." As soon as he hears this, the man is unburdened of his concern. He realizes that the abusing man is simply acting out of a mental illness. In the same way, as long as we are unenlightened, we keep thinking, "Why am I suffering so much? Why is life so hard?" But with wisdom we see that in reality this is just the way things are. Body and mind and all formations are simply this way; they are inherently changing, unsatisfactory, and not self. When you really see this, your problems are gone.

Another significant aspect of Luang Por's teaching was his skillful use of conventions. He often expanded on the theme with a play on words in Thai, using the terms *sommot* (convention) and *wimut* (liberation), pointing out that we must use conventions but also understand them for what they are. In practice, Luang Por ran a tight ship at Wat Pa Pong: the grounds were immaculately kept; the monks were composed and restrained; everything was done to order. It might seem like a strong attachment to convention, but inwardly Luang Por was light and untroubled by them. He used conventions, but he didn't carry them.

At one time there was a young American woman who had been ordained as a mae chee[11] and was living in the mae chee enclosure of Wat Pa Pong. As a layperson, she had lived in Laos for some years and so was able to converse with the other mae chee and with Luang Por fairly comfortably. For a Western woman to live with the mae chee at Wat Pa Pong was no easy task, and very few have done it. The lifestyle revolved a lot around preparing food for the monks and working in the vegetable garden, a selfless lifestyle for little recognition: the mae chee were very much the "invisible" residents of Wat Pa Pong. This mae chee had heard of Luang Por's practice, and she wanted to go and live by herself for a while, perhaps in a cave in a remote forest location, to develop her meditation. She asked for Luang Por's permission but he said no, pointing out that it would be dangerous for a young woman to live in such a way. She pleaded with him. "But Luang Por, you went tudong and lived on your own in remote forest locations for years, developing your practice. Why can't I?" Luang Por retorted, "I'm living on my own right now! I always live on my own!" It was a teaching that rang true, as Luang Por did indeed always carry himself very lightly, even surrounded by people.

In terms of practice, Luang Por did not put great emphasis on meditation technique. He placed more importance on having a right attitude. One time I was sitting under his kuti when a young Westerner arrived at Wat Pa Pong and asked if they could study meditation under Luang Por. Luang Por answered rather gruffly, "I don't know about meditation. I only know about torture."

The word *torture* here is from the Thai word *toraman*. In a monastic context, it is often used in the sense of training or disciplining, in that disciplining the mind is a kind of torture for the defilements. It is interesting to compare this with modern attitudes to meditation, which often seem to be skewed toward looking for a peaceful vibe. Luang Por's answer was an insight into what it really means to dedicate oneself to practice. It is not just sitting with a peaceful mind or even looking for a peaceful mind. Often it is enduring that which is hard to endure: heat, pain, illness, harsh words, and, for a layperson, the complexities and conflicts of living in a competitive world. As a bhikkhu, one could be lying in one's hut, surrounded by miles of jungle, the body burning with malaria, and the nearest hospital a half-hour walk, then a twenty-minute boat ride, then another half-hour car ride away. At times like this the mind has nowhere to run. When fear of death arises, there is nowhere to find solace other than to accept one's own morality. This is meditation on another level.

When I reflect on the time I spent as a bhikkhu living with the saṅgha, one word that springs to mind is *authenticity*. From my first conversations with Venerable Varapañño to my later interactions with the Western and Thai saṅghas at Wat Pa Pong, Wat Nanachat, and the branch monasteries, I found only genuine people who were striving to deal with the various burdens of delusion with raw honesty. They were not pretending to be noble—or anything at all, really—but they had taken on a noble lifestyle with the aim of training out that which is ignoble within them, with varying levels of success. As such, it is an institution that comes as a breath of fresh air for an age where cynicism and negativity have become the norm.

As almost forty years or so have elapsed since those times and dulled my recollections, I cannot share my experiences with Luang Por in great detail. There are many Western bhikkhus and ex-bhikkhus who had far more detailed interactions with Ajahn Chah than I and would have many more stories to tell, but I offer these reflections as a small window into the experience that was living with him and in gratitude for the debt I owe him.

—BRUCE EVANS

Folios from an early twentieth-century
palm-leaf manuscript of the
Girimānanda Sutta in Tham Lao script

GIRIMĀNANDA SUTTA

There is a *Girimānanda Sutta* in the Aṅguttara Nikāya, the collection of small discourses preserved in the Suttapiṭika (Collection of Discourses) of the Buddhist Pali Canon. The text presented here is not *that Girimānanda Sutta*. While the two begin with a similar scenario—Venerable Girimānanda being struck with illness and Venerable Ānanda visiting the Buddha with a request for instruction to help him cope with the pain—the two versions quickly diverge. The Tipiṭaka version has the Buddha imparting ten reflections for Ānanda to convey to Girimānanda, whereas the version presented here has the Buddha imparting only two reflections—mind (*nāma*) and body (*rūpa*)—after which the discourse embarks on a meandering journey through various reflections on heaven, hell, teaching, and realization.

The provenance of this version is unclear. As noted in the preface by the Thai translator Phra Dhammadhīrarājmahāmunī—a bhikkhu more widely known as Chao Khun Upāli, whose work is represented in the following chapter—this sutta was presented to him by a pair of lay disciples as a palm-leaf scripture, which he then translated from the "Northern Siamese" into "Central Siamese" (Thai).

Palm-leaf manuscripts, made from the talipot palm, were a common way of recording religious and other texts throughout Southeast and South Asia for many centuries, with manuscripts surviving from as far back as the ninth century. The languages used were the vernacular of the location, such as Khmer, Shan, or Lanna. Because of their fragile nature, fresh copies of the manuscripts were always required, and it became a practice for monks to painstakingly inscribe the texts onto fresh palm-leaf manuscripts. Since the advent of books, these manuscripts have become increasingly rare and are now mostly of interest to collectors, although it is still possible to see them used in village temples when monks read them as a way of giving a Dhamma talk.

I have consulted some scholars familiar with palm-leaf scriptures but have been unable to find any concrete information on this text's origins. According to Venerable Phra Khru Kittikhunsāthorn (Mun) of Wat Borom Niwas in Bangkok (the temple of the Thai translator Chao Khun Upāli), the original version was made in the Hanthawaddy era in present-day Myanmar around the year 2085 B.E. (around 1540 C.E.), in the Thai Yai (Shan) language. From there it spread throughout the nearby kingdoms into present-day Laos and Thailand and was translated into the vernaculars of those regions. David Wharton, a scholar of Buddhist manuscript cultures who previously worked for many years with the Preservation of Lao Manuscripts Program of the National Library of Laos, assures me that there are over fifty similar manuscripts in the online Digital Library of Lao Manuscripts. Samples of them contain similar versions of this sutta, so it is certainly of some age and has had a wide distribution.

As noted in the translator's introduction, the sutta is given in the *roi krong* style, a stylistic form in which Pali terms are interspersed throughout the text. The text was intended to be read out loud, and the use of Pali terms, as well as the constant reference to the Buddha and his disciple Ānanda, would have not only given the text an air of authority, but would also have imbued it with a reverential air and been a soothing balm for its listeners, who would have been faithful Buddhists already familiar with many of the terms and the cadence of Pali. The aim of the composition as a whole is not to impart nuggets of information, but to lead the listener on a journey through certain aspects of the Buddha's teachings. For that reason, it is as much a literary exercise as a source of teaching. For readers unfamiliar with the Pali, it is perhaps advisable to treat the Pali terms as simple literary devices, since they are always translated in the text wherever they appear.

The sutta has enjoyed ongoing popularity among Thai Buddhists and is praised by members of the Thai forest bhikkhu community in particular, holding as it does many similarities to a Thai forest dhamma talk, such as the very direct injunctions to put the teachings into practice and focus on awareness of body and mind.

There are a number of editions of this title in my possession. This translation is mostly based on a facsimile printing of the 2465 B.E. (1922) edition from Sueksa Thammada Press, published for free distribution on the occasion of the funeral of Princess Thanom Diskul.

I have tried to preserve the roi krong style of the original text and have thus retained the Pali words where they occur. The words immediately following the Pali phrases are invariably translated repetitions of the Pali, so in essence the Pali is only included for rhythmic effect. However, I have reformatted the paragraphing and added quotation marks to indicate the beginning and end of various speech segments. In addition, following the Venerable Chao Khun Upāli's lead, I have made further cuts to the text to reduce some of the excess repetition which, while being well suited to a listening audience, is less tolerated in written form.

GIRIMĀNANDA SUTTA

Thai Translator's Preface

The original of this *Girimānanda Sutta* was heard by the lay-women Thongdam and Thongyoi at Roi Et Province. They liked it and hired a scribe to inscribe a palm-leaf copy as a translation in twelve bundles and sent it to me. I have read and checked it in full and have found it to contain inspiring words, so I would like to offer the observation that whether these are indeed the Buddha's words or the words of another teacher citing the Buddha's words is not the point. The point is the teachings themselves, which are credible and, judging from the way they are written, free of bias (*agati*), the intention of the speaker being truly imbued with goodwill and compassion. This is the important point. I myself guarantee that they are good teachings and can greatly further knowledge and understanding. However, regarding the statement that anyone who punishes, by banishment (*pabbājanīyakamma*) or disrobing, a bhikkhu who has committed an offense less severe than a *pārājika* offense[1] has committed a great evil, tantamount to destroying the teaching, I do not agree. The teaching can be damaged not only through the four pārājika. However, I have left the text as it is. Bearing in mind all of you who are searching for knowledge and understanding, who desire happiness and wish to gain wisdom, I have endeavored to translate this teaching from the northern Siamese dialect to the central Siamese so that it can be heard on a wider scale and so become a beacon of wisdom. In my translation, I have chosen only those parts dealing with happiness, suffering, heaven, and nibbāna, which I felt would be of use to the reader. As for those parts that were repetitious, convoluted, and not practicable, I have not included them here.

Phra Dhammadhīrarājmahāmunī
(Siricando, Jun)
Wat Borom Niwat, Bangkok
Translator

The Sutta

evamme sutaṁ, ekaṁ samayaṁ bhagavā sāvatthiyaṁ viharati jetavane anāthapiṇḍikassa ārāme tatra kho āyasmā girimānando ābādhiko hotī'ti.

Now I will expound a sutta referred to by the ancients as the *Girimānanda Sutta*, which goes as follows: At the time of the First Great Council, the five hundred great elders had convened and were waiting for Venerable Ānanda, who was still practicing calm and insight meditation and had not yet realized arahantship, to join the council. Once Ānanda had attained arahantship, he entered the fourth absorption, taking the earth *kasiṇa* as his meditation object, and appeared spontaneously on his seat in the midst of the assembly, allaying all doubts as to his attainment of arahantship at the Sattapaṇṇa Cave. When he had thus declared his attainment of the state "beyond learning" (*asekhabhūmi*), the assembly of bhikkhus, with Venerable Mahā Kassapa at the head, invited him to ascend the Dhamma seat and expound the Suttanta Piṭaka. In time he came to the *Girimānanda Sutta*. Venerable Mahā Kassapa asked him, "Ānanda! This sutta known as the *Girimānanda Sutta*, to whom did the Buddha expound it, where was it expounded, and what was the occasion of its expounding? What were the details of the teaching? May the Venerable Ānanda now please make it known."

atha kho āyasmā ānando: Then Ānanda Thera, seated atop the Dhamma seat, having been invited by the assembly, recited this sutta, which begins with the opening *evamme sutaṁ*: "I, Ānanda, heard from the jewel of the Blessed One's mouth as follows."

ekaṁ samayaṁ: "At one time the Blessed One, Fully Enlightened Buddha, was staying at the Jetavana Vihāra, which had been built and offered by Anāthapiṇḍika the merchant, close to the city of Sāvatthī. At that time the venerable one known as Girimānanda Thera—*ābādhiko*—was stricken with a grave illness, more painful than he could bear. The venerable one sent word for me, Ānanda, to go to his residence and addressed me:

"'Ānanda, I, Girimānanda, am stricken with a grave illness, more painful than I can bear, and am unable to go to the Blessed One's presence. May you, Ānanda, convey the news of my grave illness to the Blessed One, so that he may have compassion on me and make the pain that now racks my body disappear.'

"Having heard the venerable one's words, I, Ānanda, went to the Blessed One and conveyed to him in its entirety the news of the illness and pain as related to me by Venerable Girimānanda."

atha kho: "At that time the Blessed One, hearing the news of the Venerable Girimānanda's illness, said to me:

"'Ānanda! Hasten back to Girimānanda's dwelling.' Then the Blessed One continued: *visuddhacitte ānanda dve saññā sutvā so ābādho ṭhānaso paṭipassambheyya*—'Ānanda, when you reach Girimānanda's dwelling, convey to him these two reflections: the reflection on physicality (*rūpasaññā*) and the reflection on mentality (*nāmasaññā*). That is to say, physicality, this entire body, and mentality, the mind and its concomitants—abandon them. Do not hold the body or the mind and its concomitants to be your self or think of them as belonging to you, any of them. In truth these things are merely externals.

"'Ānanda! If this body were really our self, then when it became old and decrepit, shortsighted, hard of hearing, wizened, loose-toothed, and racked with pain, we could force it as we wished not to be that way. But this we cannot do. Whether it becomes ill, old, or dies, the body goes about its business, and we are powerless to prevent it. When we die, there isn't one part that we can take with us. If the body really were our self, we could probably take it with us.

"'Ānanda! The mind and its concomitants, too, are not the self and do not belong to us. If the mind and its concomitants were us or belonged to us, then we could control them as we wished, saying, "May my mind be like this, may it not be like that; may it be happy and at ease at all times and never experience suffering or distress." But this is not the case. Whatever the mind wants to think, it goes ahead and thinks; it comes and goes of its own accord. Because both the body and the mind are *anattā*, neither self nor belonging to self, you should give up all attachment to them.

"'Go, Ānanda, and convey these two reflections—that is, physicality and mentality as anattā, neither self nor belonging to self—to Girimānanda in full. When Girimānanda hears them, the illness and pain will entirely disappear from his body, and quickly at that.' *Bhante Ariyakassapa*: Venerable Ariyakassapa, leader of this assembly, thus did the Blessed One address me."

Tadanantaram: "Following that, the Blessed One said to me, 'Ānanda! Be it our own body, the bodies of other people, or the bodies of animals, they are merely piles of bones, every one of them. There is no treasure, no jewel, no gold or silver ingot to be found anywhere within them. Nothing that could be a self, either within the body or within the mind and its properties, can be found. It is all anattā, void of essence. All people—women, men, laypeople, or renunciants—who contemplate and see clearly mentality and physicality, the mind and its concomitants, as not-self, will obtain immeasurable benefits, like the novice Subhadda: he simply contemplated the word *aṭṭhimiñjaṁ*—bone marrow—taking bones as his theme of meditation, and his mind became clear and bright. He developed penetrating insight into the nature of his body, attaining to the immaculate truth, all on account of maintaining the reflection on bones and seeing anattā clearly.

"'Ānanda! [When developing] *maraṇasaññā* (contemplation on death), *aṭṭhikasaññā* (contemplation on bones), *paṭikūlasaññā* (contemplation on the body as ugly and loathsome, full of worms and a great many creatures in the large and small intestines, with its sinews and putrid substances), [we see that] everything in this body is void; it has nothing within it that can be said to be ours. We think being born is happiness, but in fact it is just searching for happiness. If we were to speak correctly, we would have to say that we are born to suffer, born to be hurt, get sick and diseased, born to get old, and born to die, born to be separated from each other, born to be deprived of happiness. If we really look into this happiness, we will see that it's only a small amount, much less than the suffering. You may think that sleeping is a form of happiness, but if you care to really look into it, you will see that it is only suffering. Whoever contemplates things as explained here by the Tathāgata[2] will obtain a sign. Committing it firmly to memory, it becomes a cause for realizing the path, fruit, and nibbāna in the present moment without a doubt.

"'Ānanda! The wise, those skilled in wisdom, who develop the recollection on unattractiveness and aspire to nibbāna, take the unattractiveness (*asubha*) within themselves as their object of meditation. If they were to take outward unattractiveness as their object, they would not have full wisdom, since they would be still relying on memory. By taking the inward unattractiveness as a meditation object, they reach full wisdom, which is insight knowledge.

"'Ānanda! Those who desire nibbāna should clearly see the unattractiveness within themselves. If they are unable to see it, they should develop the perception of loathsomeness (*paṭikūlasaññā*) in themselves, thus: "This body of ours, even when it is alive, is already repulsive and loathsome. If there were no skin enfolding it, it would be positively hideous. It is only when it is wrapped in skin that we can bear to look at it. In truth, this body exists only because of the in-breaths and out-breaths. Without the in- and out-breaths, this body would quickly rot and disintegrate, becoming in turn food for various kinds of creatures such as worms."

"'Even this in- and out-breath, the lord of life, is anattā, neither self nor belonging to self. If it wants to stay, it stays; when it wants to cease, it ceases; we cannot force it according to our desires. Once our body is deprived of in- and out-breaths, its own attractiveness and the attractiveness of others, such as wife, children, and possessions, all vanish. Looking left or right we see no wife, children, or grandchildren. We are left to lie alone in the cemetery, utterly devoid of friends.

"'Ānanda! One who contemplates the thirty-two repulsive meditation objects, seeing the corpse within oneself, can be said to be aspiring to the happiness of nibbāna. The way to develop the meditation on unattractiveness in sequence is to first contemplate "hair of the head" (kesā), seeing it as unattractive and considering it as not self. Then to contemplate "hair of the body" (lomā), seeing it as unattractive and not self. Then to contemplate "teeth" (dantā), seeing them as unattractive and not self. Then to contemplate "nails" (nakhā), seeing them as unattractive and not self. Then to contemplate "skin" (taco) and so on according to the sequence until one reaches "brain in the skull" (matthake matthaluṅgaṁ), seeing it all as unattractive and not self.

"'Ānanda! The Tathāgata has here explained in detail, broadly from beginning to end, but in fact for one who is wise it is only necessary to contemplate "impermanent, suffering, and not-self" (aniccaṁ, dukkhaṁ, anattā). The wise person, when developing the meditation on unattractiveness, does not contemplate all the parts from beginning to end, because that would be too slow. One only needs to look at one of these parts, throwing it under the heading of "impermanent, suffering, and not-self," and one can thereby comfortably attain path, fruit, and nibbāna.

"'The development of the meditation on unattractiveness is in order to arouse weariness with one's body, which we see as attractive and desirable. By contemplating all things, both internal and external, as rotten and decayed, we can lift ourselves above the power of the defilement of desire.

"'The wise, knowing this, should delight neither in their own bodies nor the bodies of others, be they male or female, nor in material objects, no matter how delicate and refined they may be, because all love is a mass of defilements. If you can keep your mind from falling into this mass of defilements, you will attain happiness both in this life and the next. As long as the mind is still messed up with the mass of defilements, even if you do experience happiness, it will only be in this present life. In future lives you can expect no happiness, only suffering. The wise, when developing this meditation of the recollection of unattractiveness (asubhānussati kammaṭṭhāna) based on these thirty-two parts, should totally renounce this mass of defilements and desire.

"'Only when one knows and practices accordingly will the wholesome fruits arise. If one simply knows but does not practice accordingly, no benefit will be obtained, because one has not given up defilements and desire. It is like a man who has fallen into a fire—as soon as he realizes he is in the fire, he strives to the utmost to get out, to escape the heat. If one knows one has fallen into a fire but makes no effort to get out, how can one escape burning? In the same way, one who knows that something is harmful but does not give it up does not escape from harm.

"'Ānanda! One who knows but does not practice accordingly cannot be called "one who knows," because no path or fruit has arisen for that person. The Tathāgata allows the establishment of this teaching so that people, knowing what is harmful, will give it up. He does not establish the teaching just to be read, listened to, or recited for fun. All those individuals who are experiencing misery in the human and netherworlds are doing so for no other reason than the defilements of desire and craving. As long as one has not transcended defilements, desire and craving, one has not transcended the misery of the netherworlds. One who has not transcended defilements, desire and craving, no matter how diligently one makes merit and performs good works, can expect at most only the happiness of the human and celestial worlds, but will not experience the happiness of nibbāna.

"'If you really want nibbāna, whether you are a man or a woman, you must shave your head and go forth[3] in the Buddhist teaching. If you can do this, you will be practicing close to nibbāna. This is because the City of Nibbāna is void of defilements and desire. The human and celestial worlds are nests of defilements and desire, unlike the City of Nibbāna. The wise person, aspiring to the happiness of nibbāna, should go forth in the Buddhist teaching and devote oneself to developing calm and insight. Do not lose your way in the world. If you merely desire nibbāna but do not know the way to it, you will wind up ascending to the formless brahma realms (*arūpabrahma*),[4] which is losing your way in the world and rebirth, and straying further and further from nibbāna.

"'The making of merit and doing of good works are not for the purpose of being borne away somewhere by that merit, but simply for the sake of extinguishing defilements. Do not think that once you have made merit and skill, that merit and skill will somehow lift you up to nibbāna. It is not like that. Merit is made for the purpose of extinguishing defilements, and then you can go to nibbāna. Defilements and desire lie within us: if we ourselves do not quell them, who will? The root and source of all defilements and desire lies within us, and if we cannot quell them, it will be impossible to reach the happiness of nibbāna.'"

Tadanantaraṁ: "Following that, the Blessed One continued: 'Ānanda!—*nibbānaṁ nagaraṁ nāma*—What we call the "City of Nibbāna" is located at the world's end. Wherever the end of the world is, that's where you will find nibbāna. Nibbāna is an immense city, a place of incomparable happiness. This phrase *the world's end* does not refer to space (*ākāsaloka*) or the universe (*cakkavāḷaloka*). The lower periphery of space and the universe extends only as far as the earth. The earth is supported by water, beneath which is wind to a thickness of 940,000 yojanas.[5] Beneath the wind is infinite space. The lower extremity of the universe goes only as far as the wind. In breadth, the universe is limited by the Ananta universe,[6] beyond which is simply empty space. Thus, we say that in breadth the universe extends only to the Ananta universe.

"'The upper limits of the universe extend only as far as the formless brahma worlds. The Buddha calls these four formless brahma worlds the brahma nibbāna, or worldly nibbāna. The worldly nibbāna is still not the limit of the universe. The nibbāna of the Buddha, which is called transcendent nibbāna, is the ultimate extremity. Beyond the four formless brahma worlds there is only empty space. For this reason, we say that the upper limit of the universe extends only to the formless brahma worlds. The Buddha says that you must not understand that the wind supporting the water, the Ananta universe, and the formless brahma worlds are the limits of the world, and that nibbāna is to be found at these limits. Those places cannot be reached by physical effort or by any means of transport, such as elephant or horse. Do not think that nibbāna lies at these extremities of the world, or that it lies at this or that place, or that it lies anywhere at all. But that nibbāna does lie at the end of the world is the truth, of this there is no doubt. You should all study and see the world, know the world clearly: then you will see nibbāna. Nibbāna lies at this end of the world.

"'Ānanda! All those people who have reached the end of the world, who have left the world, can be said to have reached nibbāna and know of themselves that they have transcended suffering and dwell in constant ease and contentment, entirely free of agitation and despair. As long as one has not yet reached the end of the world and has not yet left the world, one cannot be said to have reached nibbāna and must endure the large and small tribulations of repeated rebirths and deaths and endless comings and goings.

"'Those people who desire nibbāna but who know not what nibbāna is like or where it is to be found and do not understand generosity (*dāna*), morality (*sīla*), concentration (*samādhi*), and wisdom (*paññā*), which are the path to nibbāna, will have great difficulty reaching nibbāna. It is like two people, one blind and the other clear-sighted, wanting to swim across a great river: of the two, which would you expect to reach the other shore first? The one with clear sight must arrive first. It is with extreme difficulty that the blind person would arrive at the other shore, perhaps even drowning in the middle of the river, on account of not knowing or seeing where the other shore lies. In the same way, for one who does not know and does not realize where nibbāna is or what it is like and does not understand the path leading to nibbāna, but simply desires to go there, arriving will only occur with the utmost difficulty and duress. That person might even die before seeing so much as a shadow of nibbāna. The practitioner should understand that nibbāna lies at the end of this world and that morality (*sīla*), concentration (*samādhi*), and wisdom (*paññā*) are the path to nibbāna. If you understand this, there is some hope of eventually reaching nibbāna. But even with this understanding, you will have to exert the utmost effort to get there, like the person with clear sight swimming to the other shore who still must strive to the utmost to get there.

"'Ānanda! Those people who aspire to nibbāna should first study and know it thoroughly. Once they know it clearly, whether they reach it or not is no distress to them. But if they do not know it, but merely want it, they will be in store for a lot of suffering. It is like a man who desires some object but does not know that object: even if that object were right in front of him, he would be unable to take it. Even though it is there, it does not serve any purpose, and that man's desire is unrequited; as a result he experiences great suffering. One who desires nibbāna but does not know nibbāna suffers in this way. You may think, "It does not matter if I do not know it; just by wanting it I should get it," but this kind of thinking is wrong and not at all useful. Even those who do know nibbāna and strive their utmost to attain it will attain it only with great difficulty. How is one who does not know or understand nibbāna to attain it? To say nothing of nibbāna: in all undertakings, such as silver- or goldsmithing, metallurgy, carpentry, drawing, and so on, it is necessary to know in the mind, or to see an example with one's own eyes, before one can do it. One who desires nibbāna must likewise study and know nibbāna before one can attain it. How could one possibly attain it simply through desiring and not knowing it?

"'Ānanda! People should thoroughly study and know the way to nibbāna and not be heedless. Then if they want to go, they can, and if they do not want to go, they don't have to. Once they see the way to nibbāna and the desire is there, they should practice the way to attain nibbāna with an inspired heart. Even if they do not attain it at that time, they will have developed the conditioning factors for attaining it in the future. Those who do not know, even if they want to go or they come very close to it, will be unable to get there because of their wrong understanding. They mistake it to be here and there, and so go astray following after their wrong ideas, wandering through the realm of *saṁsāra* with no chance of getting to nibbāna.

"Ānanda, those who do not know, are not clear, or do not understand nibbāna should not teach nibbāna to others. If they do insist on teaching others, they will only lead them astray, making bad kamma for themselves. They should teach only the way to human happiness and celestial happiness: teaching, for example, about generosity, the five precepts, the eight precepts, the bases for wholesome action, proper conduct toward one's parents, serving one's teachers and preceptors, and developing merit and skillfulness—things that are of use to oneself and others. With just this much, one may attain sufficient human and celestial treasures. As for the happiness of transcendent nibbāna, one who truly aspires to it must first maintain the ten precepts or the Pāṭimokkha[7] precepts in order to be considered to have come close to the way and to truly have a chance of attaining it. Even then, those who are developing the way to nibbāna should know of their teacher that they really do know the way to nibbāna before going to study with them. If they go to study in the presence of a teacher who does not clearly know or is not clear about the way, they will not attain the transcendent nibbāna, because the way to transcendent nibbāna is extremely difficult to learn. This is because beings mostly take delight in sensual pleasures, which are the enemy of nibbāna.'" *Bhante ariya-kassapa*: "Venerable Ariyakassapa, thus did the Buddha instruct me, Ānanda. May the Order so understand it."

Tadanantaraṁ: "The Buddha then continued his instruction as follows: 'Ānanda, those people who aspire to nibbāna should search for a good teacher, one who has attained to peace and is not heedless, because nibbāna is not like other things. With other things, if you make a mistake, there is a chance for correction or the repercussions are small, because those things are not particularly subtle or profound. But nibbāna is the subtlest and most profound of all things: if one makes a mistake with this, one will incur great suffering, losing one's way in the world and going far astray of happiness. One's benefit is lost on account of the teacher. If one obtains a teacher who is good and right, one will attain a result that is good and right. If one obtains a teacher who does not know, who is not good or right, one attains the wrong results and suffers accordingly. You will be lost in the world and led astray of the path, wandering aimlessly through the world of rebirth for unreckonable ages. It is like someone who is going to lead us to a certain village, but that person does not know that village. When we also do not know the way, how can such a guide take us to our destination? In the same way, a teacher who does not know nibbāna, but yet tries to lead us there, will only lead us astray, endlessly coming and going, dying and being reborn in the cycle of rebirth, with no way of reaching nibbāna, like the guide who does not know the village we are going to. There's no way we could reach it. This is how it is.

"'Many are those in this world who have met with teachers who do not really know and have attained bad results accordingly, such as Aṅgulimāla. He went to study with a teacher who had wrong view and obtained a bad result, becoming a great bandit, murdering a thousand people. It was only because the Tathāgata became aware of his condition within his net of omniscience, took pity on him, and instructed him to renounce his evil ways [that he did so] and then only with the greatest difficulty. If it were not for the Tathāgata, Aṅgulimāla would have had to suffer for countless lives in the realm of rebirth (saṁsāra).

"'Ānanda, one who does not know nibbāna should on no account teach the way to nibbāna to others. They all want to teach, but what can they teach if they do not know? It is like someone who has never been a draftsman or tradesman of some kind trying to teach others. What can they teach? They themselves do not know or understand: what are they going to teach others? All they can give is words, but they cannot set an example for others to see. What can anyone be expected to learn from them? They provide no example to see, no example to follow. The teacher must do it first. If he cannot do it, then he should not teach others. If he insists on teaching, he will only lead others to ruin, causing them to lose their way in the world, making much bad kamma for himself in the process.' Thus did the Buddha instruct me, Ānanda."

Tadanantaraṁ: "The Buddha then instructed as follows: 'Ānanda, one who is going to teach nibbāna must clearly know for oneself that nibbāna lies in such a place and is of such characteristics. One must know this clearly. If one only says the words "nibbāna, nibbāna," but one's mind is not really clear on it, one should not be believed. One must know it clearly within one's own mind before one is qualified to teach others. Anyone who clearly knows nibbāna, whether a child or an adult, is qualified to be a teacher and should be revered as a teacher. But no matter how great and eminent a person may be, if that person does not truly see or understand nibbāna; they should not be upheld as a teacher.

"'Ānanda, if you want to attain a particular kind of happiness, you must know that happiness beforehand. If you desire the happiness of nibbāna, you should know the happiness of nibbāna. If you want the happiness of the human and heaven realms, you must know the happiness of the human and heaven realms before you can attain them. If you do not know a particular kind of happiness, you will be unable to create it. This is unlike the suffering of hell. Whether you know the suffering of hell or not, if you have committed evil kamma, you go to hell just the same. The more ignorant you are of hell, the less chance there is of ever escaping it. No matter how much merit you make, you will be unable to escape.

"'This does not mean that generosity and making merit do not lead to merit (puñña). The happiness that arises from merit does exist, but it is a happiness that has not yet transcended the suffering of hell. As long as you do not yet know or see hell, you have not transcended it. If, having fallen into hell, you know the way out and you want to get out, you can escape it. You must know clearly that hell is at such and such a place and that it is like this or that, and you must clearly know the way out of it. The way out of hell is the ten precepts and the Pāṭimokkha precepts. If you know this, then when you want to get out, you can, and if you do not want to leave it, you don't have to. Both those who know and those who do not know will experience the suffering of hell just the same if they are heedless. As for happiness in the human and heaven realms and the happiness of nibbāna, you must know them first before they can be attained. If you do not know or understand them, you will have no way of attaining them. They are different in this way.

"'Ānanda, if you want to know about hell, heaven, and nibbāna, you should know them before you die, while you are still alive. If you want to escape the suffering of hell, quickly escape it before you die, and if you want the happiness of the human or heaven realms or of nibbāna, quickly strive to find those kinds of happiness before you die. To think that after you die you will be able to escape the suffering of hell, or after you die you will go to heaven or nibbāna, is useless. This will lead to no benefit.

"'Do not go thinking that while you are alive there is one kind of happiness, and that when you die there is another kind of happiness. This is truly a wrong understanding, because there is only one mind. When you are alive, it is this mind; when you die, it is this same mind. Whatever kind of suffering you have when you are alive, that is the kind of suffering you will experience when you die. Whatever kind of happiness you have when you are alive, that is the kind of happiness you will experience when you die; of this there is no doubt. If you neither see nor understand the nature of suffering and happiness in this way while you are alive, once you die you will be even worse off: how will you be able to see or understand things then?' The Buddha instructed me, Ānanda, in this way."

... "'Ānanda! The happiness of nibbāna is of two kinds: raw and ripe. When one who is still a living being experiences the happiness of nibbāna, this is called the raw nibbāna. When one dies and experiences the happiness of nibbāna, this is called the ripe nibbāna. There are only these two kinds of nibbāna. The so-called "worldly nibbāna" or "brahma nibbāna" is a deluded kind of nibbāna and is not counted here. The raw kind of nibbāna is the important kind. You should know it, see it, and attain it before you die. If you do not attain this raw nibbāna, there is no way you will attain the ripe nibbāna after you die, even more so if you do not even know or understand it. Even if you do know it and see it and strive to attain it, it is extremely difficult to do so. Those who think that there is only one kind of nibbāna and it is attained after one dies are deluded. The raw nibbāna cannot be considered such a profound kind of happiness as the ripe nibbāna, but it is an incomparably subtle kind of happiness. It is just that it is still touched by the "smell" or "taste" of suffering, and so is not as subtle as the ripe nibbāna. Ripe nibbāna is unadulterated by the smell or taste of suffering and is void of all things. Even so, you must attain the raw nibbāna first.

"'Ānanda, consider the raw nibbāna as like the great earth. Whatever the great earth is like, we must make ourselves like that. If we can do so, we can be said to have reached the raw nibbāna. If we cannot do so but simply talk about attaining, no matter how much we talk about it, we will not be able to attain it. If we wish to attain nibbāna, we must make our minds like the great earth, and that is not easy to do. One must strive with the utmost difficulty in order to do so. The great earth is such that no matter what harmful things people or animals may do or say, it is unmoved by anger or bitterness. Making the mind like the great earth means to let go of the mind; do not attach to or cherish one's mind as one's own, but reflect that one has only come to live with it temporarily. Whatever it wants to think or feel, one need not follow it. One should understand that we are only living here in waiting for the day we die: of what use are material possessions and the body, which are externals? Even the mind, which is important and an internal thing, must be let go of and not held to as belonging to a self. I have given here a brief explanation sufficient for your understanding.

"'Ānanda, the phrase *let go of the mind* means to relinquish greed (*lobha*), anger (*kodha*), and delusion (*moha*), to give up the good and bad that people talk about, such as gain and loss, status and loss of status, praise and blame, happiness and suffering—to neither delight in nor sorrow over them. In regard to our supports and requisites, such as food, clothing, shelter, and medicine, we should give up greed and delusion in them. Be content with little in these supports. This does not mean we are prohibited from eating, wearing clothes, or using shelters and medicines. No, it means to give up indecision over those supports. That is, when one obtains fine things, one uses fine things; when one obtains coarse things, one uses coarse things. One uses according to what one obtains, and does not let the mind become clouded by greed, anger, or delusion. This is what is called "letting go of the mind." If you are still choosing your supports, allowing greed, anger, and delusion to dominate you on account of one or another of the four supports, you are still clinging to your mind and cannot attain nibbāna. If you can relinquish greed, anger, and delusion in regard to the supports, you can be said to have made your mind like the great earth and to have reached nibbāna.

"'The question arises here: why are we told to not hold on to the mind? If we do not hold on to it, then where do we put it, since it is no one else's mind but our own? We live right now because we have this mind, and without it we would simply die. If we let go of this mind, what would we be able to see or know? The answer is that those who believe that the mind is really their own are deluded. In fact, it is not our own mind. If it were our mind, we could probably control it as we wished, to prevent it from aging, from dying, or from anything else, because it was ours. In fact, the mind is only a wind that arises for the world. It is not *our* mind. The world was established before us, and only later have we come into it with this "wind" of the mind. If it were our mind, we would bring it into birth, but once we die, that mind would be gone; then who would be born after that? It is not anyone's mind, but something belonging to the world. When a person is born, one brings this wind with one, and then it becomes one's mind. Actually, it belongs to the world. What we call a person's mind is only the knowing of merit, skillful actions, evil, unskillful actions, and the knowing of suffering, happiness, heaven, and nibbāna. It is made use of only so far as the achievement of nibbāna. Once one has achieved nibbāna, the mind must be returned to the world. If one cannot let go of the mind, that is harmful and one will not be able to reach nibbāna. This is the answer here.'"

Tadanantaram: "The Buddha then continued, 'Ānanda, those people who have mistakenly wound up in the formless brahma realms, which are void of awareness, were all of them aspiring to nibbāna, but they simply did not know how to let go of their minds and be done with suffering. They did not know how to let go of the mind that they had lived with in the world. They thought the mind was their own and that nibbāna existed up above. They wanted to take the mind up there and enjoy happiness there. Once they died, this idea led them up to the place where there is no form, in accordance with their mind's preconceptions.

"'Ānanda, those who have strayed into the formless brahma realms will only attain transcendent nibbāna after a very long time, because the lifespan of the formless brahmas is extremely long. You cannot say how long it is, and that is why it is called the mundane nibbāna. It differs only in that consciousness (*viññāṇa*) has not yet ceased. If consciousness were quelled, it would be transcendent nibbāna. As for the happiness and well-being in the two different kinds of nibbāna, they are equally exalted, but the mundane nibbāna is simply not the final nibbāna. Once the power of the *jhāna*[8] is depleted, there will once more be birth, aging, sickness and death, good and evil, benefit and fault, happiness and suffering in full measure. For that reason, there is no one who desires the brahma nibbāna; they all without exception aspire to the transcendent nibbāna, but because they do not know how to let go of their consciousness, they mistakenly end up as formless brahmas. Transcendent nibbāna is void of consciousness. Wherever there is consciousness, there will be birth, aging, sickness, and death. Transcendent nibbāna is void of consciousness, and so has no birth, aging, sickness, and death. It has only happiness and well-being void of objects (*āmisa*). There is no happiness comparable with the happiness of nibbāna. Birth, death, good, evil, merit, sin, benefit, harm, happiness, unhappiness, difficulty and distress, misery, illness, and pain do not exist in nibbāna.' Thus did the Buddha address me, Ānanda."

Tadanantaraṁ: "The Buddha then continued his instruction as follows. 'Ānanda, those who aspire to nibbāna but who cannot yet let go of their minds, who still yearn for happiness, thinking that nibbāna is here or there, and that they will have their minds go live there in happiness, are afraid that if they let go of their minds there would be nothing left to experience happiness. They hold on to their minds through coveting happiness, and so they do not rise above the brahma nibbāna.

"'Ānanda, in instructing to let go of the mind, the Tathāgata gives the ultimate, essential point in order to make it easy to understand. Letting go of the mind is letting go of happiness and suffering, letting go of sin and merit, benefit and harm, letting go of greed, anger, and delusion, letting go of gain, rank, blame, and praise, as if you had no heart. That is what it means to make your mind like the great earth. If you cannot do this, do not expect to attain transcendent nibbāna. Whenever you can make your mind like the great earth, then you can expect to attain the transcendent nibbāna, and you will certainly attain it at that very moment. Nibbāna is something extremely difficult to attain. Within a hundred thousand people it would be extremely difficult for even one to attain it.

"'Ānanda, those who have not fully developed the practice of the noble path, who are still worldlings (*puthujjana*) thick with defilements and lacking in wisdom, will be incapable of letting go of the mind and making it like the great earth. The reason they cannot let go of the mind is because they still think of the body and mind as being their own, and so they must endure suffering in the world, being born and dying in endless repetition. Ānanda, only the wise and the worthy can let go of the mind and become like the great earth, because they do not cling to themselves. They can settle their minds like the great earth and so attain nibbāna. As for those who hold on to their minds and cannot let go, they are all fools. The worthy ones see not-self (*anattā*) clearly. They hold on to their minds only as far as it takes to know merit and sin, benefit and harm, what is and what is not useful, to know morality, generosity, the skillful and the unskillful, to know the way to happiness and suffering in the human and heavenly realms and nibbāna. Once they reach the final destination, they let go of all those things as being not-self (*anattā*). Fools hold on to themselves, seeing their body as being themselves, and so they cannot let go.

"'Ānanda, if you aspire to the happiness of nibbāna, leave your mind with all worldly things. The happiness of worldly things exists only in the six sense faculties (*indriya*). Of those six sense faculties, the mind is the master. The remaining five senses of eyes, ears, nose, tongue, and body are the five sense pleasures. The five senses are what fabricate happiness for the Great King Mind. The eye sense sees various beautiful visual objects and brings the happiness to Great King Mind. The ear sense, hearing words and sounds that are pleasant and soothing, brings happiness and pleasure to Great King Mind. The nose sense, when it smells odors that are fragrant, brings happiness to Great King Mind. The tongue sense, when it partakes of foods that are tasty and fine, brings happiness and pleasure to Great King Mind. The body sense, when it makes contact with feathered pillows and fine beds and bedecks itself in beautiful clothes and jewelry and partakes of sense pleasures, brings happiness and pleasure to Great King Mind. Great King Mind is simply the mind. The mind is the master, the only one who receives the happiness and pleasure. It is the duty of the other five senses to bring happiness to the mind. The five senses are therefore called sense pleasures (*kāmaguṇa*). The happiness in this world consists only of these five sense pleasures. Whether you are a king of a large or small country, or even in the heavenly world (*devaloka*), you have only these five sense pleasures.

"'Ānanda, those who wish to take themselves to the happiness of nibbāna must let go of worldly happiness. If they cannot let go of it, they will not attain the happiness of nibbāna. If they cannot let go of worldly happiness, they won't be able to transcend suffering, because worldly happiness is a happiness that is tainted with suffering. When you take up happiness, you are simply taking up suffering. If you don't let go of happiness, that means you're not letting go of suffering. If you think that you can just take up happiness and not the suffering, this is not possible, because happiness and suffering are interconnected. If you do not let go of happiness, that means you have not transcended suffering.

"'Ānanda, extremely rare are those people who know that happiness and suffering are attached. There is only the Tathāgata, endowed with the tenfold gnosis (*dasabalañāṇa*). Those people who are still foolish worldlings believe that happiness is one thing and suffering is another, and that when we take up happiness, we get only happiness, and if we don't take up suffering, we won't have suffering. Because they do not know that happiness and suffering are attached, they do not transcend suffering. Whoever wants to transcend suffering must lay down happiness; in so doing they will also lay down suffering. Who would have the ability to split happiness and suffering? Even the Tathāgata does not have such a marvelous power. If the Tathāgata were able to split happiness from suffering, why would I wish to enter nibbāna? I would just take up happiness and enjoy only happiness in the world. That would be sufficient for me. But it isn't like that. I searched for only happiness, but there was no way to get it. So I laid down happiness. Once I had laid down happiness, there was no need to lay down suffering—it was already gone, it could not stay. Thus I attained nibbāna and transcended the mass of suffering.

"'Ānanda, worldly happiness, if you examine it closely, is simply a mass of suffering. They are bosom friends; no one is able to split them apart. The Tathāgata was deathly afraid of suffering and could find no way to overcome it. I therefore desired to enter nibbāna because of that fear of suffering.' Thus did the Buddha instruct me, Ānanda."

Tadanantaraṁ: "The Buddha then continued his instruction as follows: 'Ānanda. Skillful conditions (*kusaladhamma*) and unskillful conditions (*akusaladhamma*) are simply the mass of 1,500 defilements (*kilesa*). The neutral condition (*abyākatadhamma*) is nibbāna. Once you are able to transcend the skillful and unskillful conditions, that is a factor of arahantship and true nibbāna. If you cannot yet transcend skillful and unskillful conditions, then you have not reached neutrality (*abyākatadhamma*), and there is no factor of arahantship, no factor of nibbāna. Ānanda, skillfulness is happiness, and unskillfulness is suffering. The masses of happiness and suffering arise together, and no one can take them apart. When you take up skillfulness, the mass of happiness, you get unskillfulness, the mass of suffering, even though you did not actually take it up.

"'Ānanda, a person who aspires to nibbāna should first let go of worldly happiness or skillfulness in order to attain it. If one is not yet able to do so and cannot yet realize nibbāna, one should first take up skillfulness in order to attain the happiness of the human and heavenly worlds. But with only this much one will not be able to transcend suffering. If you know that you cannot yet transcend suffering, then hold on to the skillful as a bridge to happiness. If you know that you cannot transcend suffering and then go and discard skillfulness, you will be even worse off: you will only go to the mass of unskillfulness, the mass of evil. Once you fall into the mass of unskillfulness, that unskillfulness will lead you to the painful feelings of the four nether realms, where no worldly happiness can be found. For that reason, as long as you have not yet reached nibbāna, practice merit and skillfulness to give yourself some happiness in this world and the next.' Bhante Venerable Ariyakassapa, thus did the Buddha instruct me."

Tadanantaraṁ: "The Buddha then continued his instruction as follows: 'Ānanda, the Tathāgata will teach you the ultimate points in brief, for ease of understanding. The ultimate is the mind (*citta*) and desire (*taṇhā*). The mind can be further analyzed into skillfulness, the mass of happiness, while desire can be analyzed further into unskillfulness, the mass of suffering. The root of suffering is the mind and desire. The mind is the one who thinks of the good and experiences happiness, while desire arises in response to that. The more happiness the mind has, the more desire creates suffering in response.

"'Ānanda, in the beginning, when the Tathāgata did not know that happiness and suffering were attached, I held on to the skillful mind, hoping to experience only happiness at all times and not allow the suffering. I applied myself to cultivating the skillful mind, but no matter how much happiness I attained, suffering would always follow in equal measure. Later I examined the matter with direct knowledge of the eye of wisdom and saw clearly that happiness and suffering are attached. Once I saw this, I examined further and searched for a way to separate happiness and suffering from each other, but it was so difficult, beyond my power. I was at my wits' end and could find no way to do it. So the Tathāgata laid down happiness, and left it with suffering. That is, I lay down the mind and left it with desire. Once I had let go of the mind with desire, the happiness of nibbāna came in and led me to the raw nibbāna at that very moment. Ānanda, once I had laid down the mind, there was neutrality; it is called "taking neutrality as mental object," which is a factor of arahantship. I entered nibbāna in this way.'

"Then the Buddha instructed me, Ānanda, as follows. 'Ānanda. The word *arahaṁ* applies not only to the Tathāgata; it is something that belongs to the world, for the purpose of saving all sentient beings. It is not the exclusive possession of the Tathāgata or of any one person. Ānanda! The Tathāgata is one far from defilements; thus I am called arahaṁ. All those who are without defilements have equally attained the status of arahaṁ. Those who are not yet without defilements, no matter how much they plead with the Tathāgata, saying *"arahaṁ, arahaṁ"* till the day they die, will not be able to attain the status of arahaṁ. They are merely reciting the words, thinking that the presence or absence of defilements is not important, but simply by praying for arahaṁ with their mouths or in their minds, the arahants will come and lead them to nibbāna. If you think like this, you are truly deluded. When you have not yet transcended the vulgar stain of defilements and you implore the arahants who are free of the stain of defilements to come and establish themselves within you, who are soiled with the vulgar stain of defilements, what chance is there of them coming? It is like a pond full of all kinds of rotten and putrid water, truly an object of loathing, and a man has fallen into it. If that man were to cry out to you, Ānanda, to go down into the stinking pond and join him, would you go? Ānanda, I tell you, if you were likely to go down into that pond with that man soiled by the putrid, stinking water, then perhaps an arahant would be likely to become established in the mind of a person soiled with defilements.

"'The arahants are pure and have transcended suffering (*dukkha*); they are not inclined toward any individual. Those who desire happiness should incline themselves toward the arahants, and they will freely give happiness to all. Do not disparage the arahants by saying that they choose among people. Whoever transcends the defilements and the objects of the senses has inclined toward the arahants. The arahants will help lead them to nibbāna to experience happiness with the arahants. The arahants do not choose or discriminate between people: it's just that those who are sunk in defilements do not incline themselves toward the arahants.

"'Ānanda, the Tathāgata inclined toward the arahants, and the arahants helped the Tathāgata to become the teacher of the world that he is today, because the arahant is a good person. You cannot expect them to associate with evil people; that would be against the custom. It is only fitting that the vulgar and inferior incline themselves toward the virtuous and superior person.' Venerable Mahā Kassapa, thus did the Buddha instruct me."

Tadanantaraṁ: "The Buddha then continued his instruction as follows: 'Ānanda, that which causes worldly beings to spin around in birth and death in the realm of saṁsāra, repeatedly enduring torture in the hell realms and being born in animal realms with no respite, is none other than defilements and desire, which deceive the minds of beings, preventing them from transcending the dangers of saṁsāra and attaining nibbāna. Whoever is ignorant of the mass of defilements will encounter only danger and experience endless suffering in the four nether realms.

"'Ānanda, you must catch desire. If you can catch it, when you experience suffering you will be able to see that you are not a self (*anattā*). If you cannot catch it, you will not be able to see yourself as not-self. All those people who have become students of the Tathāgata aspire to nibbāna. Whether they are superior or inferior is decided by their defilements. Nibbāna is a place devoid of defilements and desire. Whoever is diminished in defilements and desire is superior to one who is still thick with defilements and desire. Whoever is established in regular morality, which is the five precepts, is still thick with defilements, but can nevertheless be said to have reduced the defilements on one level. Whoever is established in the observance (*uposatha*) precepts, that is the eight precepts, can be said to have diminished the defilements on two levels. If established in the ten precepts, one can be said to have diminished the defilements on three levels. One who enters the morality of the Pāṭimokkha, that is the 227 precepts, can be said to have reduced the defilements on four levels. The rewards are greater in accordance with the level of morality. Whoever has little morality has few rewards; whoever has much morality receives much reward in proportion to that morality.

"'Whoever is not established in the five precepts, no matter how learned and clever one may be, should not disparage one who maintains the five precepts. One who has the five precepts should be contented with one's own level of morality and should not disparage one who has the eight precepts. One who has the eight precepts should be content with one's own morality and should not disparage one who has ten precepts. One who has ten precepts should be content with one's own level of morality and should not disparage one who holds the precepts of the Pāṭimokkha. Any person who insists on disparaging one whose morality is higher than one's own is deluded and far from the path to happiness of the human and heavenly worlds and nibbāna.

"'Ānanda, a person who has no morality (*sīla*), who is void of any moral training, should not utter words of disparagement to one who has morality. Living outside of morality, one thinks that one is better than one who has morality and so utters careless words of disparagement—such people have much wrong view, have gone astray of the path, and are far from the happiness of the human and heavenly worlds. Ānanda, those who are established outside morality can be said to be sunk in defilements and still thickly bound by defilements. No matter how learned, knowledgeable, and clever they may be, they should not exalt themselves above those who have morality, because those who have no morality are still very far from nibbāna. One who has morality can be said to be close to nibbāna. Even though one knows nothing except the morality one adheres to, one is still better than one who has no morality, because one has fewer defilements. One who is still thick with defilements, no matter how much one knows and how conversant with the teachings one may be, should be respectful and reverent toward one who has morality in order to be conforming with the path to nibbāna. It would be a mistake and is very far from the path to nibbāna if one who is moral were to be reverential toward one who has no morality and who is thick with defilements.

"'Ānanda, you cannot judge only by knowledge and ignorance: we must take the renunciation of defilements as the gauge, because the attainment of nibbāna is entirely dependent on the renunciation of defilements. Once you have renounced defilements, even if you do not know much and know only that you have given up the defilements, you can attain nibbāna, which is free of the suffering of hell, and enjoy the happiness of heaven and nibbāna simply on account of having renounced defilements. That which causes us to experience pleasure and suffering these days is defilements. Once the defilements have been extinguished, that is the cause for experiencing happiness and becoming free of suffering. If you cannot renounce defilements, you will not attain happiness and neither will you become free of suffering.

"'Ānanda, the attainment of happiness is dependent on the renunciation of defilements. To have knowledge but to have not given up defilements is of no use whatsoever to that knowledgeable person. Even if one knows a hundred thousand texts or has infinite knowledge, it is simply knowledge and cannot be used for any purpose; there is no merit or skill (*puñña kusala*) or enjoyment of happiness on account of that knowledge. The Tathāgata does not praise one who has great knowledge but no morality. One who knows little but who is established in morality—that one I praise and acknowledge as a good person. Those who revere people who have defilements above those who have no defilements can be said to have placed the practice of morality around the wrong way, taking high for low and low for high. To believe in this way goes astray of the path to nibbāna. It is to be one who has wrong view (*micchādiṭṭhi*). The Tathāgata does not praise the exaltation of one who is thick with defilements above one who is void of defilements. The Tathāgata praises and approves reverence to those who are diminished in defilements and are close to nibbāna. Making merit, giving offerings, and doing that which is skillful, hoping that the merit and skillfulness will take you to nibbāna, is in vain if you do not know that the making of merit and practice of skillfulness are for the purpose of helping to extinguish defilements. You will be one who is lost in the world and gone astray of the way to nibbāna.

"'I do not say that the skillfulness that arises from practicing cultivation is not attained. In fact, it truly is skillful and meritorious, but it is simply a diversion from nibbāna. Any kind of practice of effort, cultivation, and making of merit, no matter how great, should be understood to be for the extinguishing and reduction of your own defilements and desire, so that you can transcend the mass of defilements. This is to walk the right path to nibbāna. Ānanda, practice according to the teaching I am giving you. Whoever does not practice accordingly should be understood as "outside the teaching of Buddha." Thus did the Buddha address me, Ānanda.'"

"The Buddha then continued, . . . 'Ānanda, a son of good family who goes forth in the Buddha's dispensation, who is a disciple of the Tathāgata, does so in order to quell the defilements, desiring not to be born into the world again. This is because defilements are the germ of continuation of the world. They cause the mind to delight in worldly things. Once there is birth, then there is pain, illness, aging, death, and separation; there is love and hate, abuse, fighting, hunger, deprivation, suffering, and destitution. The manifestations of defilements being thus, the Tathāgata allows the going forth for the quelling of defilements, in order to not allow them to be a germ for continuing the world. Knowing this, concentrate on maintaining morality for the quelling of defilements, and reflect in order to find a means for destroying defilements at the root.

"'Whether it be maintaining the Pāṭimokkha precepts or maintaining one of the thirteen *dhutaṅga* (austerity) practices, they are all contained within the word *sīla*. It isn't that you have to maintain every single kind of practice: maintaining the Pāṭimokkha precepts or the dhutaṅga practices is for no other benefit than extinguishing the defilements. When you know that the defilements are the root of the mass of suffering, the mass of harm, the mass of bad kamma (*pāpa*), then whatever practices are for lifting oneself out of that mass of defilements, you should perfect those practices. If practicing the Pāṭimokkha precepts and the dhutaṅga practices is not understood as being for the purpose of extinguishing the mass of defilements, it can be said to be empty practice. When we know that the practice is for the extinguishing of defilements and maintain [the precepts] for no other purpose, even if we only practice a little, not the full extent of the Pāṭimokkha precepts or dhutaṅga practices, we can be said to be maintaining the precepts in full, because we have grasped the root of defilements. It is like a man cutting down a tree: if he cuts it at the taproot, then the branches and twigs, while not directly cut, will die of themselves. If he cuts only the branches and twigs, but not the root, that tree may grow again.

"'Ānanda, a person who goes forth in this dispensation can be compared to that man cutting the tree. The going forth is not intended for any other purpose: it is only for extinguishing defilements. If you do not aspire to the extinguishing of defilements, then it's better not to go forth. If you go forth without the intention to extinguish defilements, any knowledge you have, no matter how grand it may be, is only empty knowledge. I do not say that being a clever and learned person is not good, meritorious, or skillful—the knowledge is good and meritorious and skillful—but it is knowledge that has gone astray of the path to nibbāna.

"'Ānanda, the Tathāgata gives this teaching in many a form in order to allow foolish, unenlightened beings to be inspired by it, so that they will be filled with belief and faith. Foolish people who do not see it as inspiring will not have belief and faith in the qualities of the Tathāgata. If I were to state it only in brief, they would not understand, unlike those who have much merit and good fortune, whose understanding would become great and extensive even with a brief teaching. Normally, for those who have real wisdom, they know for themselves with their own wisdom even without having to say anything. You don't have to go to much trouble explaining things. The Tathāgata has been put to so much trouble just on account of foolish, unenlightened beings. If I only give a little teaching, they don't understand because they think they are already fine.

"'In reality the knowledge of fools, no matter how much they have, is good only as far as their in- and out-breaths. Once the breath is gone, all that's left is putrefaction, and they lie prone on the earth with no essence to be found, full of only unclean things. You think that you are a learned and virtuous person, and having learning and virtue, you will not die? No matter how much knowledge you have, you cannot escape death. No matter how special your knowledge is, it all goes to death. No matter how much knowledge and virtue you have, it is all based on the earth. Your knowledge and virtue cannot escape the earth. When you still have breath, you are above the earth. Once the breath is gone, you are still on the earth. You cannot escape the earth. Why do you hold on to yourself? That you are filled with rotten and noxious things you do not know or see. You just see yourself as knowledgeable and virtuous and hold on to yourself. The Tathāgata is well and truly fed up with the knowledge and virtue of foolish, unenlightened beings.

"'Ānanda, normally those who are sages, who are wise, do not hold on to themselves, saying, "I am knowledgeable in this and that way." No matter how much knowledge they have, they do not hold on to themselves as do foolish, unenlightened beings. Foolish, unenlightened beings are far from nibbāna for the reason that they hold on to themselves. The more they hold on to themselves, the further they stray from nibbāna. This is because the doorway to nibbāna is extremely narrow. If you were to slice a strand of hair into three slivers, just to get one sliver through the doorway to nibbāna would be very difficult; it would not be able to pass. Therefore, if you want nibbāna, you should not hold on to yourself as being someone knowledgeable and virtuous, as an important person of high position. The more you hold on to yourself, the narrower is the doorway to nibbāna. That is why I say that foolish, unenlightened people are far from nibbāna: because they hold on to themselves.

"'Ānanda, a person who goes forth as a disciple of the Tathāgata and still allows oneself to suffer, I say, is a foolish, unenlightened being, a stupid person. Such a foolish person cannot be called a disciple of the Tathāgata. One who has gone forth and conducted oneself to be happy at all times: that is a true disciple of the Tathāgata. The Tathāgata hoped for happiness, that is why I went forth. If a person has gone forth and then proceeded to make oneself suffer, that person can be said to be incomparably foolish and of no wisdom. A wise person does not make suffering for oneself. It is the person without wisdom who makes oneself suffer. Not only those who have gone forth, but also householders who have no wisdom will also have trouble and suffering. The wise person, who is clever, having gone forth, considers and sees clearly what is of benefit and what is not of benefit. That person, considering and seeing clearly the moral precepts and practices, both the major and the minor, does not have to keep a whole lot of precepts in great number, but chooses just a few to keep and so is comfortable in body and mind. A foolish person keeps a great number of practices of various types and suffers through trying to keep too many. The wise person, choosing only that small number of practices that are true and real, receives happiness. It is like a clever man who goes into the forest to cut a tree to use for some task or other. Having felled the tree, he shaves off the bark and sapwood, leaving only the part he desires. Then he measures and cuts only that part that is appropriate to the work. He does not have to trouble himself with carrying. A person who is not clever, not fully understanding the task that needs to be done, having cut the tree, does not shave off what is not needed, afraid that he will lack something, because he doesn't understand the task. He then proceeds to carry it all, the bark, the sapwood, and pith, in full length, and is more and more wearied and troubled, because he is foolish and lacking in wisdom.

"'Ānanda, keeping jewels that are not good or of no value, even if you have them in the thousands, is not as good as keeping only one jewel that is good and precious. A jewel that is not good and has no value can't be sold, and keeping it would be of no use. You end up just looking after it to no purpose. A jewel that has value can be sold for a lot of money. If you keep it, it is useful to you. Studying sacred words and verses that are not good or auspicious, even if you study hundreds or thousands of them, is not as good as studying one sacred verse that is good and auspicious. It is the same with keeping the precepts and practices. When you know the benefit of morality and the observances, you don't have to follow a whole lot of them. When you do not know or understand, you keep so many that they are endless, and so you must suffer, like the man who doesn't understand the work and has to carry the whole tree, the bark and the sapwood, in its entire length. One who is clever observes the *vinaya* and the practices in moderation but receives sufficient reward, like the person who looks after just one gem or the person who studies just one good and auspicious sacred verse and so receives the benefit in full.

"'Ānanda, the Tathāgata wants you to go forth into homelessness in order to attain merit and skillfulness. What is merit and what is skillfulness? Merit and skillfulness are none other than the extinguishing of defilements. Observing any kind of practice or training rule (*vinaya*) that extinguishes many defilements is of great merit. If it extinguishes only few defilements, it is of little merit. If it does not extinguish defilements at all, it is of no merit at all. Sin and unskillfulness are none other than defilements and desire. However much you can extinguish defilements and desire, that is how much merit you obtain. If you cannot extinguish defilements and desire, then you have not attained merit or skillfulness at all. Those who do not know merit and sin understand that by going forth and maintaining the practices and precepts they will obtain merit, that merit is something outside of them, floating in the air. Having gone forth and keeping the practices, that merit will float in to them from various places such as the heavens above and transport them to heaven and nibbāna. Seeing wrongly in this way, they are all deluded.

"'Ānanda, those who do not know evil understand that evil is something outside of themselves. When an evil deed is committed, that evil will rise up to them from hell, under the earth, and they will be captured and taken down to hell. Understanding in this way, they are all deluded. Ānanda, happiness, suffering, merit and sin, benefit and harm, all lie within us. Even if you believe for a hundred or a hundred thousand lifetimes that merit and evil are outside of us and that, having made merit, that merit will come and take us to a happy place, it will not happen. Merit and demerit, happiness and suffering do not exist outside of us. Merit, skillfulness, and happiness are our own minds. Evil, suffering, and harm are the retinue of desire. Where else will desire exist other than our own minds? Merit and sin are in our minds. If you do not like suffering and want to obtain happiness, you should try to fix your mind. If we ourselves do not want to search for happiness and escape suffering, who else will help us to attain happiness and escape from suffering?

"'Ānanda, those who understand that someone else will make merit and skill, heaven and nibbāna for us, and that someone else will take us to sin, suffering and harm, hell and the animal realms, are all lost in the world, have gone astray of the path, and are lost in the realm of rebirth. These people, no matter how much merit and skill they make, even to the extent of going forth as renunciants in the Buddhist teaching, will find no happiness. They will experience only suffering.

"'Ānanda. Merit and happiness are one and the same thing. When there is merit, you can say there is happiness. Sin and suffering are one and the same thing. When there is sin, you can say there is suffering. If you don't know sin, you cannot let go of it. If you don't know merit, you won't know how to find it. It is as if we want to obtain some gold, but we don't know what gold looks like. Even if that gold were right in front of our eyes, we could not obtain it because we do not know that it is there. It is the same with merit. If we don't know merit, we cannot find it—and not only merit, which is an abstract quality, even with other things that are material, if we don't know them, we can't obtain them.

"'Ānanda, the Tathāgata does not say that those who do not know merit or happiness do not obtain merit or happiness when they make merit. When merit is made, it is indeed meritorious, and happiness results. But if one does not know, does not understand, it is just empty merit and happiness. Ānanda, it is truly pitiable when merit is made by those people who desire happiness but do not know that merit is happiness When merit is made, happiness is attained right there. It is not that it will be attained some long time afterward. When you make it, you get it right then and there. But they do not know this. They are sitting and lying on top of merit in vain. They do not receive the merit, the happiness, because they do not know it. That is why they are said to have missed the opportunity of having been born as a human being and encountering the Buddha's teaching.' Thus did the Buddha instruct me, Ānanda."

"Venerable Mahā Kassapa, the Buddha continued to instruct me as follows. 'Ānanda, those who understand that by making a lot of merit, whether you know it or not is not important, that merit will lead you to happiness, this is called being a truly deluded person. Why would merit lead you to happiness, since merit and happiness are one and the same thing? If you do not know happiness, you do not know merit. When you know happiness, when you see happiness, then you know merit and see merit. Why would anyone be leading anyone anywhere?

"'Ānanda, no one can help us with happiness and suffering. No one can lead anyone to hell, heaven, or nibbāna. Whether you go to hell, to heaven, or to nibbāna, you must go by yourself. You absolutely cannot take anyone else with you. Whoever wishes to escape the "ripe hell" in the land of ghosts must first free oneself of the raw hell in this very human world. If you want to obtain happiness in the future, you must first attain the raw heaven in this human world. If you have not attained the raw heaven in this human world, when you die you will not obtain that ripe heaven. If you do not attain the raw heaven, when you die there will only be hell waiting for you. As for the happiness in heaven, it is still not free of suffering. It is not that there is suffering only in the raw heaven in this human world. Even the ripe heavens in various celestial levels all have both happiness and suffering. It is the happiness that is not void of suffering, unlike nibbāna, which is *ekanta-paramasukha*: sheer happiness, unstained by suffering.

"'Ānanda, the raw heaven in the human world is when you become a powerful person, an owner of possessions, status, retinue, and fame. When someone becomes such a big person in this way, that person is said to be partaking of the happiness of raw heaven. One who desires happiness in the future should obtain happiness while still alive and not be concerned with any physical difficulties. All levels of heaven, be it the raw heaven in the human world or the ripe heaven in all the levels of the sky, are tainted by suffering. They are no different, and no greater nor less. The happiness of heaven is indeed happiness—you cannot say it is not happiness—but it is happiness that is tainted with suffering. Even so, it is certainly better than falling into hell.

"'Do not doubt, Ānanda, whether the raw heaven in this life and the ripe heaven in the next life are different, even though they may differ in some small ways. If you want any particular kind of happiness, you should strive to attain it while you are still alive in this human world. Do not just sit or lie around waiting for happiness to come to you. It is unlike nibbāna. For the happiness of nibbāna, you don't have to make a lot of effort. Once you grasp it properly, you can sit and recline in happiness. If you say that the happiness of nibbāna is difficult, it's as if it's easy; if you say it's easy, it's as if difficult. It's difficult in that you don't see it. Fools and unenlightened beings who are blind grasp it wrongly and see it wrongly. So they must make a lot of effort in many ways, and it is all for nothing. As for those who are wise, who consider it rightly and grasp it correctly, they do not have to do much. Just sitting and reclining, the happiness of nibbāna always arises for them. For that reason, the happiness of nibbāna is a happiness that is untainted by suffering.

"'Ānanda, if you want to know whether you will attain the happiness of heaven or the suffering of hell, just look at your mind while you are still alive. Does your mind have a lot of happiness or a lot of suffering? Suffering is the raw hell. When you die, you will fall into the ripe hell. Happiness is the raw heaven. When you die, you will rise up to the ripe heaven. While you are still a person, however much happiness or suffering you have, you will probably have that much happiness or suffering when you die; it is no different. Those who desire happiness in this world and the next should look after their minds so that they obtain happiness. The outer body is not so important. Never mind however much happiness or suffering it receives. When you die, it is discarded onto the earth and has no value. As for the mind, it follows you into the future, because the mind is deathless. When you say "death," it is only the body, the dissolution of the elements, the cessation of the *khandhas*. If the mind died, then there would be no more birth: that would be the attainment of nibbāna.

"Ānanda, in past lives the Tathāgata was lost and wandered for ages through this realm of rebirth (*saṁsāra*), for hundreds, thousands of lives and many more. I made merit and performed skillful deeds, hoping to transcend suffering and attain happiness in the future. I believed that when I died I would escape suffering. When I actually died, it was only the elements, the khandhas, that died. The mind did not die and had to go to rebirth. When I was reborn, I had to die again. If it was like this, how could I escape suffering? When people say "die," they mean dying as in rotten, as in stinking as understood these days. It is just play-dying, incomplete dying, dying and then being born, being born then dying. There is no beginning and no end. Really dying, true dying, is both the form and khandhas ceasing and the mind as well. It is only the Buddha and the arahant disciples, the vanquishers of the outflows (*khīnāsava*), who do not have to return to be born again.

"Ānanda, in my past lives, when I still did not know, I understood that when I died I would escape from suffering. When I made merit and performed skillful actions, I aimed for happiness in the future. When I died, I did not escape suffering as I had wished. Now in this, my last life, I realized that heaven and nibbāna are within us. So I hastened my practice to be able to attain them while still a person and so transcended suffering, and experienced the happiness that is void of material things, becoming the ultimate teacher for trainable beings that I am today.' Venerable Mahā Kassapa, thus did the Buddha instruct me."

Tadanantaraṁ: "Following that, the Buddha continued his instruction as follows: . . . 'Ānanda, you cannot take the body with you if you fall into hell or go up to heaven. You can only take the mind. That mind, no one can grasp. It is like a wind. Because the mind is subtle, it cannot be held. When the mind falls into hell, who could help pull it out? If the mind had substance, help would be possible. Those people who are waiting for someone to help them out of suffering and lead them to happiness are all fools of no wisdom. Even the Tathāgata, who knows heaven and hell, suffering and happiness, and searched for a means to escape suffering and experience only happiness, had the utmost difficulty. How could I possibly lead anyone else's mind out of suffering? It is the same for the buddhas who will be enlightened in the future. They can only point out happiness, suffering, heaven, hell, and nibbāna. Whoever desires any kind of happiness or suffering, that depends on their temperament, but they must first study and really and truly know in their minds that the suffering in hell is like this, the happiness in heaven is like that, the happiness of nibbāna is like that. Once they know, then there is a way for them to achieve it and they won't have to wander too long in the realm of rebirth. If they are still not clear on it while they are still alive, they will not be able to escape, and they can be said to have wasted their lives being born as a human being, and lost their original desire, meaning they have been born for happiness but have allowed themselves to miss out on it. What's more, they have fallen into hell, causing them to break their aspiration, which is extremely piteous.' Venerable Mahā Kassapa, thus did the Buddha instruct me."

Ito paraṁ girimānandasuttaṁ anusandhiṁ bhasissāmīti: And now I will continue to expound the *Girimānanda Sutta*, beginning with Venerable Ānanda's words *Bhante ariyakassapa*: "Noble Sirs, with Venerable Mahā Kassapa at the head. *Bhagavā*: The Blessed One. *desesi*: did instruct me, Ānanda, as follows: . . . 'Ānanda, the countless beings who have fallen into hell are packed into hell like a sack of rice grains, beans, or sesame, but they cannot see each other, because they do not know or see hell; they do not know happiness and suffering, merit and sin, benefit and harm. They do not know that their own mind is suffering and happiness. Their minds are obsessed with sensual desire, greed, and defilements, and so they are fallen into hell, pressed together like grains of rice, beans, or sesame seeds in a sack. They call out to each other, but they cannot see each other. That is, they do not see each other's happiness or suffering.

"'Ānanda, we cannot see each other's minds. Only the Buddha and the arahants can see the minds of others. That the Buddha can see and know the minds of others is through his arahant knowledge. If you cannot relinquish the crafty defilements, the qualities of the arahant will not arise in your heart, and so you cannot know the state of mind of other beings. The Tathāgata himself is able to know the state of mind of all beings through being free of defilements—that is, through being an arahant. Why should we believe those who have not escaped defilements, who have not accomplished arahantship, and who say they know and see the minds of others? Even if they do know through some means, such as through *samādhi*, their knowledge does not extend very far. Their knowledge is hit-and-miss. They do not have the clear knowledge that appears in the qualities of the arahant. If a person who has not yet escaped from defilements were to know more than the Tathāgata, who is an arahant, then my giving up my wife and child, my wealth and happiness to go into homelessness would mean I was more stupid than those people, because even though they are still sunk in defilements their knowledge would exceed the Buddha, who is an arahant, far from defilements. Because of the fact that they have not yet relinquished defilements—that is, they have not achieved arahantship—it is impossible that they would have more knowledge of the minds of other beings than the Buddha or the arahants, or have equal wisdom. Those who have not yet given up defilements, who have not yet attained arahantship, and who say that they know and see the minds of others are simply boasting. Such knowledge is not yet free of hell, and they should not be believed. Whoever believes them can be said to be one who is outside the teaching. Truly, they are just hiding behind our miraculous teachings to deceive the world. These people, no matter how much merit they make, do not escape hell, and those who believe in them are bound for woeful realms in the future.

"'Ānanda, those who boast of knowledge or attainments will be the ones who stain our teaching and bring it to decline. When they appear, they harass the great elders and the young novices with words that are not uplifting. Those who are gullible and of little wisdom will be impressed by them and disrobe from the teaching. Thus will our teaching decline.

"'Ānanda, any group who harms and decries the elders, the monks, and the novices of the Saṅgha, who are disciples of the Tathāgata and who have incurred a wrongdoing that is less than a wrongdoing of defeat (*pārājika*), and who forces them to disrobe from the holy life, or who banishes them from that place (*pabbā-janīyakamma*), those people have incurred heinous bad kamma and will not escape hell. Any group of people who has faith and belief in the virtues and teachings of the Tathāgata and who praises them and does not disparage them, those people will have only prosperity and happiness, both in this world and the next. Whatever kind of happiness they aspire to that is not beyond their abilities, they will attain that happiness in accordance with their wishes. Those who disparage and mock disciples of the Tathāgata who have wrongdoings less than offenses of defeat incur a fault that is many times greater than those who destroy Buddha images, stupas, and *cetiyas*. Those who destroy Buddha images and so on have made much bad kamma, it is true, but it is not considered to be destroying Buddhism. Those who disparage [the Saṅgha] can be said to have destroyed the Buddhism of the Tathāgata, because those who have incurred wrongdoings of a lesser weight than offenses of defeat can still be said to be disciples of the Tathāgata. Once they have committed an offense of defeat, they are then stripped of the status of a disciple of the Tathāgata. If they have incurred such an offense, then it is not wrong to punish them or banish them. Rather, you can be said to be helping the teaching. There is still a way that destroying Buddha images, stupas, or cetiyas can be called a skillful action, such as when a Buddha image is not good or beautiful and you destroy it in order to make a better one. It is the same for a cetiya or a bodhi tree. If a bodhi tree is growing in a place that is not appropriate, such as close to a permanent structure that it might grow to damage, then to cut it down is not wrong. If it is cut down for one's own benefit or cut down out of jealousy or envy, then that is indeed bad kamma. Even so, it is not said to be destroying the teaching. Those who disparage and harm members of the Saṅgha who have incurred offenses that are less than the final level and cause them to leave the holy life are said to be really destroying Buddhism.' Venerable Mahā Kassapa, thus did the Buddha instruct me."

"He then further instructed me, Ānanda, as follows: 'Ānanda, a person who aspires to heaven and nibbāna should quickly arouse effort and attain those things while still alive, because everything is within our own mind. It is only really difficult when it comes to nibbāna. One who desires the happiness of nibbāna needs to make oneself like the great earth or like someone who has died—that is to say, one must let go of both happiness and suffering. The important point is that they must destroy the 1,500 kinds of defilements. The 1,500 kinds of defilements can be boiled down to five: greed (*lobha*), hatred (*dosa*), delusion (*moha*), pride (*māna*), and wrong views (*diṭṭhi*). Lobha is the aspiration and desire to attain sensual pleasures—forms, sounds, odors, tastes, bodily sensations—and to obtain sensual objects—material possessions, both sentient and nonsentient. This is called lobha. Dosa refers to aversion, aggression, harming others. Moha is delusion, such as being deluded by love, deluded by hatred, deluded by possessions, deluded by rank, and so on. Māna is attachment to the self, pride, looking down on others. Diṭṭhi is attachment to wrong views, such as *ucchedadiṭṭhi* (annihilationist view) and *sassatadiṭṭhi* (eternalist view), being unable to let go of one's views. If you can extinguish these five kinds of defilements, then you can extinguish the 1,500 kinds of defilements. If you cannot extinguish the five defilements, then you cannot be said to have extinguished the defilements.

"'Ānanda, that it is so hard for dense worldly beings aspiring to nibbāna to attain it is because they do not know how to extinguish the defilement of desire. They understand that by making lots of merit and doing many skillful actions merit will float down from above and take them up to nibbāna. As for where nibbāna is actually located, they have no idea. They are just guessing. And so it is difficult for them to attain. In reality nibbāna does not lie in any far-off place: it is within the mind. When lobha, dosa, moha, māna, and diṭṭhi are fully extinguished, then nibbāna has been reached. If you do not know and have not yet extinguished the defilement of desire but simply hope to attain nibbāna, even after ten thousand or a hundred thousand lifetimes you will not reach it, because the defilements and desire all lie within us. As long as you do not know how to extinguish all the defilements and desires that are there, you cannot attain it or reach it. That merit and skillful actions will help you extinguish your defilements is not something you can reasonably expect. Merit and skillfulness are ourselves. We ourselves must be the ones to get rid of defilements in order to attain our objective.

"'Ānanda, it is difficult for foolish worldlings to attain nibbāna because they simply wish for it, and so they do not attain it. They do not know that nibbāna is within their own minds. They simply think that they will go and get it in the next life. They do not know that hell, heaven, and nibbāna are within their own minds. For that reason, they fall into even more suffering and hardships, spinning around in the realm of birth and death, taking rebirths in small and large births endlessly.' Venerable Mahā Kassapa, thus did the Buddha instruct me, Ananda."

"Then he instructed me further thus: 'Ānanda, those who are wise should consider themselves and conquer their own minds to be free of suffering and hardship and to be free of Māra's trap.[9] If they do not consider thus, even though they have wisdom, it is empty wisdom; they cannot be counted as wise ones. The action of transcending suffering and hardship and being free of the trap of Māra is to be free of the defilements and desire. Once we have escaped the defilements and desire in this way, we can be said to have escaped suffering and hardship completely. If we have not yet escaped them, we can be said to have not yet escaped suffering and hardship. As long as you have not yet escaped, you should not teach others, because you yourself have not escaped.

How can you teach others to escape? It is like a person who wishes to cross a river. If we ourselves have already crossed the river, then it is truly fitting that we can call out to other people and help them across. Once we have called them across, whether they agree to follow or not is up to them. We ourselves have already crossed the river in accordance with our objective. In the same way, one who is to teach others to escape suffering must first lead oneself out of suffering. Then it is fitting to teach others, just like the person crossing the river. If one has not yet rid oneself of the mass of defilements and wants to free the beings in the cemeteries and ghosts, they will just laugh: "Ha-ha ha-ha. You have not yet escaped suffering. How will you lead us out of suffering? You and we are the same; we have not yet escaped hell. How can you lead us out of hell?" . . .

"Ānanda, any group of people who allow the ghosts in the charnel grounds to ridicule them in this way, if such a group arises, will be a cause for disease and pestilence of many a kind; there is no happiness or prosperity to be found. Ānanda, any householder or renunciant who states that they know and see and can talk with spirits, should be known as not a disciple of the Tathāgata. They are of wrong view and are outside the teaching. They should not be upheld as teachers, because they are tricksters, fraudsters, magicians. Only the Buddha and the arahants truly know and see and can speak with ghosts. Apart from that, no one truly sees or knows. They are all simply boasting.

"Ānanda, I will make a prediction about the future. There will arise groups of wrong view, who are outside the teaching, boasting that they know and see and can talk with ghosts. When this group of people arises, they will harm our teaching and cause it to decline with damaging and critical words. The monks and novices will be disturbed and have no comfort. They will teach strict views on practices and adhere to the forest ascetic practices like Devadatta. Then there will arise town monks and forest monks, and they will split up into groups and not be harmonious. Each will boast of their own virtues, and our teaching will go into decline because of these people with wrong view and a desire for wealth. They will have no happiness, and the path, fruit, and special dhammas will not arise for them. They will study only a little of the knowledge and morality that have been taught by those of wrong view, then go on to boast. In truth, this knowledge is only good for going to hell. They will not escape the four nether realms.

"Ānanda, this is what will be in the future, of this there is no doubt. One who knows about these doctrines, having seen them, should practice to forsake them and so attain happiness. To extinguish the defilements, you must reduce two kinds of consumption. Those two kinds are robes and dwelling places, the external consumable. That is one kind of consumption. Then there are food and medicines: these two are considered to be internal consumables. This is the other kind of consumption. These two consumptions are defilements; they are suffering and happiness, all of them. The more you consume these things, the more suffering there will be. If you consume less of these two things, suffering will be less and happiness will increase. That is to say, the less bad kamma there is, the more merit there will be. Merit and skill all lie within the individual. One who gives up consumption of these two things will escape hell and will attain heaven and nibbāna.

"Ānanda, if one has gone forth and does not know how to extinguish the defilements—that is, these two consumptions—or reduce them, and thinks that by going forth and keeping the precepts and undertaking the practices one is gaining merit, but does not seek out a means for reducing the defilements of these two kinds of consumption, where will they attain merit and happiness? If they think like that, even if they observe the precepts, including all the Pāṭimokkha precepts and the ascetic practices (dhutaṅga), it will be for nothing. Their observance will only lead to hardship and exhaustion, and they will not attain merit and skill. The Pāṭimokkha precepts and dhutaṅga practices allowed by the Buddha are tools to be used for reducing the defilements and desire of these two consumables. If you cannot reduce them, there is no merit or skill. One who thinks that the Pāṭimokkha and dhutaṅga practices will help raise them up to heaven and nibbāna is a fool of little wisdom. They will not escape suffering. The two consumables are called palibodha, which translates as "worries." Observing the Pāṭimokkha precepts and the dhutaṅga ascetic practices is in order to cut off worries, to reduce them. The more they are reduced, the more merit and skill, heaven, and nibbāna there are. The Buddha summarizes the whole of the teaching as ultimately down to two palibodha. A student is not praised on the basis of having more or less knowledge. Whether one has much or little knowledge, if one can extinguish the palibodha, then that is good. If one cannot extinguish the two palibodha, whether one lives in a village temple or a forest temple, that is not good.' The Buddha gave this instruction."

"Following that, he continued to instruct me as follows. 'Ānanda, this teaching is called the Phrayā Dhammikarāja, because it is bigger than all teachings. When one has listened to the teachings that the Tathāgata has given here, pointing out hell, heaven, and nibbāna, the defilement of desire, and utterly realized them, and wishes for any kind of happiness, one can choose and practice accordingly.'

"When the Buddha had instructed me thus, he then gave permission for the final ordination as follows: 'Ānanda, in the end times, when it is impossible to find a quorum of bhikkhus to confer ordination, even if there is only one bhikkhu, if a son of good family has faith in the Tathāgata and wishes to go forth as a bhikkhu in that bhikkhu's temple, then let him go forth. Moreover, even if one bhikkhu cannot be found, if a son of good family has the faith to go forth and continue the dispensation of the Tathāgata, then let him study and understand the four rules of defeat (pārājika) and the two consumables, then approach a Buddha image or a stupa or a cetiya, or even, if such an object of worship cannot be found, just to think of the Tathāgata, and then go forth as a bhikkhu. He should determine as follows: *imaṁ pabbajjaṁ samādiyāmi dutiyampi imaṁ pabbajjaṁ samādiyāmi tatiyampi imaṁ pabbajjaṁ samādiyāmi,* and then undertake the four rules of defeat as follows: *pathamaṁ pārājikaṁ samadiyāmi, dutiyaṁ tatiyaṁ catutthaṁ pārājikaṁ samadiyāmi,* and then go forth as a bhikkhu.

"'If the Saṅgha still remains, even if it is only one bhikkhu, one must not go forth by oneself. If one does so, this is to disparage the dispensation and is very bad kamma. Do not do this. If one has gone forth in this way and someone should say that it is not proper and is very bad kamma, I have permitted this only for end times.' Venerable Mahā Kassapa, the Buddha did instruct me, Ānanda, in this way. May the noble Saṅgha know accordingly with their own knowledge in this way that, I, Ānanda, have presented it.

"Then the Buddha stopped and gave no further instruction. Having heard this, I paid my respects and returned to the residence of Venerable Girimānanda and conveyed to him the two reflections—that is, the reflection on body (*rūpa*) and the reflection on mind (*nāma*)—so that he could hear it in full as the Buddha instructed. Venerable Girimānanda followed the Dhamma teaching and was enlightened to arahantship at the moment that he laid down body and mind. The illness that ailed him, the painful feelings, disappeared in that moment. Venerable Mahā Kassapa, to call this sutta the *Phrayā Dhammikarāja Sutta* as I was instructed may convey the wrong picture, because it was given in relation to Venerable Girimānanda. This sutta was given by the Buddha at Jetavana Forest Hermitage, with the sick bhikkhu Venerable Girimānanda as cause, and so it is called the *Girimānanda Sutta*, with content as herein expounded."

CHAO KHUN UPĀLI

Chao Khun Upāli (Jun; 1857–1932) is widely known and revered among Thai Buddhists and members of the Thai saṅgha. A contemporary of the eminent meditation master Luang Pu Mun, he is considered to be a rare combination of *pariyatti* (learning) and *paṭipatti* (practice), having progressed far in Buddhist studies as well as devoting himself to seclusion and meditation practice, in which he is generally acknowledged as having attained great proficiency. Due to his many talents he was also called upon to perform various administrative duties and fulfill ecclesiastical positions, often in remote areas, where his steadfast establishment in the teaching and practice made him a safe choice to take on such challenging environments. He served, for example, as abbot of a monastery in Champasak Province (present-day Laos) and as regional ecclesiastical chief of Ratchaburi Province.

Born in Ubon Ratchathani Province,[1] he became a novice monk when he was thirteen. He left the robes when he was nineteen in order to help his mother while his father was conscripted to fight in the Haw Wars. He ordained as a bhikkhu when he was twenty-two and spent his first few years studying scriptures.

In his tenth year as a bhikkhu, he made a determination to delve more deeply into the Buddha's teachings, as related in his autobiography: "I became inspired by the Buddha's teaching *attāhi attano nātho*: one should be a refuge unto oneself. When I was still not clever, I thought that this body and mind were my self, and so I devoted myself to study, and strived to constantly maintain good conduct, with shame and fear of wrongdoing at all times. Later, as I studied more, reading the

Saṅkhittovāda of Somdet Wanarat of Wat Sommanat Wihan,[2] which states, 'No, there is no-one who is born, no-one who gets old, no-one who dies. It is only mind and body, the elements, the *khandhas*, and the sense bases that arise and pass away,' I devoted myself to the practice."

As a result of this devotion, he saw to it that his administrative and ecclesiastic duties did not become obstacles to the practice, taking the time to seek seclusion and develop his meditation. In 1922, for example, he traveled to Keng Tung State (the present-day Shan State in Myanmar) to visit the Jomyong Pagoda (a journey that in itself was no mean feat in the days before trains and accessible roads), where he stayed for one rains retreat.[3] During the rains retreat he had sufficient seclusion to be able to make good progress in his meditation practice. After the rains, the local prince invited him to the capital where the royal entourage was inspired by his teachings.

He developed a reputation as a skillful and erudite teacher, and many of his talks, as well as his more formal writings, have been subsequently recorded by hand and published in Thai. In 1915, during World War I, he penned *Dhammavicāyanusāsana*, an article decrying the "wrong knowledge" that leads to war. Because Thailand was aligned with the Allies and actively engaged in the war, the article clashed with government policy at the time, and as a result he was punished by the stripping of the ecclesiastical title he held at the time (Chao Khun Phra Debmoli) and confinement to Wat Bowonniwet in Bangkok for one year. He was released the following year and awarded a new title of Phra Dhammadhirarājmunī.

His teachings, even the more informal talks (which, before the days of tape recorders, were preserved by a court stenographer and then revised by Venerable Chao Khun Upāli himself for publication) tend to be rather formal and offer a window into the style of teaching of a hundred years ago. The teachings are imbued with his own insights, resulting in some unusual perspectives on traditional themes, as is shown in the following translations. The first talk in this collection, *Kāyanagara*, is a good example of this, being very traditional in some ways but also containing some thought-provoking reflections. The second talk is the *Dhammavicāyanusāsana* mentioned above.

KĀYANAGARA (THE BODY CITY)

Kumbhūpamaṁ kāyamimaṁ viditvā
nāgarūpamaṁ cittamidaṁ thaketvā
Yodhetha māraṁ paññāvudhena
jitañca rakkhe anivesano siyāti[4]

NOW I WILL OFFER for the benefit of listeners who are followers of the Buddha a clarification of the Buddha's words recorded in the Dhammapada, as fitting for the occasion. The content of the Buddha's words is cited above: *"Kumbhūpamaṁ kāyamimaṁ viditvā*: a person should know clearly of one's own body that it is not enduring, like a dish, a clay bowl, or pot." In explanation, dishes made of clay, be they small, large, raw or fired, deep or shallow, thick or thin, will always become broken up in the end. In the same way, this body that we take to be our self, be it large or small, fat or thin, tall or short, black or white, robust and strong or frail and weak, will become broken up and destroyed in the end.

"Nāgarūpamaṁ cittamidaṁ thaketvā: establish this mind in the body containing the nine doorways,[5] which can be compared to a mighty city replete with gateways and towers strong enough to repel enemies." In explanation, whenever enemies confront a city, the city's governor or generals, from their base in the mighty city with its ramparts, gateways, and towers, should go forth and fight their enemies. If they lose the advantage, they should retreat to the city and steadfastly guard the gateways and towers, and enter into and rest therein. When the brave soldiers have fully replenished their forces, they should then go forth once more to fight, and do so frequently. They should not let

77

their enemies increase in strength. Once they are victorious and have taken the enemy's territory, they should establish a base to protect their advantage and not lose it.

Moreover, they should not be content with just that. They should quickly go forth, conquering until they have subjugated the whole of the enemy's lands. As in this analogy, a yogi who sees the harm of the realm of rebirth, having obtained a body that is replete with the six doorways such as the eye doorway, being free of disadvantages such as muteness, mental illness, blindness, and deafness, can be said to have a good "city."

"*Yodhetha māraṁ paññāvudhena*: seeing that one has obtained a good 'city' in this way, one should resolve to fight with the defilement demons using the weapon of insight knowledge." If one finds that the defilements are more powerful and one cannot defeat them, one should retreat into the city to rest and recuperate, and work to strengthen one's weak insight using the concentrated mind, then to go forth into battle again.

"*Jitañca rakkhe anivesano siyā*: whenever you have a victory, then establish sense restraint and maintain it well; do not give up the advantage to the enemies. But do not be content with merely that." The important point is that nibbāna is a place that is surrounded by the enemy, it is behind enemy lines. We have to resolve to break through them before we can be really safe and victorious and no longer have any enemies to oppose us, like a universal emperor. The analogy is the same as for the brave regiments having victory over the lands of the enemy.

Now I will explain how the Body City is said to be surrounded by enemies. Those enemies are none other than the *upakkilesa*, the mental impurities, of which there are sixteen, as follows:

moho: delusion, not knowing good from bad;
ahirikaṁ: lack of shame in regard to bad actions;
anottappaṁ: lack of fear of wrongdoing;
lobho: greed and desire to obtain the belongings of others;
diṭṭhi: distorted view that has strayed from the right way;
māno: conceit;

issā: jealousy, not wanting to see others do better than oneself;

macchariyaṁ: miserliness, not wanting to share one's excess belongings;

kukkuccaṁ: annoyance;

thīna: torpor;

middha: sleepiness;

vicikicchā: doubt;

makkho: concealing the goodness of others;

pasāso: boastfulness;

māyā: deceit;

sātheyyaṁ: concealing one's own faults.

These, or the fourteen unskillful mental qualities, all have the same nature: they are all defilement demons (*kilesamāra*), because these unskillful conditions, having come into contact with a person's mind, cloud and defile the mind. If you cannot calm the mind itself, the unrest spreads outward into the external, causing blemishes in body and speech, revealing to the world that one is conducting oneself improperly, and one will have to receive consequences of various kinds. At the very least, one will be criticized and disparaged. At worst, one will be sentenced by the government to jail terms or execution, and this may cause suffering to those who are under one's protection.

Thus, they are called *māro*, demons. It would be wrong to say that these defilement demons are always within one, but also to say that they do not lie within one is incorrect. When they arise, it's because of a cause, which is sense contact, with ignorance as a supporting factor. As for sense contact, if it is supported by knowledge, these unskillful mental concomitants will not arise. Therefore, for one who has conquered the demons, these six bases of sense contact such as eye contact are still there, but when supported by knowledge, the unskillful mental qualities cannot touch them. Their minds are always clear.

One who has determined to look after the Body City so that it is calmed and abides happily must be prepared to face the enemy, which is these defilement demons, so that they cannot infiltrate the city. The way to do so is not difficult. It is to conquer the armies of Māra on the lowest or coarsest level with the weapon of morality, to conquer the armies of Māra on the middle level with the weapon of concentration, and to conquer Māra's general, which is the foundation of rebirth (*upadhi*), with the weapon of wisdom. The battlefield is the six doorways to this city—namely, eyes, ears, nose, tongue, body, and mind. To fire those three kinds of weapons, you must take aim at the target with mindfulness and clear comprehension; do not waste your ammunition through uncertainty. With just this much you can overcome the enemy, the defilement demons. These defilements have little power. They are no match for the noble path of morality, concentration, and wisdom. To give another analogy, the defilements are like bandits, because they can only bully foolish people who are lacking in mindfulness. Faced with those who have mindfulness, they no longer have any power.

There is another type of enemy about which we should be concerned, and that is birth, aging, sickness, and death. This group of four enemies surrounds us on all sides. The sages of this world, those who are recognized as having true wisdom, headed by the Lord Buddha, who leave their homelives and renounce their wealth and sensual happiness to practice austerities and lead the holy life, do so on account of seeing the danger of falling into the trap of these four enemies.

If we clearly focus on the truth, we will see that birth itself is suffering, because it is the base upon which aging, sickness, and death stand. The sorrow, lamentation, difficulty, distress, and despair that fill the world these days are all on account of birth. Aging is another important kind of suffering, because as aging progresses it manifests various kinds of physical defects, such as loss of vision, loss of hearing, broken teeth, sunken cheeks, and loss of energy. Whatever activity one wants to undertake, it is all obstructed and thwarted, and one experiences suffering, sorrow, and despair of various kinds, all on account of aging.

As for illness, it is also an important kind of suffering because of the painful feelings that arise within the body, such as headaches, stomachaches, fevers, and chills. One is subject to all kinds of suffering and sadness, all on account of illness.

As for death, it is also another important kind of suffering because we cherish life and the body. Continuing to live is pleasing to everyone.

Death is supremely unpleasing. When something that is unpleasing arises, it has the effect of causing suffering, sadness, and distress. Therefore, death is another kind of suffering.

If we were to speak truthfully, these four groups of suffering should be referred to as an inheritance from our parents. In fact, our parents do not like them. They like only birth. As for aging, sickness, and death, they hate them passionately. So why do they bequeath those other things to us as well? It's a real mystery. If you were to say they loved us dearly, that's correct, because they look after and tend to us with the utmost care. If you were to say they hate us a lot, that would be right too, because they know full well that aging, sickness, and death arise contingent on birth.

It's like a man who has leprosy. He knows that if he has a wife and fathers a child, then that child may well develop leprosy just the same as he has. "Better if I just be patient and accept the results of this kamma on my own so that it comes to a halt with me. Let this disease not spread to a child." Thinking in this way he refrains from having a wife and so does not allow that disease to spread onward. In that case, would he not be worthy of praise as someone who had thought out the matter well?

Is the "disease" of aging, sickness, and death not worse than the disease of leprosy? Let's put aside whether our parents have been stupid or clever, and let's just talk about ourselves. Will we allow ourselves to pass on this evil bequest, which lives within us, to our children? The matter of our own parents is in the past—there's nothing to be done about it now—but we here in the present moment have a chance to do something about it.

Those who are wise should reflect on this matter. You may think, "If everyone agreed on not having husbands or wives, who would there be to continue our traditions?" There is no need to ask this. It would be like the old saying "Harvesting grass to roof the field." The wise—those who see the danger of the round of rebirth—reflect only on themselves. No matter that the world is everywhere in sorrow, they will not cry and sorrow.

Birth, aging, sickness, and death are the cycle of suffering. Now we can be said to be surrounded, are we not? Birth is the beginning, and we have already been born. Death is the end. Aging and sickness are on either side. Which way do we go to get out? Those who see the fault of the cycle of suffering have sought various ways out, giving rise to different views. One group is known as the *sassatāsaya*: they believe that birth is permanent, that whatever you are born as you will be continually born in that way—but one does not escape death. Another group is known as the *ucchedāsaya*: they see that after death there is nothing, that the knowledge and thought that arise today are merely a spark of earth, water, wind, and fire coming together. Once the four elements break up, that thought and knowledge utterly cease. This is called *ucchedadiṭṭhi*—but one still must die. Another group is called the *anulomikkhantāsaya*. They have an indefinite view and just follow others. Whether after death one must be reborn, they're not sure; whether after death there is nothing, they're not sure. They just follow along with what others say. This is called *anulomikadiṭṭhi*—but one still must die.

These three views cannot lead one out of the siege, and one must still die: die under siege, die in the trap, die in assumptions. So they are called wrong views.

Another group is known as *yathābhūtāsaya*: those with views in accordance with the truth. How is their view in accordance with the truth? As to this, previously, with ignorance as a condition, one saw birth as being in the past—that is, one has already been born—while aging, sickness, and death are in the future—they have not yet arrived. So one saw that there is no birth, aging, sickness, and death in the present moment, and this is the foundation of the three kinds of desire. Birth, which is in the past, is sensual desire. That which is the present moment, which does not have birth, aging, sickness, and death, is desire for becoming. Aging, sickness, and death, which are in the future, are desire for cessation.

When one considers this, one clearly sees that we fall within the power of these three kinds of desire. These three kinds of desire are known as the cause of suffering (*dukkha samudaya*). Because we do not know that birth, aging, sickness, and death are the cause of suffering, then birth, aging, sickness, and death become suffering. Once we carefully examine and clearly come to see the face of suffering and its cause, then we must search for the way to lay them down, to let them go, to find a way out of those desires.

Where can we give them up, let them go, and escape? The ancients said that once you have climbed to the top of a tree, where can you go? The answer is that whichever way you went up, that is the way you must go down; whichever way you came, that is the way you must return. So we, having come by way of birth, aging, sickness, and death, cannot escape by any other way. We must leave by way of birth, aging, sickness, and death in order to follow the direct path.

When this is clear with certainty in our minds, we must examine birth. To what exact point does the word *birth* refer? Where can we draw the line that "this is birth"? If you don't understand, then think of the *paṭiccasamuppāda*, where it says "*bhavapaccayā jāti*: with becoming as a condition, birth arises." The word *bhava* indicates the presence of the physical body. Once there is a physical body, then there can be said to be becoming. Once there is a becoming, a place for birth, then birth will take place at that becoming. We can see that we are the becoming and the birth. To whatever extent becoming arises, birth appears to that extent. That we eat food or shift our physical postures is for maintaining our birth. We will see that we are always being born, with every breath we take.

Whenever birth in the present moment, which is the truth, clearly appears in our minds, then birth in the past, as we had previously understood it, ceases at that moment. When we see birth, the arising in the present moment, clearly, then we will see that aging, sickness, and death in the present arise along with it. They exist together and cannot be separated. When this vision is clear, the aging, sickness, and death that we had understood to be in the future will cease. All that remains is the birth, aging, sickness, and death that exist in the present as the path.

The action of seeing that birth, aging, sickness, and death are in the past or in the future and seeing yourself in the present, empty of birth, aging, sickness, and death, is suffering and also the cause of suffering.

The action of seeing birth, aging, sickness, and death as the present moment—that is, our self—or seeing that our self is actually birth, aging, sickness, and death, that is cessation and also the path.

At the moment when the development of the path by a yogi has progressed fully, when it has fully become purity of conduct, purity of mind, and purity of view (*sīlavisuddhi, cittavisuddhi, diṭṭhivisuddhi*), then the knowledge and vision that analyze into "this is the world, this is dhamma, this is supposition (*sammatti*), this is concept (*paññatti*)," will arise within the yogi. This is the attainment of liberation. Then it is said that one has well escaped from birth, aging, sickness, and death through knowledge and liberation. That person is therefore called *khemī*, one who is securely delivered from the fetters; *averī*: one who is peaceable; *abhayo*: one who is without danger. "*Paṇḍitoti pavuccati*: the wise of the world confer on these people the title *pandit*, or sage." These people are said to be *yathābhūtañāṇāsaya*: they have escaped from the enemy's siege through knowledge and vision into things as they are. They are liberated. They do not die within suppositions. Because of this, they are truly worthy to be followed by we Buddhists.

We must understand that the way to retreat and the way to attack will become clear to us through knowledge of the task to be done (*kiccañāṇa*), practicing the things that need to be cultivated so that there is development of the path—that is, by fully developing the noble eightfold path within oneself.

I have herein expounded in brief on the verse about the Body City in accordance with the Buddha's words and my own explanations, sufficient to provide some reflections for you who are followers of the Buddha.

DHAMMAVICAYĀNUSĀSANA[6]
(DHAMMA ADMONITION)[7]

Suvijāno bhavaṁ hoti duvijāno parābhavo
dhammakāmo bhavaṁ hoti dhammadessī parābhavo

I WILL NOW EXPOUND a Dhamma teaching on the Buddha's verse that appears in the *Parābhava Sutta* for the benefit of Buddhist followers, as appropriate to the occasion. You are all gathered with a skillful intention with the thought of listening to a Dhamma teaching out of faith arising from knowledge. Truly, the words of the Buddha come with three benefits: benefit in this life, benefit in the next life, and the ultimate benefit, which is nibbāna. Those three benefits can apply to both personal benefit and the benefit to others.

At this time we are all endowed with a human birth, which is the doorway to good and bad destinations, in that a being that is to be born into hell must first take a human birth and a being that is to be born into heaven or the brahma realms or nibbāna must first take a human birth, as a man or a woman, and be endowed with that status. This is because the human birth is a neutral one. Having been born as a human being, whatever level of happiness or suffering you aspire to can all be attained.

But we human beings mostly search for happiness along the pathway to suffering. Why is that? It is because of our knowledge. Whatever we know, we are content with that. Whatever art we have knowledge of, we are content with that kind of art. That is to say, if we know gardening, then we are content with gardening. If we know farming, we are content with farming. If we know selling, we are

85

content with selling. If we know draftsmanship, then we are content with drawing. If we know law, then we are content with being a lawyer. It all depends on what kind of knowledge we have; we are satisfied in accordance with that knowledge. If we know brickmaking or pottery, we are content with brickmaking and pottery, which is where our knowledge lies.

In our personal conduct it is the same: if we know how to kill animals, then we are content to kill animals. If we know the art of stealing, then we are content to steal. If we know the art of adultery, we are content to commit adultery. If we know the art of lying, we are content to tell lies. If we know the art of drinking intoxicants, we are content to drink intoxicants. If we know the art of gambling, we delight in gambling in accordance with our knowledge. And if we know how to play chess, we will like playing chess in accordance with the level of our knowledge.

With good conduct it is the same. If you know the value of giving, then you delight in giving. If you know the value of morality, then you like to live morally. If you know the value of meditation (*bhāvanā*), then you like to meditate. If you know the value of the path, fruit, and nibbāna, then you delight in the path, fruit, and nibbāna. If you know the value of the Buddha, the Dhamma, and the Saṅgha, then you incline to showing respect to the Buddha, the Dhamma, and the Saṅgha. It all depends on your knowledge and aptitude: whatever knowledge or art you know, then you are content with that.

Therefore, the Buddhist sages have stated in the Maṅgala Gāthā, "To avoid fools and to associate with the wise": not mingling with fools but associating only with wise persons is a great blessing, a supreme blessing. This is because association is the doorway to knowledge. If we begin by associating with those who are wise, we may come to learn good arts. If we first meet with fools, we may come to learn evil arts. If we know evil arts, then we will become content with that knowledge, and that will be a difficult thing to rectify.

For this reason, as explained above, the Blessed One, the ultimate teacher, gave us this Buddhist verse in the *Parābhava Sutta* that I have stated as the beginning of this talk, as follows:

Suvijāno bhavaṁ hoti: Good knowledge is a pointer to prosperity.
Duvijāno parābhavo: Bad knowledge is a pointer to ruin.
Dhammakāmo bhavaṁ hoti: Love of the Dhamma is a pointer to prosperity.
Dhammadessī parābhavo: Hatred of the Dhamma is a pointer to ruin.

In brief, the teaching of this verse is that good knowledge is a bridge to prosperity and bad knowledge is a bridge to ruin and decline; love of the Dhamma is a bridge to prosperity and hatred of the Dhamma is a bridge to ruin. The teaching does not expand on the factors of good knowledge and bad knowledge or love and hatred of the Dhamma. If we were to look at it impartially, good and bad knowledge are *saccañāṇa*:[8] these two kinds of knowledge must be known and understood. The Buddha himself knew these two kinds of knowledge. He knew what was good, and so he expounded on it to his followers. He knew what was bad, and so he expounded on it to his followers. The important point is *kiccañāṇa*, which is action, the practice. If one conducts oneself outside of the way of goodness, one will surely receive no happiness.

In order to maintain good conduct, one must know its causes, its results, and its power or value. And so we cannot get away from knowing good and knowing evil. Knowing good and evil is the important matter and something that should be talked about in particular, being the real bridge to prosperity and decline.

Now I will expand on the matter of good and bad knowledge according to my view for the reader's consideration. First, *suvijā*: good knowhow or knowledge. What kind of knowledge constitutes good knowledge? In worldly terms, it is whatever knowledge or art presents no harm; that is to say, any knowledge or art that is imbued with goodwill, compassion, sympathetic joy, and equanimity is good knowledge. Let us take as an example the knowledge of reading. If you believe that knowing how to read is a pathway to happiness, it follows that if you want happiness, then you need to learn how to read: this is a manifestation of goodwill. Wanting oneself to be free of the ignorance of illiteracy, and so attending to learning, is a manifestation of compassion. When one is able to read and feels glad within oneself, this is a manifestation of sympathetic joy. When one makes one's mind neutral—that is to say, at a time when one should be established in goodwill, one is established in goodwill; at a time when one should be established in compassion, one is established in compassion; at a time when one should be established in sympathetic joy, one is established in sympathetic joy; at a time when one should be established in equanimity, one is established in equanimity—this is a manifestation of equanimity. Thus is the knowledge of reading imbued with the four divine abidings (*brahmavihāra*). When goodwill, compassion, sympathetic joy, and equanimity arise within one, there is a way by which they can then spread out to others without limitation. Whatever kinds of knowledge are imbued with the brahmavihāra in this way are classified as good knowledge.

In terms of the Dhamma, we have the teachings on the *sappurisadhamma* (the qualities of a good person), which are given as: (1) knowing the Dhamma, (2) knowing the qualities of the Dhamma, (3) knowing oneself, (4) knowing one's moderation, (5) knowing one's time, (6) knowing the company, (7) knowing the person. These are called the best kinds of knowledge; they are suvijā. Anyone who knows this and conducts oneself regularly within these seven conditions will be a good person and can be said to have good knowledge.

But knowledge in Buddhism points out the source of things: this means that knowing oneself is the ultimate knowledge. For example, the paṭiccasamuppāda describes knowledge (*vijjā*) and ignorance (*avijjā*), meaning knowing oneself and not knowing oneself. Knowing oneself involves some good and some bad.

As for knowing the bad self, I will take this up in the section on bad knowledge (*duvijā*). Here I will discuss only knowing the good self. It is knowing that one has taken birth as a human being, be one a man or a woman: that is something we cannot change. As a man, one performs the duties of a man; as a woman, one performs the duties of a woman, as per the ways of the world. But in terms of Dhamma practice there is no distinction between man and woman: we all have the same duty.

It is only that in these times a woman cannot take on full ordination.[9] Even so, there are still ways to practice the holy life (*brahmacariya*).

Knowing oneself to have been born as a human is to know that this is the most excellent, unequaled birth. It is the doorway to all kinds of births. Whether a being becomes a deva, Indra, a brahma, or a demon, one must always obtain a human birth beforehand. In terms of the highest path, called the transcendent—beginning with the stream enterer and moving on to the once returner, nonreturner, and ultimately the arahant—these all must be attained from birth as a male or female human being.

The human birth is the birthplace of all kinds of knowledge in the world, except if you are deficient, e.g., mute, insane, or imbecile, or have a physical disability such as being deaf or have deformed limbs,[10] or one is overwhelmed by greed, hatred, and delusion as a result of being born with an *ahetukapaṭisandhi citta*.[11] These latter lack the full human endowment and are incapable of perfecting the human qualities, which are three kinds of good bodily conduct, the four kinds of good verbal conduct, and the three kinds of good mental conduct. They are not counted as having a full human birth because they cannot be receptacles for all kinds of knowledge in general. As for those who are fully endowed with human qualities—that is to say, their natures are not overwhelmed by these faults—they are capable of fully developing the human endowment, achieved by the two causes and the three causes,[12] and are said to have the true human birth in this sense.

If you have a true human status, then you must truly be the master of knowledge; that is, you are capable of learning any branch of knowledge you study. However, worldly knowledge is no small matter. The human lifespan is only seventy or eighty years. Even if you do nothing else but devote yourself solely to learning the branches of knowledge that the world has to offer, your limited lifespan will be spent and you will not have learned all the branches of knowledge there are in the world. For that reason, you must consider carefully, look into what branch of knowledge will be sufficient for making a comfortable living, and learn only those one or two branches of knowledge. But you must do it properly so that it becomes something you can rely on. You must understand that whatever branch of knowledge you are happy with, that must be completed, because this human status is the master of all the branches of knowledge in the world.

This human status, if you were to compare it to the kinds of vehicles used in the world these days, must be said to be the worthiest vehicle. On water there are ships. On land there are motor vehicles. In the air there are flying machines. They also use motors. The flying machines can only travel in the air by the power of the elements of earth, water, fire, and air. When their nutriment is spent—that is, they are out of fuel—they must fall down to earth. Motorboats can only travel on water. As for motorcars, they can only travel along the smooth roads that have been made for them. They aren't so special, because they are all fabricated out of this body vehicle.

The body vehicle—that is, the human body—is supported by four "wheels": standing, walking, sitting, and reclining. It uses food and the various consumables rather than petrol. It can be driven anywhere, and doesn't choose over water, land, mountains, forests, near or far. It can lead you to becoming a king, a general, a tycoon, a merchant, a philosopher, or a sage, all depending on your aspiration. If you aspire to heaven, the brahma realms, or transcendence, it is possible to attain those things, because we have the example of those who have gone before us, who have "driven" to all those places. They have pointed out the way to these three kinds of happy places with this one path endowed with the eight factors, commonly known as the eightfold path: right view, right thought, right speech, right action, right livelihood, right effort, right mindfulness, and right concentration. These eight factors are called the noble path because they are the path traveled by the body, speech, and mind of the noble ones.

If you do not wish to be a noble one, but wish only for the treasures of heaven, then you can practice according to the morality section of the path (*sīlakhandha*): right speech, right action, and right livelihood. Do it properly and you will surely attain heaven. When we reach heaven, we can be said to have driven our body vehicle to the heaven realm. If you want the treasures of the higher level of the brahma realm, you should add firm practice of the concentration leg of the path: right effort, right mindfulness, and right concentration. If your absorption (*jhāna*) does not deteriorate, you will attain the brahma realm and can be said to have driven your body vehicle to the brahma realm. Having attained the brahma realm, if you wish to go further, to aim for the transcendent, then you should practice according to the wisdom leg of the path—right view and right thought—using insight knowledge and vision to destroy distorted views, and you will attain the transcendent treasure. Having attained to transcendent deathlessness, it can be said that you have driven the body vehicle to the other shore, which is nibbāna, and have done with birth, aging, sickness, and death. It is the one ultimate happiness.

This body vehicle is an inheritance from being born. It can be driven to any happy realm one aspires to, as it has in the past driven many others to all those places. Having attained this "motorcar," this human body, we should not use it in wrongful ways, allowing it to decay and break down to no purpose. If it has not yet led us to the happy realms, then we can be said to have wasted it, having attained a good thing but failed to use it properly. Instead we go around creating harm for ourselves. Knowing that one is capable of attaining all the branches of knowledge in the world, up to and including the transcendent, is to know oneself well; it is the pathway to prosperity.

Now as for the second statement, *duvijāno parābhavo*, "bad knowledge is a bridge to ruin," this is explained as any knowledge that is rooted in greed, hatred, and delusion. That is, having learned it, one aims only to harm others, to take advantage of them for one's own benefit, such as the arts of swindling, stealing, and robbery. One aims to create ruin for others, to take only for oneself. Some of these bad kinds of knowledge are necessary to learn, but some are not necessary at all. For instance, the knowledge of soldiering and training to shoot guns is called *duvijā*, a truly evil kind of knowledge, because it lacks goodwill and compassion for others. The knowledge of making guns and swords and weapons of all kinds, such as fighting vehicles, flying machines, submarines, artillery shells, and torpedoes, these are all counted as bad knowledge, a bridge to ruin, decline, and destruction. Even though we know these kinds of knowledge to be bad, we must still know them and be clever in relation to them, but we must know them as bad knowledge, as bridges to ruin.

There is a clear example of this that we can see in the occurrence of the Great War that began in Europe in July 1914. It has caused massive destruction. Human beings should live together with love, should protect and look after each other, in order to be worthy of the name civilized beings.

According to the news, the cause of what has occurred is not a very big thing. Apparently a Serbian national, acting in the way of brutish people everywhere, assassinated the royal heir of Austria and his wife while they were touring through Serbia. As a result, the two countries had words with each other and turned to the great powers to help them resolve the issue. Russia sided with Serbia, while Germany sided with Austria. England and France sided with Russia. Having brought great powers to the meeting, neither side had any intention of reaching a resolution; instead, each wanted to show their strength, and so all declared war and began attacking and murdering each other. It has spread over the whole world. Countless people have been killed by weapons, and countless other people have died as a result of starvation or disease. It's not only the soldiers who are dying. The aged, women, and children who have uprooted their families to flee the enemy are without food, and countless have died. The number of people who have died in this war is not in the millions: it looks like we'll have to count them in the tens of millions (*koti*). It's tragic. There must be separation of husband, wife, and child; people are widowed and orphaned; there's no one to make a living; and they must endure relentless poverty.

It's impossible to describe it all. I've only pointed out a little bit of it in order to show the power of evil knowledge and how much damage it causes. Each side considers itself to be the owner of the knowledge. "I can make flying machines. I can make submarines. I have lots of battleships. I can make artillery shells and bombs." Because each side brags about owning its branches of knowledge, they dare to go into battle, completely devoid of kindness, and look on each other as animals or fish.

Bad knowledge is the cause of ruin. Whether that ruin is great or little is measured by the power of the knowledge. For instance, the knowledge of making spears and swords does not lead to massive effect. The damage from those weapons is not that great. With big knowledge, there is a big effect, such as the knowledge of how to make artillery shells and bombs. The resulting harm is great, as we can see in the present day. You must understand that knowledge that is imbued with greed, hatred and delusion, and jealousy and vengefulness is called duvijā, as fits the Buddha's words *duvijāno parābhavo*: bad knowledge is a bridge to ruin and destruction.

What I have described so far is external bad knowledge. There is also internal bad knowledge. Seeing oneself badly has many forms. For instance, seeing ourselves as being filled with greed, hatred, and delusion, that one is still behaving badly, killing animals or stealing and so on, is knowing the bad self. If you know that you are bad in this way, then you must quickly fix it and not allow those bad things to remain in you, and that becomes a pathway to happiness and prosperity. If you know that you are bad but you continue to behave badly, that is truly the pathway to decline.

There is another way, and that is intending not to do bad and feeling that it isn't a bad thing: the intention is skillful and you feel that it is in accordance with the path to insight and peace, but it can still become bad knowledge. For instance, someone who develops the meditation on the three characteristics or the meditation on loathsomeness or the meditation on death: they contemplate the body according to the instruction to look on it as impermanent, suffering, and not self, that it is unclean, unbeautiful, and ugly, that it has no use, that it is only for discarding on the earth. Seeing in this way is a cause for the arising of *saṁvega*.[13] It is one way of getting rid of love and infatuation within oneself and prevents delusion in perceptions, and so it is taught as a form of insight meditation. It has incalculable benefits. But it also has many drawbacks, as for example the group of bhikkhus who developed their meditation on death and became so wearied and disgusted with their bodies that they used their bowls and robes to hire the hunter Migalaṇḍika to deprive them of life. The story is related in the backstory to the third offense of defeat (*pārājika*). This is an example of the harm that can arise from seeing oneself as bad or knowing oneself as bad.

And not only that: of those who contemplate impermanence, suffering, and not-self, many go crazy, developing the nihilist view (*ucchedadiṭṭhi*) and seeing that there is no merit or sin, that after death there is nothing. In fact, their seeing in this way is not really their own knowledge; it is mostly knowledge heard from others. That is, there are two groups: the first group is foolish; they don't know anything. They just listen to what others say. For instance, they may say that thinking is reliant solely on the brain. When you die, there is no brain, so what is there to be reborn? Birth lies solely with the parents. Most people just see things this way.

That birth is dependent on a father and mother is not in dispute. It is not only birth that one relies on them for. Once born, you must depend on your parents until you are grown up. Our parents are of so much benefit to us it is impossible to describe it all. But you must consider what it is that our parents have created. If you look at it carefully, it seems to be something that has happened entirely of its own accord. To say that your parents were your origination is not the full picture. It's like a potter who makes pots for sale. You could say that the potter is the originating factor, but that is still a bit shallow, because the clay that the potter uses to make the pots was already there. In the same way, the conditions that lead to the arising of a child were there before the parents. Since this is the case, for someone to see only the parents as the origination is not quite right. They are looking only on the level of conditioned things (*saṅkhatadhamma*). They have not yet seen the unconditioned. They have not yet used their own knowledge and vision, but are simply believing what others have said. They are separating the elements only on account of their belief in what others have said. Their separation of the elements is only in form. In fact, can you deny that one needle does not contain all four elements? Even air, which is even subtler than a needle, you cannot deny that it does not have all four elements within it. Air being so subtle, the elements can't be separated. If this is so, how can they talk about separating the elements?

Another group is those who are too smart. They focus too much on contemplation of not-self (*anattānupassanā*) and contemplation of emptiness (*suññatānupassanā*) so that they develop perception of not-self (*anattasaññā*) and perception of emptiness (*suññatasaññā*), seeing that there is no self, that everything is empty, and they take that emptiness as their focus. Then they think that emptiness is nibbāna. This kind of emptiness is just ignorance. So it can be said that they take ignorance as their refuge. They are *moghapurisa*, empty people. They are ingrates (*akataññū*), not recognizing the benefits of the Triple Gem, the benefits of their parents, the benefits of their teachers, the benefits of their king and advisors; such recognition is not to be found in them.

These people, whether believing that after death there is nothing or that after death you are reborn, fall into the category of wrong view, and they are incapable of making goodness for themselves and so blame the teachers, saying, "They know the truth in full, but they make a living based on deception. They say, 'Doing this is meritorious, doing that is bad kamma,' intentionally deceiving others to make a living. Where is there any merit or sin?" This is how they speak. These people tend to heap the blame on those who are benefactors, exalting themselves and disparaging others in various ways. As for themselves, they do not make merit or keep the precepts, and moreover, they criticize others. They ruin both their own benefit and the benefit to any others who come into contact with them. It is like this on account of seeing not-self as emptiness, a form of wrong view. They know wrongly and believe wrongly, so they have wrong view. They study Buddhism, but they unknowingly become a danger to it. There are hundreds and thousands of people like this.

Students of Buddhism should consider very carefully and not fall into error. Impermanence, suffering, and not-self are not toys. If you get it right, you'll go straight to nibbāna. If you get it wrong, you will fall into the abyss of hell. Thus, in terms of knowing or seeing oneself as something bad, it is said to be a bridge to ruin and decline, in accordance with the Buddha's words *duvijāno parābhavo*.

The third stanza, *dhammakāmo bhavam hoti*, "love of the Dhamma is a cause for prosperity," should be studied until one clearly understands the Dhamma, to know what it is that we refer to as the Dhamma. The Dhamma, if you were to describe its features and forms, is endless. For instance, it can be divided into learning, practice, and realization, or into wholesome dhammas, unwholesome dhammas, and neither wholesome nor unwholesome dhammas. This may not be clear. For that reason the meaning is summarized as *svākkhāto bhagavatā dhammo*: "the Dhamma that is well taught by the Blessed One." This means that all of the teachings given by the Blessed One are Dhamma. If that's the case, then there is also no end to it, because the teachings of the Buddha are very extensive.

We can summarize the Dhamma into three kinds, described as *ādikalyāṇaṁ, majjhekalyāṇaṁ, pariyosānakalyāṇaṁ*: the teaching of the Buddha is good in the beginning, that is morality; good in the middle, that is concentration; and good at the end, that is wisdom. In summary, morality, concentration, and wisdom are the Dhamma, because they are the teaching of the Buddha. If that's the case, then we must search for and find morality, concentration, and wisdom, because the teaching of the Buddha is to be witnessed each person for oneself.

If we do not know morality, if we do not have morality, how can we observe morality? It's like a person who does not know cattle and has never seen cattle. How can such a person look after cattle? If you want to see morality or know morality, you must first know your body, speech, and mind. The meeting of the six elements is known as body. The sounds emitted from the mouth, relying on the body, are speech. Reflection, thought, and moods in general, contingent on the body, are known as mind. Morality is defined as this body, speech, and mind. As for the mental aspect, it refers to the kamma of intention. When we talk of morality, we cannot leave out the mind. The one who watches out is the mind; the one who looks after is the mind. What is it that it watches out for? It watches out for actions and speech. What does it look after? It looks after actions and speech. So, in short, it's the self watching out for the self, the self looking after the self, because actions are oneself, speech is oneself, and mind is oneself.

Watching out for and looking after the body mean to not kill living beings, steal things, commit sexual misconduct, or take intoxicants. Watching out for and looking after the speech mean not to speak falsely, speak harshly, to gossip, or to speak frivolously. When body and speech are free of these harmful things, it is called right speech, right action, and right livelihood. It means one is endowed with morality. Seeing that one has morality, one can say that one is Dhamma, is it not so? Because morality is the teaching of the Buddha.

The teaching of the Buddha is called Dhamma. When you see that you have morality and the morality is Dhamma, then you can be said to be one can who has attained the Dhamma on the level of morality. One who observes morality is one who observes the Dhamma; one who looks after the Dhamma is one who observes morality. Whatever is morality can lead to samādhi and wisdom.

One who loves the Dhamma on the level of any part of morality, concentration, and wisdom will receive the results of growth and prosperity, more or less, depending on the level of the Dhamma that one has attained and loves, in accordance with the Buddha's words *dhammakāmo bhavaṁ hoti*, "Love of the Dhamma is a cause for prosperity."

The phrase *dhammadessī parābhavo*, "hatred of the dhamma is a bridge to ruin," should be understood in the same way. Knowing that we are Dhamma and that the Dhamma is us, but continuing to conduct ourselves in unskillful ways—that is to say, allowing ourselves to fall into the power of greed, hatred, and delusion, continuing to create bad conduct and bad kamma through body, speech, and mind—this is called "hating Dhamma."

Whoever conducts oneself as an enemy to oneself is someone who hates the Dhamma. The phrase *an enemy to oneself* should be understood as follows: the six internal sense bases of eye, ear, nose, tongue, body, and mind are one's features. If one has all six in full, then one is ready and replete with the qualities that could lead one to every kind of aspiration. If one is lacking in one or two of these, then one is an *abhappapuggala* (disabled) and may not be able to realize the higher benefits. But even if one has the six senses in full, if one is overpowered by foolishness and makes these sense bases into one's enemy—that is, when one sees a sight with the eye, hears a sound with the ear, smells an odor with the nose, tastes a flavor with the tongue, feels a sensation of touch in the body, or cognizes a mental object in the mind, if it's a pleasant sensation, one wants to obtain it, wants to delight in it, and likes it excessively to the point that suffering and misery arise, causing one to experience all kinds of sorrow and despair; if one experiences an object that is unpleasant, then excessive aversion arises, so that one experiences all kinds of sorrow and despair as a result—this is called making oneself one's own enemy. Such a person cannot realize their own higher benefit. Understand that whoever is still suffering, who still has despair, aversion, and distress in the mind on account of eyes, ears, nose, tongue, body, and mind, is their own enemy. One who is one's own enemy is what we refer to as *dhammadessī*, one who hates the Dhamma. Such a person will truly receive decline and ruin as supported by the Buddha's words *dhammadessī parābhavo*, as herein explained.

In summary, these statements of the Buddha—that is to say, good knowledge, bad knowledge, loving Dhamma, and hating Dhamma— are four in number, but if we were to condense it down to just one— good knowledge is to know the good self,[14] bad knowledge is to know the bad self,[15] to love the Dhamma is to love oneself, to hate the Dhamma is to hate oneself. So it all comes down to one, which is oneself. For that reason, one who knows oneself, who sees oneself, is regarded as possessing the highest kind of knowledge, as explained herein. Readers who consider this carefully will not fail to attain real benefit.

AJAHN BUDDHADĀSA

Few Thai Buddhist masters can claim as large a public profile as Ajahn Buddhadāsa (1906–1993), whose larger-than-life persona and extensive body of work have already become familiar on numerous platforms in the West. His unique takes on Buddhist teaching and perspectives on other religions and teachings (including Christianity and Zen Buddhism) were a result of a dedication to spirited inquiry and a prolific output of teachings and writings over many decades.

He was born Ngueam Phanit to Chinese parents in Phum Riang Subdistrict, Surat Thani Province, in Southern Thailand. He became a bhikkhu in 1926, initially simply to further his studies, but he quickly showed an aptitude for teaching. He traveled to Bangkok to go deeper in his learning but soon became disillusioned with the saṅgha establishment and ended his Pali studies at level 3, after which he returned to his home village with the intention of devoting himself to practicing the Dhamma. He established a temple in a forest setting near Chaiya, which eventually became his famous Suan Mokkh (Garden of Liberation) temple.

Not having a meditation teacher, he turned to the Tipiṭaka for guidance in his practice and, as a result, studied the texts extensively. This led to his work as a translator and writer. He adopted the epithet Buddhadāsa (Slave of the Buddha) as part of his impassioned campaign to revive interest in the core Buddhist teachings as recorded in the suttas rather than the later commentaries, and he sought to bring the teachings to life with expositions on central Buddhist teachings such as the four noble truths, mindfulness of breathing, and emptiness.

He was endowed with a keen sense of curiosity and searching for truth. This led him to take an interest in various practical matters such as photography and, in the early days, gramophone records, which he used to study English. As his command of English developed, he began to read texts from other traditions, such as Zen and Western writings on Buddhism, and he translated *The Zen Teachings of Huang Po* and *The Platform Sutta* into Thai. He later stated that while his understanding of English was not perfect, he was able to rely on his understanding of the Dhamma to complete the translations.

In 1954 he translated the regular Buddhist chanting, which had traditionally been done in the Pali language, into Thai, and his book of chants in translation became a staple of many monasteries throughout Thailand. In 1962 he built the Spiritual Theatre at Suan Mokkh and established a program of practice for his bhikkhu disciples to create Buddhist artworks.

Ajahn Buddhadāsa was a prolific Buddhist writer and thinker. His brother adopted the name Dhammadāsa (Slave of the Dhamma) and established a small publishing house to help spread the teachings. Its output included a quarterly Buddhist magazine, which carried translations of Mahayana Buddhist teachings, and numerous writings such as *The Noble Truths in the Buddha's Words* and *Treasures from the Buddha's Mouth*. Ajahn Buddhadāsa's writings are monumental in extent and pivotal in their impact. Few are the members of the Thai saṅgha who have not been influenced by his writings.

Although he is known in the West for some of his less orthodox writings (such as *Christianity and Buddhism*), the bulk of his writings are very orthodox, being collections of translations from the Pali (such as *The Buddha's Life in His Own Words*) or commentaries on various suttas. His aim was to present the Buddha's teachings in ways that were accessible to a wider audience and strip away the erroneous misconceptions prevalent in Thai society early in his career, such as the belief that it is impossible to realize the Dhamma in this day and age.

The translation presented here is an example of such a work: an exposition on the *Dhammacakkappavattana Sutta*, probably the most important sutta in the Pali Canon, in which many of the Buddha's core teachings, including the middle way, the four noble truths and the eightfold path, are outlined. It is recorded as the first discourse given by the Buddha after his enlightenment.

THE DHAMMACAKKAPPAVATTANA SUTTA[1]

NOW I WANT TO FURTHER CLARIFY what is known as the *dhammacakka*, to show how it can be used as a weapon for destroying suffering, both on the personal and social levels. First, let us all consider the purpose for which the Buddha gave this teaching. In the Pali it is said that the Tathāgata arises in this world for the happiness, for the prosperity, for the benefit of all beings, both devas and humans. This means that if there is no need for this benefit, then there is no need for a buddha to arise. We would only need to have arahants who free themselves from suffering on a personal level. That a buddha arises in the world is for the purpose of helping worldly beings.

When the Buddha arose, he gave the Dhammacakka as his first teaching. Why is that so? The word *dhammacakka* has many meanings that are broad and profound, but in essence it is to reduce human problems. That is why the Buddha gave this as his first teaching following his enlightenment.

Now let us examine what is known as the *Dhammacakkappavattana Sutta*. First, let us examine the title. This sutta is known by three names. This first is the *Paṭhamadesanā* (First Sermon). The second is the *Anuttaradhammacakka*. The third is the *Dhammacakkappavattana*.

The first title is self-explanatory. It was the first teaching that the Buddha gave to the world. But looking a little more deeply, I'd like you to consider that by *first*, we mean it's the first thing that all people should know at all times in all ages. All people must know this first. It is not the first simply in the sense that it was the first teaching for the Buddha and the five first disciples. I want you to see it as the first thing that *all* people should understand. And it is also the first thing for all times in all ages for however far in the future.

What is the first matter for all people? We can ascertain this from the content of the teaching. These days we are not very interested in clearly understanding the teaching of this sutta, and we don't really understand the meaning of this "first matter." Today we will consider this and see how it is so.

The second title is Anuttaradhammacakka. This means that it is the "unexcelled *dhammacakka*." That is, there is no *cakka* superior to this one. Thus it is called the Anuttaradhammacakka. The dhammacakka is a tool or weapon for cutting off problems and cutting off suffering. There is no better tool or weapon than this.

We can also define the word *cakka* in another way, as "wheel." A wheel, such as a cart wheel, is a symbol of progress and prosperity. The wheel is universally acknowledged, even in India during the Buddha's time, as a symbol of progress. And regarding progress, there can be no better wheel than the wheel of Dhamma. The Dhamma acts as a wheel leading to prosperity. That is, it leads easily, just as a cart or car wheel facilitates the movement of the cart or car. The Dhamma is the same. In addition to being a weapon, it can also be looked on as a wheel, which leads to quick progress toward prosperity. There is no wheel better than the dhammacakka. And there is no weapon better than the dhammacakka. Thus it is called *anuttara*, unexcelled.

The third title, Dhammacakkappavattana, means "releasing" the dhammacakka, or more literally it is "setting in motion the wheel of Dhamma." The Buddha released the dhammacakka; that is, he announced the realm of the Dhamma, as it is said in the Thai translation, *anuttaraṁ dhammacakkaṁ pavattitaṁ*: the Blessed One has set in motion the matchless wheel of dhamma—*apattivattiyaṁ samaṇena vā devena vā brāhmaṇena va brāhmuṇā vā kenaci vā lokasamin'ti*—that Dhamma wheel that no one can resist, no one can turn back. Be one a recluse, a brahmin, a brahma (god), or deva, no one can resist it or force this wheel to turn back. This is the meaning of Dhammacakkappavattana.

There may be those who wonder how you can explain the fact that nowadays there are those who resist the Dhamma, take no interest in the Dhamma, who disparage the Dhamma, and neglect the Dhamma. How can you explain this? This is looking at it too superficially. Why don't they consider whether the opposition to the Dhamma of those people is successful or not? Wherever there is opposition to the Dhamma, there is destruction then and there for that person. Think about it and you will see.

This is all in relation to the titles *Paṭhamadesanā*, the First Sermon; *Anuttaradhammacakka*, the supreme wheel; and *Dhammacakkappavattana Sutta*, the teaching that sets forth the Dhamma wheel into the world. Carefully considering the meaning of these three titles may increase our appreciation and understanding of the *Dhammacakkappavattana Sutta*.

Now let us consider each title in more depth. First let us consider how it is the first matter that should be known. According to the sutta, the first thing that should be known is that which is called the two *anta*, or "extremes," together with that which lies between—that is, it does not veer to either of those extremes. Let us suppose the two sides as left and right. The left extreme is following after sensual desires. This side is called *kāmasukallikānuyogo*, blindly indulging in pleasant feelings through the senses. This is one extreme. The other extreme is the torturing of the body by foolish people who think that if they oppress the body until there are only bones remaining or they die, they will be able to give up defilements. This is a practice that goes to the opposite extreme. You can call them the left extreme or the right extreme, it's up to you, as long as we understand that it is veering to two opposite extremes.

Worldly beings fall into these two extremes. When you look at it, you can see that they mostly veer toward indulgence in sensual pleasures. There are very few who veer toward the extreme of self-torment. We could probably explain why this is so, but please understand that there is this veering toward these two extremes. No one finds the right balance. Thus, it is said that this is the first thing that should be noted: that worldly beings are divided into these two extremes of practice, and mostly it is toward the side of indulgence in sense pleasures.

As for the middle way, which does not veer to either of these two extremes, this is the way of the noble disciples who have heard the teaching from noble ones or the Buddha and who know how to maintain themselves in the middle. There are even fewer of these. Almost the entire world is veering toward the extreme of indulgence in sense pleasures. There are a few who are stuck on the foolish way of self-torment. As for those who are on the middle way, they are the remainder, and there are very few of these. Anyone who can do this is classed as a noble disciple.

This middle area is known as the *majjhimā paṭipadā*, the middle way. It has many different explanations and systems. The system that is well known is the one expounded on in this sutta, known as the eightfold path: right view, right aspiration,[2] right speech, right action, right livelihood, right effort, right recollection, and right concentration. These eight limbs, together known as the path (*magga*), were said by the Buddha to be teachings never before heard, meaning no one had taught them to him. It was something he was directly enlightened to.

He taught the benefits of this path in a way that is really noteworthy: practicing this eightfold path leads to vision (*cakkhukaraṇī*), leads to direct knowledge (*ñāṇakaraṇī*), leads to knowledge, and ultimately leads to nibbāna. Everyone should know how to use this eightfold path for their own benefit, to begin to develop the eye of correct knowledge until they attain supreme knowledge and ultimately realization of nibbāna. This is the benefit of being in the middle and avoiding the two extremes. This is the first thing that you need to know.

What is the benefit of having avoided the two extremes and taken the middle way? It is, as I said, the arising of the eye of knowledge and direct knowledge, specifically knowledge of the four noble truths (*ariyasacca*). These are the truths that one should know, or to put it more directly, they are the truths that one *must* know. If you don't know them, then you will certainly suffer.

Let us take a look at this word *sacca*. It translates as "truth." If something is true, then it does not deceive. In the Pali it is described rather quaintly as *yaṁ saccaṁ taṁ amusā*: "that which is true does not lie." That is sacca.

Things that are sacca are all true, but some are noble and some are not. The truth that results in the cessation of suffering is what we call a noble truth. Truths that are simply truths according to nature but not of benefit to human life are not called noble truths. Please understand the meaning of this word *ariya*, or noble, as leading to the cessation of suffering and being of benefit.

These noble truths were things that the Buddha had not learned from anyone else; he became enlightened to them by himself. As with the middle way, he declared that he had not heard this teaching before. It was a direct result of the Buddha's enlightenment.

There are four noble truths: suffering, its cause, its cessation, and the path, putting it briefly in just four words. They are words that include everything that human beings should know or must know.

The first truth is *dukkha*, suffering. It refers to the suffering that is a major problem for human beings. It is that which is hard to endure and causes trouble and agitation. No matter how many kinds there are, they all have the same meaning in that they cause hardship for human beings. This is the first truth.

The second truth is called *samudaya*: it means the cause of suffering. This is hard to see and hard to understand. It's not obvious to ordinary people. It needs someone with the highest wisdom—that is, a buddha—to teach it. It refers to the defilements springing from ignorance, which cause us to cling to this and that as being self or belonging to self, and the arising of foolish desires in accordance with clinging. This is the cause of suffering's arising, the second truth.

The third truth is called *nirodha*, the remainderless cessation of suffering. Please do not think that this is something easy to see or easy to understand. Some people have the wrong understanding. To end suffering, they turn to things that cannot end suffering or that are not the cessation of suffering. They're always deceiving themselves, and so they never experience the true ending of suffering. They do not know cessation. If they do not know the cause, there is no way they can know cessation. These things must occur together. You must know that defilements are the cause of suffering before you can end defilements and end suffering.

Nowadays people think that money is the end of suffering, so everyone is looking for money. Thinking that rank or honor is the end of suffering, they seek rank and honor, looking for power and prestige. Or they make offerings to spirits, devas, or holy objects to help end suffering. These are the actions of fools. They do not know that suffering arises from defilements. The cessation of suffering must be at the cessation of defilements, cessation of desire and clinging. This is how the Buddha taught. It is the teaching of nirodha, the third truth.

The fourth truth is called *magga*: it is the explanation of what we need to do to end defilements, and that comes back to the noble eightfold path, the middle way. Practicing according to the noble eightfold path leads to the cessation of defilements; suffering ceases and our problems are gone.

These four things are interconnected, as can be clearly seen. When there is suffering, there is a cause of suffering. It is something that must cease, and that is through right practice. The noble truths are therefore separated into four in this way: as suffering, the cause, cessation, and the path.

All people, be they householders or renunciants, should take an interest in this and see it properly; otherwise there is no benefit in us being followers of the Buddha. But it seems that people have not shown as much interest in understanding this to the best of their abilities due to various kinds of misunderstandings, so that the matter is all confused. The truth that we must know is the four noble truths. They answer the questions: What is that? It is suffering. Where does it come from? That is the cause (*samudaya*). What is the aim? It is for the cessation of suffering (*nirodha*). How is that thing accomplished? It is by the noble eightfold path, or the middle way.

There are statements of the Buddha that these four noble truths are fixed. You cannot add to them, and you cannot take away from them. There must always be four. This is what we must know and what all people must understand.

Let us look further into them and we will see the criteria for knowing the practice of the noble truths. This is explained in the Pali in the same sutta, following on from the explanation of the four noble truths.

It is the three kinds of direct knowledge (*ñāna*), which are referred to as *saccañāna, kiccañāna*, and *katañāna*. Put like this, it might be hard to understand, so let's just put it into simple language: they are the things that you must know in relation to the practice of the four noble truths. First, it is to know the nature of those truths. What is the nature of suffering, what is the nature of the cause, what is the nature of cessation, and what is the nature of the path? We don't know how these things exist in nature.

Suffering refers to birth, aging, sickness, and death, as well as other kinds of suffering that exist naturally. When foolish people cling to things as themselves, suffering arises.

As for the cause, which is defilements, these have their natural causes and conditions. When a foolish person clings to things and does not know them in accordance with their nature, the chance for mental fabrication arises, leading to defilements and suffering. It doesn't matter who you are—child or adult, female or male. If you're foolish in this way, there is the chance of fabricating defilements into the mind, leading to suffering.

With cessation it is the same. This truth tells us that defilements are something that can be extinguished. There is nothing that is born that does not cease. There is birth, then there is cessation in accordance with the laws of nature. This is knowing what the causes and conditions for cessation that exist in nature are like.

And for the eightfold path, it is a natural fact that when this kind of practice arises, then the results follow in such and such a way. For instance, if you maintain yourself on the noble eightfold path, the result is the cessation of defilements or protection against defilements in accordance with nature.

All in all, this is called knowing how things exist in nature, and it is termed *saccañāna*: seeing as it is what suffering is like, what the cause is like, what the cessation of suffering is like, and what the path leading to the cessation of suffering is like.

The second kind of direct knowledge is to know what we human beings need to do in relation to those things. The tasks that we need to do in relation to these things are: in relation to suffering, to know it; in relation to the cause of suffering, to give it up; in relation to the cessation of suffering, to realize it; and in relation to the path leading to the cessation of suffering, to cultivate and perfect it. This is knowing the duties that we must perform in relation to those things. In brief, the task for suffering is to know it; the task for the cause of suffering is to give it up; the task for the cessation of suffering is to realize it; and the task for the path is to perfect it.

When we do not perform these tasks, we don't know that suffering is something that needs to be known. We sit bawling our eyes out, but we don't know that this is suffering. We don't know suffering even though we are drowning in it. Because we do not have this knowledge, we do not know the cause of suffering, and we do not know that which is more profound than that, which is the cessation of suffering. And so we sit there crying, or have mental illnesses, or go crazy—all because we do not know one thing, which is suffering.

Please note that these things are all interconnected. If we really know suffering, we will know the cause of suffering, and we will see the cessation of suffering and the way leading to the cessation of suffering, because they are all interconnected. If you don't know one of these things, then you don't know any of them, and it all starts with not knowing suffering. If you know suffering, you will notice that this is suffering. Then you will look into it and see its root, that from which it arises. On the opposite side, there is the cessation of suffering, and there is the method by means of which suffering cannot arise. Knowing this is knowing the task in regard to those four noble truths, known in brief as *kiccañāṇa*.

The first set of knowledges is saccañāṇa. The second set is kiccañāṇa. The third set, known as *katañāṇa*, is the acknowledgment that these duties have been well carried out—knowing that suffering has been well-known, that the cause has been well-abandoned, that the cessation of suffering has been well-realized, and that the path has been well-cultivated and perfected. Knowing this is to know whether you have completed these knowledges or not, and also knowing that, if it is not yet completed, what it is that we are still stuck on, what obstacles still remain. Knowing in this way is called katañāṇa. Thus, there are these three direct kinds of knowledge, the things that must be known in regard to the practice of the four noble truths as I have already explained.

The passages that follow in this sutta refer to the Buddha himself, stating that the Buddha became the Fully Self-Enlightened Buddha (*sammāsambuddha*) through knowing these noble truths in full in accordance with these three kinds of knowledge. There are four noble truths, and for each truth there are three things to be known. With these three kinds of direct knowledge applied to each of the four noble truths, that gives twelve facets.

Knowing this in full means knowing all things, or knowing the whole world or whatever it is that we must know, and knowing it truly. Putting aside the noble truths, to know anything in this world it must be known according to these criteria: know the thing itself, know what we must do in relation to that, and know that we have done that task. For example, a rice farmer must know what a rice paddy is, what task needs to be done, and how it is to be completed. This is knowing about farming. It is the same with other things. And so this same principle is applied to the four noble truths.

If we know in this way, then we will be without doubts; we will be without remorse, attachment, and longing. We will know the whole world, knowing suffering is in the world of defilements. Knowing in this way, we no longer doubt whether there is anything remaining in the world that is worth longing for, and so we no longer have any aspirations or attachments to things that are suffering in this world. To put it briefly, knowing the four noble truths is knowing the whole world in all aspects, to the point that we have no doubts and no longer expect anything from the world. We no longer delight in or attach to the world.

Now let us consider how it is that we should know this, or what it is that we know with, and that is knowing with superknowledge (*abhiñña*), or to name it according to the texts, it is right wisdom according to the truth (*yathābhūta sammappaññā*). It is not knowing according to the ten wrong kinds of knowing outlined in the *Kalama Sutta*.[3] That is to say, we don't believe merely on account of having heard it from others, through guesswork, through logical analysis, on the basis of things written in the Tipiṭaka or other texts, or simply because our teacher says so, and so on. Knowing according to yathābhūta sammappaññā is tasting the flavor of suffering, seeing how it arises from defilements, how it ceases if defilements are extinguished, seeing the causes and conditions for defilements, and extinguishing those causes and conditions. Knowing in this way is called knowing with abhiññā, superknowledge in accordance with the truth.

The Buddha knew these four noble truths through this superknowledge. Being a fully enlightened buddha means knowing these four noble truths, knowing the whole world as it really is. The world is the birthplace of suffering. What we refer to as the world is described in a very interesting statement: *sadeva ke samāra ke sabrahma ke*, which translates as "in the world with its deva realms, its māra realms, and its brahma realms." This "deva realms, māra realms, and brahma realms" refers to worlds that are distinguished by their level of happiness. Devas have the happiness of devas; māras, the highest level of devas, have the happiness of māras. Some people may not understand how *māra* is called "the highest level of deva."[4] Normal devas are simply called devas. The highest level of devas are called *māras*, referring to the *paranimmitavasavattī*, which have the highest level of happiness among beings on the sensual realm. They are māras because they attach to the mind more than any other level. The māra who challenged the Buddha on the night of his enlightenment, known as Payāvasavattī Māra, came from this highest deva realm.

Now the brahmas have the happiness of brahmas. So the world is divided up into *devaloka, māraloka, brahmaloka*, distinguished by their respective levels of happiness.

Then there are the words *samaṇa brāhmaṇīya pajāya sa deva-manussāya*: "the world with its *samaṇa* (recluses) and brahmins": here the level of mind is the criterion.

All in all, it is the world in all its various levels. Regardless of the criteria by which it is classified, it is all the world—a receptacle for suffering. The cessation of suffering lies with cutting off the cause of suffering. When the cause is extinguished and one is no longer foolishly attaching to the world, one is no longer counted as the world or a worldly being. One is not considered to be a deva, a māra, a brahma, or anything at all. There are no defilements remaining to cause clinging. By knowing these four noble truths, the Buddha declared himself to be a sammāsambuddha. This is said to be completing the holy life, as the Buddha declared, *ayamantimā jāti natth'idani punabbhavo'ti*: "This is my last life. There is no further rebirth." The words *completing the holy life* refer to knowing the noble truths in the manner referred to as "fully realized and penetrated," so that suffering can no longer arise. It is referred to as "the last life (*jāti*), . . . no further birth (*jāti*)." The word *life* (*jāti*) here refers to suffering.

The Buddha became the Buddha by his enlightenment to the four noble truths as I have explained here: that is, knowing according to those three cycles and twelve facets. He knew the world in full, such that he no longer had any doubts that there is anything worth longing for and clinging to. He knew this with sharp wisdom that was capable of cutting off any delusion. He peeled away the terms *deva, māra, brahma*, or whatever, and all that nonsense, and so he is said to have completed the holy life.

As shown in the Pali of the *Dhammacakkappavattana Sutta*, this teaching resulted in one of the five people listening to the teaching—namely Venerable Añña Kondañña—gaining the Dhamma Eye (*dhammacakkhu*). He declared *yaṁ kiñci samudaya dhammaṁ sabbaṁ taṁ nirodhadhammam*: "Whatever is of the nature to arise is of the nature to cease." Listening to the Buddha's teaching of the four noble truths as I have explained, he attained the Dhamma Eye. Seeing the Dhamma here means seeing the way to nibbāna. Seeing the way to nibbāna is seeing the path that leads out of suffering and to the cessation of suffering, to nibbāna. He had not yet fully reached nibbāna, but he saw the way to nibbāna, from suffering to the utter extinguishing of suffering. Seeing in this way is called having the Dhamma Eye (*dhammacakkhu*).

Having the Dhamma Eye is a guarantee that one will no longer take the wrong path. One will not regress, but only progress toward nibbāna. The Dhamma eye sees the law of cause and effect and sees the law of arising and ceasing. Seeing the law of cause and effect refers to seeing that causes and effects lead to the fabrication of things and the arising of suffering. This is the law of cause and effect. It can also be looked at as the law of arising and ceasing, the reasons that things arise and cease. This is seeing the law of dependent origination (*paṭicca-samuppāda*), which I will talk about in detail at a later time. For now, I will just say that having the Dhamma Eye is to see the law of cause and effect and to be no longer subject to credulity. It is seeing the law of arising and ceasing to the point where one can stop the arising and ceasing. This is the Dhamma Eye. When the Buddha taught the *Dhammacakkappavattana Sutta*, one person attained the Dhamma Eye.

Following this it is described how the teaching pervaded throughout all world systems. This is not the Buddha's words. These are words stated at the end of the sutta. They are the words of the later teachers who compiled the suttas into written form, dealing with what happened after the Buddha taught the Dhammacakka: "All ten thousand world systems were shaken." Briefly, the effect of the teaching pervaded throughout all world systems. The words used are *ten thousand world systems*. It's up to you how you interpret that. It's not something that we have to look at in detail. Just know that there is not just one world but many—"ten thousand world systems." You could say it is the variations in ways of existence of various beings, or even within one person there are tens of thousands of kinds of suffering, and that these are ten thousand world systems within one person. To put it in general terms, as normal people would say, we can say that there are many other worlds apart from this one. Whatever way you say it, if it is useful for the purpose of extinguishing suffering, then so should you take it.

I would like to interpret it as follows: the four noble truths dominate the ten thousand–fold world system. The entire ten thousand–fold world system lies under the domination of this highest law of the four noble truths. When the noble truths are taught, then the ten thousand–fold world system must shake, because it lies under the rule of these truths. Or you could say that the ten thousand–fold world system had never before heard this teaching given by the Buddha, this teaching on the four noble truths, and there is no other person apart from a buddha who could give this teaching. So the world system shook when the Buddha gave this teaching.

I have related this because this content occurs at the end of this sutta. You could put it very briefly that this talk of the ten thousand–fold world system is just a manner of speaking, meaning it permeated throughout the land in every direction. It is the highest teaching in many aspects. For instance, in terms of amazement, it is the most amazing; in terms of benefit, it is the most beneficial; in terms of excellence, it is the most excellent. But what is of particular interest is that it is something that is opposite to the world. The world or worldly system is all to do with ignorance. Beings exist through ignorance and arise from ignorance. So once this matter arose, it was the opposite; it caused a clash. When opposites meet, there is a clash, just like when you mix acid with alkaline: there is a strong clash, a struggle for domination until one or the other wins out. So this was in direct opposition to the world, such that it caused the ten thousand–fold world system to shake, as stated at the end of this sutta.

This then is the *Dhammacakkappavattana Sutta*. It tells about the extremes that are the wrong ways and the middle way that is the path to the cessation of suffering. If you are on the middle way, you will see the four noble truths: suffering, the cause, the cessation, and the path. And you will see the nature of those things, how they exist in nature, what our task is in relation to those things, and also whether we have completed those tasks or not. If you can do this completely, then you can be said to know the noble truths in full. If you know like a buddha, then that is a buddha; if you know like a follower, then you are a follower.

Once the Buddha had given this teaching, there was one person who gained the Dhamma Eye, and that was Venerable Añña Kondañña. When the teaching had been given, ten thousand world systems shook.

This concludes the matter of the *Dhammacakkappavattana Sutta* as it appears in the Pali. Now let us consider how it applies to us. I ask you to take an interest in this teaching. This sutta is the deepest heart of all the Dhamma. We can see that the teaching explains the problem: that the normal existence of worldly beings is filled with suffering. How we should relate to this or know it is explained in full. This is the deepest heart of all Dhamma. Or we could look at it in another way as the primal point of the Dhamma, which should be taken up, studied, and put into practice. And it is a matter that concerns everyone, something that all people must have, must deal with.

The Dhamma has many different qualities and can be looked at from many different perspectives, as I said earlier today: the Dhammacakka can be seen as a weapon, which one must have and know how to use. If we look at it another way, we can see it as like an eye for healing stupidity, following Venerable Añña Koṇḍañña, who was the first. Or it can be seen as like a medicine for curing illnesses, because there is no illness worse than the illness of defilements. Or it can be seen as like a wall, a shelter or roof, a protection against the arising of things that are enemies. But the best way to see it is as a path. It is said that the most important aspect of this teaching is it points out the path known as the noble eightfold path. This is the Buddha's true meaning or objective in giving this teaching. So please take this sutta as an explanation of the path for living your life.

Now we know the heart or the meaning of this *Dhammacakka-ppavattana Sutta*, which is the teaching the Buddha gave on a day like this: that is, the full moon of the month of Asāḷha. We have now performed the ceremony known as Asāḷha Pūjā as a way of commemorating the Buddha's giving of this *Dhammacakkappavattana Sutta* to bring light into the world. I hope that everyone will take a growing interest in it until they truly receive its benefit, in accordance with the Buddha's wish: "A Tathāgata arises in this world for the benefit, for the happiness, for the support of beings in this world, both devas and humans." The exposition of the *Dhammacakkappavattana Sutta* is sufficient for now. I now bring this discourse to a close.

BHIKKHU P. A. PAYUTTO (SOMDET PHRA BUDDHAGHOSĀCĀRIYA)

Venerable P. A. Payutto is widely regarded as the foremost Buddhist scholar in Thailand at the present time. His writings are extensive and many have been translated into English. A bhikkhu who embodies that rare combination of broad learning and profound wisdom, in person he is also a humble and warmhearted presence, which is, in its own way, as inspiring as the teachings he gives.

The subjects of his talks can vary, ranging from Buddhist perspectives on social themes such as science, economics, or education (in titles such as *Buddhist Economics* and *Towards Sustainable Science*, both published by the Buddhadhamma Foundation in Bangkok) to detailed expositions of traditional Buddhist teachings. The latter is embodied in the author's magnum opus *Buddhadhamma*, a grand and expansive exploration of the entire Buddhist teaching based on the Pali Canon and commentaries. My condensed translation of this text was published by Shambhala as *The Essential Buddhadhamma*.

Venerable Payutto was born Prayudh Arayankura in 1939 in Suphanburi Province in Thailand. He became a novice monk (*sāmaṇera*) at the age of thirteen and studied Pali and *vipassanā* meditation. He completed the highest level of Pali language studies (Parian 9) while still a novice and was consequently granted royal patronage for his ordination as a bhikkhu in 1961, with the ordination name "Payutto."

Venerable Payutto completed a bachelor's degree in Buddhist studies from Mahachulalongkorn Rajavidyalaya Buddhist University in 1962. He served as secretary-general of the university from 1964 until 1974, when he was appointed abbot of Wat Phra Phiren in Bangkok. After three years he left that position to further his academic studies. In 1972 Venerable Payutto lectured on Buddhism and Thai culture at the University of Pennsylvania; in 1976 he lectured on Buddhism at Swarthmore College; and in 1981 he was a research fellow in world religions at the faculty of the Divinity School, Harvard University.

He has received numerous awards, including honorary doctorates from universities in Thailand and abroad, and the UNESCO Prize for Peace Education in 1994. Honorary degrees include doctorates in Buddhists studies, liberal arts, education, philosophy, and science, reflecting the broad scope of his writings.

Buddhadhamma represents the venerable author's most famous work, but his publications in Thai are extensive, numbering in the hundreds and touching on subjects as diverse as economics, science, politics, law, and social commentary, as well as clarifications of traditional Buddhist subjects such as the correct understanding of kamma and the proper kind of faith for a Buddhist.

In the following talk we see something less formal. It is a talk given at a private function: a merit-making session for a deceased relative. It offers a delightful introduction to some of the techniques of Buddhist meditation, explained in a simple and lucid way for his listeners. The talk was previously published for free distribution in Thailand in 1990 and has been reprinted a number of times. It is included in this collection with gracious permission from the venerable author.

HELPING YOURSELF
TO HELP OTHERS

THE CEREMONY OF MAKING MERIT in the name of a deceased is one way of showing appreciation for our benefactors. Even many years after they have passed away, their children and relatives still take their benefactors' goodness to heart and express their appreciation with an annual act of almsgiving, dedicating any merits arising from the occasion in their memory. This is one way of acknowledging their goodness, enabling their memory and worthiness to live on in the hearts of their children and relatives. It is also an opportunity for the sponsors to develop skillful qualities.

In the Buddhist religion it is said that when people perform meritorious actions in the name of a deceased, they should make their minds calm and clear. When the mind is so cleared and composed, that act of dedicating merit is said to be most efficacious.

Looking at it in one way, the act of merit-making seems to be done simply for the sake of the deceased, but if we look more closely, we will see that really the results arise within ourselves. When we are performing an act of merit to be dedicated to another, we must first calm and clear our own minds, and then consciously dedicate the fruits of our good actions. When the mind is so established, our dedication of merit is most thorough and fruitful. So merit or goodness must first arise within our own heart before it can be dedicated to another.

Therefore, in the practice of the Dhamma, even if one specifically looks to the benefit of other beings, the results that are most assured are those that arise within oneself. Thus it is said that by helping oneself one helps others, and by helping others one helps oneself.

There is an analogy regarding this related by the Buddha in the story of the two acrobats. One form of acrobatics performed in the Buddha's time involved the use of a long bamboo pole, which was balanced on the head and shoulders of one acrobat, while another acrobat balanced himself on top of the pole. They would perform various tricks and balancing acts in this way. Two of these acrobats, master and apprentice, were traveling around the country performing their art.

One day the master said, "Now you keep your eye on me, and I'll keep my eye on you and so keep you from falling off."

The apprentice replied, "Oh no, Master. You should look after yourself while I look after myself. In this way we can perform our act and earn a living in safety."

The meaning of the story is: in looking after yourself you also look after others, and by looking after others you also look after yourself. In practicing the Dhamma we are cultivating virtue, which first arises in ourselves. That virtue can then extend to others, even without our knowing about it. Specifically, when practicing the Dhamma we are cultivating morality (*sīla*), concentration (*samādhi*), and wisdom (*paññā*). When our moral conduct is pure, we don't harm others. This is one result of Dhamma practice. Although we have developed that virtue within ourselves, its good effects extend to others in that we no longer present any danger to them. Again, if we help others, for example by exercising forbearance (*khanti*), not harming others through anger, but exercising goodwill (*mettā*) and compassion (*karuṇā*), we are practicing the Dhamma, the fruit of which also arises within ourselves. Thus, it is said that in looking after ourselves we look after others, and when looking after others we look after ourselves. The practice of the Dhamma is coproductive in that its effects extend to all beings.

The Dhamma, when well practiced, is like a medicine for treating the ills of life, enabling us to live our lives well. The Buddha, as the proclaimer of the Dhamma, is like a skillful doctor who prescribed particular medicines for particular illnesses. If a doctor is not skillful, even though he may have good medicine he may prescribe it wrongly. His treatment will then not be very effective. A skillful and wise doctor will be very effective in treating his patients, because he thoroughly understands the properties of the various medicines.

Sometimes we hear it said, "Buddhism has been with us for thousands of years, and yet we still see people fighting and in conflict. Evil still abounds. Buddhism seems incapable of dealing with it; it's useless. We may as well dispense with it." Some people see it like this.

Do you think this is true? They say that even though we've had this Buddhist religion for so many years, people are still corrupt; they still live in conflict. Religion seems powerless to stop these things. We can see no concrete results from religion at all. Better to do away with it.

To these people I say, "Well, the science of medicine has been with us for many thousands of years. Medicine is plentiful, and there have been doctors curing illnesses throughout the ages, for thousands, even tens of thousands, of years. And yet we see disease and illness still abound. If what you say is true, then we must also say that the science of medicine is redundant; we may as well throw that out, too."

This leads us to consider that this body of ours is by nature a breeding ground for illness and subject to pain and aging. We have to procure medicines and exercise the body in order to maintain our strength and live as free of illness and pain as we can. Therefore, the science of medicine and the profession of doctor are still very valuable things. As long as there are people in the world, there will be pain and disease, so there must also be treatment for them.

Similarly, in regard to religion, as long as there are people in the world, there is also "mind." Like the body, the mind can be weakened and damaged. Problems arise in the mind and cause discontent. The quality that disturbs the mind is what we call in Buddhism *dukkha* (suffering). As long as there are people living in this world, there will be suffering, so we must also have a treatment for it. When one person is cured, there are still countless others to follow.

So religion can be compared to the science of medicine, and the Buddha to a great doctor. Having cured many people in his own time, he also left us his teaching so that we who follow after him can treat our own illnesses.

In our lives we have both body and mind. As for the body, the doctors usually deal with its illnesses. It is the Dhamma, however, that we must use for dealing with our lives as a whole, particularly the mind.

What is the disease that incessantly hounds the mind? It is the disease of defilements (*kilesa*). Whenever greed, hatred, or delusion arise within the mind, they cause discontent and suffering to arise. Such a mind can be called an ill or diseased mind. When diseases such as greed arise, they stifle and oppress the mind, causing it to become obsessed with some object or other. The mind is not spacious or clear. When hatred arises, it heats and agitates the mind. This is another disease that unsettles the mind, as do all other kinds of defilements.

The healthy mind should have the qualities of lightness, radiance, clarity, and calm. Whenever defilements arise, these qualities disappear. Clarity becomes murkiness; calm changes to excitement and agitation; the quality of lightness gives way to oppression and conflict. These are the symptoms of the diseases of the mind, which are all caused by defilements. So we say that defilements are a disease that must be treated.

In this regard the Buddha's teaching is like a handbook of medicines. Some of the medicines are for specific illnesses. The cultivation of goodwill, for example, is for treating the disease of anger. Apart from goodwill, which acts like a refreshing, cool shower on the mind when it is oppressed and disturbed, there is also patient endurance to aid in driving annoyance and irritation from the mind, or compassion (*karuṇā*), for counteracting destructive thoughts, or wisdom (*paññā*), for brightening the mind and making it clear and light.

There are many different types of Dhamma medicine, and they must be used appropriately. One who aspires to skillfulness in using these medicines should follow the example of the Buddha, whom we revere as the greatest "Dhamma doctor," in that he prescribed medicines with the greatest skill. If a teacher is unable to use these medicines skillfully, his teaching may become like so much hot air. Those listening to such teachings would have to rely on their own wisdom to choose the teachings appropriate to their needs, and if they weren't skillful, they might not obtain much benefit from the teaching.

All of the above refers to the Dhamma as a collection of specific medicines for use with specific illnesses: the diseases of the defilements. Now there is another kind of disease that is even more pervasive. Just now I spoke of the troubled and disturbed mind. Now this very mind, as well as the body, which together we call a "life," being composed of the five *khandhas*,[1] are all conditioned things (*saṅkhārā*). All conditioned things have certain characteristics. They are unstable or unenduring, suffering and not-self; they do not come under anyone's power other than as the natural process of cause and effect. All conditioned things conform to these three characteristics, known in Pali as the *tilakkhaṇa*.[2] That all conditions are unstable, suffering, and not-self is another kind of disease, one that is inherent in all saṅkhārā. It is the disease of their imperfection, of their deficiency. Being imperfect, they are naturally hounded by conflict, struggle, and change.

This imperfection also causes problems in the mind, so people suffer not only as a result of the workings of the grosser defilements, which we can clearly see arising from time to time in the mind, but also from the subtler defilement of not knowing the true nature of life.[3] Suffering arises because of the very imperfection of conditions, of their being subject to the three characteristics. This is a more profound kind of disease, one that we must cure in order to really transcend suffering. It is not enough to simply try to cure the greed, hatred, and delusion that are constantly arising in the mind: we must also clearly know the nature of life, that it is bounded by these three characteristics.

If we don't understand this, we will cling to the five khandhas as being a self or belonging to the self, demanding of them not to change, but no matter how much we cling to them, they won't conform to our wishes but simply follow causal conditions. Clinging to them only causes disappointment and suffering.

Thus, on the deeper level, we could say that beneath the greed, hatred, and delusion, the real cause of suffering is the imperfect nature of conditions, ignorance of which causes the defilements of greed, hatred, and delusion to arise in the mind.

We must therefore study the diseases of our lives on two levels. The disease that is most apparent is the disease of the various defilements: greed, aversion, delusion, conceit, stubbornness, jealousy, stinginess, and so on, which we see all around us. However, looking more deeply, we find that all disease is caused by the nature of conditions, which are bound by impermanence, stressfulness, and insubstantiality.

We must find a way to treat these diseases by not allowing the defilements to arise. But how do we prevent the defilements from arising? First, we must look on a broader scale. Just now we looked at things in terms of ourselves, seeing the disease as something that arises in our own minds, in our own lives. We saw defilements arising in our own minds, while conditions, which are impermanent and imperfect, we saw as ourselves. But if we look on a broader scale, we will see clearly that the disease (*roga*) is based on contact with the world (*loka*).

The spiritual disease and the world are connected. What is the connection? Why do greed, hatred, and delusion arise within us? How do these things come about? Generally speaking, defilements arise from contact with the world. The world makes contact with us, and we make contact with the world. How do we make contact with the world? We do so through our everyday experience, in sense contact, from receiving sense impressions through the eyes, ears, nose, tongue, body, and mind. Sensations that arise through the eyes are called sights; those entering through the ears are called sounds; those entering through the nose are called smells; those entering through the tongue are called tastes; those entering through the body are called tactile sensations; those entering through the mind are thoughts and feelings. We experience our selves through these sensations. Whenever we experience no sensations, such as when we are in deep sleep or unconscious, we are not aware. When we are aware, it is through these sensations.

From where do these sensations arise? They come from the world, our environment. Our environment manifests itself to us through the eyes, ears, nose, tongue, body, and mind, which in Buddhism we call the six sense bases. Any experience that appears to us must appear to us through these avenues, as sights, sounds, smells, tastes, bodily feelings, and thoughts.

Now these sensations or experiences appear to us, and there is contact, after which follows an immediate response. All these experiences can therefore be seen as bases for greed to arise, for hatred to arise, or for delusion to arise. If we have no Dhamma medicine, we will fall under the power of sensations, and the corresponding reactions will take place: when a sensation that is a base for greed arises, we want to possess it; if a sensation that is a base for hatred arises, instead of seducing us into desire, it upsets us and taunts us into anger. This is how defilements arise in response to sense impressions.

In the case of the ordinary, untrained person (*puthujjana*), whenever a sense impression arises, there will initially follow a feeling of pleasure or displeasure, depending on whether the sensation is agreeable or not. If it is agreeable to us, there is a feeling of pleasure, and there follows a reaction of liking or approval. Seeing a pleasant sight or hearing a pleasant sound, we feel approval. If it's a sight that offends our eyes or a sound that grates our ears, one that we perceive to be unpleasant, there is a reaction of disapproval.

From these initial reactions of approval and disapproval arise mental fabrications: thoughts about sense objects that become problems in our mind and cause it to become stained and dull. The disease arises. So this disease arises within the mind, it's true, but it comes as a result of experiencing sensations or the world as it appears to us through our senses.

We must know how to function correctly in this world. If we know how to function properly, the disease won't arise. To function properly in regard to the world is to function properly toward sense impressions. In this regard, the Buddha taught the initial practice of sense restraint, *indriyasaṁvara*: restraining the eyes, ears, nose, tongue, body, and mind so as to prevent sense impressions from overwhelming us and causing greed and hatred to arise. This entails using mindfulness (*sati*) to know things as they are when they arise. Whenever a sensation arises, *vedanā*—the feeling of pleasure, displeasure, or indifference—is there. When a pleasant feeling arises, the unmindful person delights in it. When an unpleasant feeling arises, the mind untrained in mindfulness flows down the stream of fabrications to disapproval, anger, displeasure, hatred, and so on.

The mind of the average person will be in this state all the time, constantly flitting from delight to aversion, and in the Tipiṭaka these two words *delight* and *aversion* crop up frequently.

Whenever we experience a sense impression, there is a resulting reaction from the mind. So I say we experience life through the awareness of sensations. Thus, the experience of sensation is a very important aspect of our everyday lives. If we don't practice correctly in relation to our experience of sense contact, defilements will arise, resulting in problems.

The first defilements to arise will be delight and aversion. Therefore, it is said to cut the stream at its beginning by using mindfulness to guard the senses. In the beginning, we recollect whenever a sensation has arisen. Whether it is to our liking or not, we should not allow that sensation to overwhelm us, leading us to fabricate under the influence of delight and aversion and from there to further harmful thoughts. This is how to practice properly in relation to sense impressions, which is also the proper relationship toward the world. When we practice like this, the diseases won't arise.

This is one aspect of the matter: the disease that arises within through sense contact. However, if we look more deeply, we see that this interaction between ourselves and the world, what we call *life*, is all conditioned phenomena (*saṅkhārā*). The world consists of saṅkhāra, which all come under the domain of the three characteristics: they are all impermanent, stressful, and not-self. The whole world is therefore just the same as our individual lives: all changing and ephemeral. It is not within our power to force it to be any other way than as conditioning factors direct it; it is *anattā* (not-self).

Even though the world is anattā, people still attach to it. The word *world* here refers to everything we come into contact with, not only our bodies but all our possessions, both living and nonliving. They are all impermanent, stressful, and not-self, just as are our very lives. The wrong way to conduct oneself is to perceive sensations with clinging. Seeing sensations as ourselves or belonging to us, we expect them to obey our commands. When we cling to the world in this way, wanting everything, especially our possessions, to conform to our desires, to belong to us; then when those things change according to the natural laws of cause and effect, our minds manifest a state of turmoil and distress. Suffering arises. Thus, in the final analysis, the world causes disease to arise within us because it is subject to the three characteristics.

Summarizing, we can say that there are two distinct factors that cause the disease of suffering. First, there is kilesa, the unskillful interactions with the world through the influence of delight and aversion, as well as the many other kinds of defilements. The second way is by the very nature of the world itself being impermanent, stressful, and not-self, which causes conflict to arise in the mind of anyone who clings to it.

However, the arising of problems, regardless of whether we look on the level of our own lives or outward to the world in general, must ultimately stem from one and the same source. The arising of problems in the most elementary sense occurs on a moment-to-moment basis, as the mind interacts with the various sensations and becomes, as a result, spoiled, agitated, and tricked by greed, hatred, and delusion.

If one has mindfulness and can cut the flow of defilements by not allowing the mind to indulge in delight and aversion, then one can maintain the mind in a clear, calm state. The disease won't arise. However, on a deeper level, one must also understand the true nature of this world and our lives in their entirety as impermanent, stressful, and not-self. One can thus relax the grip of attachment. Once the grip of attachment has been relaxed, one's mind is no longer swayed or overwhelmed by the world. No matter how things go, they can no longer rule over the mind. Not following those conditions, the mind detaches itself freely from them. This is an important point. In the end, we must be able to free our mind, to make it liberated, clear, and calm at all times.

What I've been talking about here is the practice of the Dhamma on various levels. First, I explained the practice of the Dhamma as a medicine for specific illnesses. This includes the various techniques for counteracting such defilements as selfishness or stinginess. When this arises, we would use one particular technique. If anger or envy arise, we may use other techniques. On the deeper level, eventually we must know the true nature of conditioned things. Just by knowing the true nature of conditioned things we can thereby simultaneously cut defilements in all their forms, because we see that they are not worthy of holding on to. When we don't cling to things, they no longer spin us around because we've seen their ultimate nature.

So on the higher levels of Buddhist practice we talk about the training or cultivation of the mind (*bhāvanā*). This training also has various levels. Initially one may train the mind simply to be calm by developing samādhi (concentration). The aim of samādhi is to focus the mind at one sensation or object of awareness. The everyday mind is rarely at rest; it's like a monkey jumping from one impression to another. One moment it has one object of awareness, then in an instant it flies off somewhere else, then somewhere else again. The more it jumps around following sensations, the less it is its own master, and the more it is enslaved by those sensations and caught up in greed, hatred, and delusion.

If we are able to bring our mind to rest on one object, not jumping around after countless sensations, the mind will become manageable. So we must take one particular impression—anything will do that is wholesome and not outright harmful, such as a meditation theme. For example, one object that is quite neutral and doesn't cause the mind to fabricate in unskillful ways is the in- and out-breathing. Another is the qualities of the Buddha, which are a very good theme for keeping the mind from wandering around.

When the mind rests with a meditation object, we don't have to bother with sensations arising from the outside world. Defilements resulting from value judgments about externals do not arise.

This is the most elementary level of meditation practice: concentrating the mind on a harmless object. With the mind coming to rest on that object, we can be said to have accomplished our aim, the mind is in samādhi, being firmly fixed on one object. When talking of samādhi, the word *ekaggatā* (one-pointedness) is used, meaning that the mind rests with one particular object. When it rests on that object, it is calm and undistracted. This is samādhi.

Samādhi has just this much as its initial requirement: bringing the mind to a focus on one particular sensation. The defilements are subdued and unable to arise. If the mind goes on to more refined levels of concentration, it may enter the absorptions (*jhāna*), but no matter how refined the concentration becomes, it still retains the same basic qualities—having one sensation for its object and fixing on that.

When the mind is one-pointed, it is said to be like a magnifying glass that is used to concentrate the sun's rays. Using a magnifying glass, a concentration of energy occurs that can even ignite an object in its path. Again, the mind can be compared to water that is released from a great height, such as a mountain. If the water has no channel, it dissipates, but if a pipe is used to channel the water, it flows down in a torrent, sometimes so strong as to sweep all obstacles, such as branches and trees, from its path. Yet again, the calm mind can be compared to still, limpid water, which is completely free of ripples, perfectly smooth. If one were to look into the water one would clearly see a true reflection of one's features. In the same way, the calm mind sees things without distortion.

To put it even more clearly, when water is still and calm, any dust or impurities in the water tend to sink into a sediment, leaving the water above clean and clear. Anything in the water—such as fish, snails, rocks, and so on—is readily visible. Similarly, in calming the mind by practicing samādhi, there is a further benefit to be derived, apart from making the mind unperturbed and unmolested by defilements, and that is the arising of wisdom. Usually, when the mind is restless, we don't see things clearly. It is like trying to look at an object while it is swinging back and forth. No matter how hard we look, we won't be able see it clearly. In fact, the more closely we try to inspect the object, the more blurred it becomes. If we want to see that object more clearly, we must hold it as still as possible.

Our minds are like this. We are always having to deal with arising sensations, but usually our minds are not calm. When the mind is not calm, it is as if its object were being blown about by a strong wind. More refined things, such as particular problems we may want to resolve, are even harder to see clearly if the mind has no samādhi.

So we calm the mind. Calming the mind is like holding that object firmly and still so that we can examine it as closely as we wish. Samādhi is a prerequisite for wisdom. It is said, *samāhito yathābhūtaṁ pajānāti*: when the mind is firm and calm, wisdom functions clearly and we can see the truth.

However, simply having samādhi doesn't mean that one will automatically develop wisdom. If one does not know how to rightly use samādhi, one may simply settle for the calmed mind. Or one may think, "Oh, when I've calmed the mind, maybe I'll be able to develop some psychic powers." One gets a desire for mental powers, such as divine sight, divine hearing, and so on. These are all by-products of a concentrated mind. Samādhi that is practiced simply for its own sake is called *samatha* practice. It flies off in the direction of the refined absorption states (*jhāna*) and psychic powers. These are all fruits of mind-power.

If you want to understand samādhi correctly in the Buddhist sense, you must see it as it is described in the scriptures, as the mind that is malleable, fit for work. The mind that is malleable is one that is ready for work in that it is firm and still, as I've just explained with the comparison of holding an object still in order to see it clearly. This means we use samādhi to facilitate the arising of wisdom.

Wisdom is of many types and can arise in many ways. For instance, in our everyday lives there are countless things demanding our attention and consideration, but if our minds are not calm, we don't see them clearly. At some later time, having calmed the mind, these things may arise once more into consciousness so that we can review them more clearly. This is one type of wisdom that can be derived from samādhi: seeing the events or experiences of our lives more clearly in retrospect. Cases where wisdom was initially not apparent become clearer.

In addition to this one can also use samādhi as a tool for looking at experiences as they arise in the present moment. For example, a meditator practices samādhi to the level of jhāna, then proceeds to examine the various qualities of jhāna—*vitakka* (initial thought), *vicāra* (sustained thought), *pīti* (rapture), *sukha* (happiness), and *ekaggatā* (one-pointedness), bringing them up for scrutiny so as to see their true nature as impermanent, stressful, and not-self. This is a function of wisdom. Wisdom can thus be used to examine an event from the past or to examine experiences in the present. In either case, the result is the same—seeing things as they really are.

The real value of samādhi lies with wisdom. The difference between samādhi and wisdom is that samādhi renders the mind calm and undefiled for only a limited time. When the mind leaves that state of calm, it experiences various sensations that proceed to influence the mind as before. Sensations that are the bases for greed, hatred, and delusion arise once more. You see, the mind is still the same as before, except that when the mind enters samādhi it rests with a harmless sensation so that defilements don't arise. As soon as the mind encounters harmful sensations once more, the defilements arise as before.

Therefore, the results of practicing samādhi on its own still leave us prone to problems. Suffering still arises; the disease is still with us. Samādhi in itself does not give us a real, lasting result. One who transcends the influence of defilements temporarily, by using samādhi, is said to have experienced transcendence through suppression (*vikkhambhana vimutti*). The illustration is given of grass covered by a rock. As long as the rock is there, the grass is suppressed and cannot grow, but once the rock is removed, the grass grows as before.

How can we cure the problem once and for all, so that even when the mind experiences various sensations, no harm or problems arise? One must delve deeper into the problem by destroying the seed of defilement in the mind, so that the mind does not react with defilement to the various sensations. This is called abandoning the defilements through true knowledge and vision of the way things are—that is, by using wisdom. Wisdom on this level is called *vipassanā* (insight).

Thus, when we talk of the higher levels of Buddhist practice, it is said to have two main branches: on one hand, samādhi in itself, which we call samatha (calm), and on the other hand, the use of wisdom, seeing the true nature of things, which is called vipassanā. If one develops samādhi and then uses that calm mind in the development of wisdom, one will achieve what in Buddhism we would consider to be comprehensive results.

Now there is another technique that is often stressed, and that is called sati (mindfulness). Sati is a very important factor of Dhamma practice. We often hear of the four foundations of mindfulness. Sati is the crucial factor of this practice. Here the development of a calm, still mind is not emphasized. What is emphasized is the use of sati to bring about the arising of wisdom. Sati is a factor that can greatly assist in the development of wisdom.

Moreover, if there is no sati, samādhi cannot arise. In the eightfold path, sati is one of the last three factors—right effort, right mindfulness, and right concentration—that are placed together to form the section on samādhi.

Now how does sati differ from samādhi? The analogy is given of tying up a wild animal, freshly caught from the jungle. The animal runs about in a frenzy. Without the rope to hold it, it would surely escape. So we must tie the animal to a stake, so that instead of escaping, the animal can only run around the vicinity of the stake. The rope is comparable to sati. Sati is that which pulls the mind back, or pulls a particular sensation to the mind, or pulls the mind to a particular sensation. It may also be said to hold the mind to, or force it to stay with, a particular sensation. That which holds or forces the mind, preventing it from wandering too far, is sati.

Now if we restrain the mind until it calms down and stays still of its own accord, this is samādhi. Like the wild animal, once it is tied it can't roam about because it is held by the rope, which we compared to sati. After a time, the animal tires and lies down calmly. The animal lying calmly is like the mind that has samādhi, being firm and still. Thus, sati and samādhi are closely related. Sati is a factor that helps to develop samādhi.

Now in addition to aiding in the development of samādhi, sati is also a factor that can influence the mind to develop wisdom. All things that we can think of or reflect on are called sensations (*ārammaṇa*). If all sensations disappeared, we would no longer have anything to reflect on, because there would be nothing there. In order for a sensation to stay with us, there must be something to hold it down. Sati is what holds the theme of contemplation to our attention, so that wisdom can consider it and develop understanding. Thus wisdom (*paññā*), too, cannot function without sati. There must be sati to hold things to awareness so that we can see them and reflect on them. We must have, before anything else, mindfulness.

The practice of vipassanā meditation emphasizes the use of sati. If there is no sati, wisdom cannot arise. Sati itself has many different functions. First, it allows us to be aware of the sensations that enter our consciousness as they arise. Usually our minds are trapped by delight and aversion. When a sensation arises that produces a pleasant feeling, we feel happy and we like that sensation. If another type of sensation arises, one that produces an unpleasant feeling, we don't like it and give in to aversion. Whenever our mind delights or is averse, or likes or dislikes anything, it gets stuck on that sensation. The mind fixes itself to the sensation but, being temporary, in a moment the sensation has passed, becoming a past experience. Immediately there follows a new sensation, but the mind, being stuck on the sensation that just passed, does not follow the new sensation that is arising. That which has just passed becomes the past, so it is said that the mind that fabricates has fallen into the past.

Just as the mind falls into the past, it can also float off and begin projecting fantasies about the future. The mind that is not aware in the present moment is the mind that delights and feels averse. The mind, either delighting or feeling averse, must clutch some particular sensation. As soon as it clutches any particular sensation, it falls into the past, even if only for a second.

Delight and aversion arise dependent on some particular sensation. For instance, if we see something we like, the mind fabricates around that liking. If aversion or dislike takes over, the mind fabricates in a different way. In other words, the mind doesn't see things the way they are. When we say the mind doesn't see things the way they are, we mean that the mind is under the influence of delight and aversion, which make the mind either fall into the past or float off into the future. Saying that the mind falls into delight and aversion or saying that the mind doesn't see things the way they are is to say one and the same thing. Either way the mind does not have awareness with each sensation as it arises.

Now if we experience a sensation in the present moment, but do not attach to it with delight or aversion, then the mind will simply follow each sensation with awareness. Delight and aversion do not have a chance to arise, because of sati, which causes the mind to stay with the present moment.

When the mind doesn't fabricate under the influence of delight and aversion, then we do not see things through the "colored glasses" of our likes and dislikes. We see things as they are. It is said that all things in this world are simply as they are in themselves, nothing more. But the mind defiled by delight and aversion proceeds to paint things into something more than what they are. We don't see things as they are. Without the staining effect of desire and aversion, we see things as they are.

Thus, sati facilitates the arising of wisdom, helping our mind not to fall into the past or float into the future with delight and aversion, but seeing things as they are, which is a function of wisdom.

The practice of the foundations of mindfulness is said to help eradicate desire and aversion and to see things as they are. Now when we are more adept at seeing things as they arise, we will notice their arising, existence, and cessation. When we perceive the various sensations coming and going as they do, we will be seeing the process by which they function, seeing that they are constantly arising and ceasing. They are impermanent. Seeing impermanence (*anicca*), we will also see dukkha (suffering) and anattā (selflessness), the three characteristics. So the practice of the foundations of mindfulness on deeper levels enables us to see the arising, changing, and dissolution of all things. This is seeing the three characteristics of conditioned existence, which is the arising of wisdom. The mind will then no longer grasp or be influenced by external sensations. The mind becomes its own master and breaks free, and that freedom is the fruition of wisdom development.

As I said in the beginning of this talk, if the mind knows the truth of life, the disease of ignorance will not arise. The disease of the mind is caused by ignorance, which causes the mind to fabricate.

This is the practice of Buddhism. Notice that it all relates to us. The practice I've been talking about here is based on this fathom-long body. The truth can be seen right here. Living in this world, we experience the environment as sensations. If we don't practice appropriately toward those sensations, we experience problems.

In one sense, it's almost as if we "lie in wait" for sensations to arise and relate to them in such a way as to not give rise to defilements. It is as if we were a passive receiver of sensations. In this sense we may feel we should sit and wait for things to happen and do our best to avoid getting involved in anything. This is one way of looking at Dhamma practice.

Another way is to use our practice to improve the world, by training to see it in a more skillful way. So the initial practice is not only to be a passive experiencer, but also learning to get up and go outside to meet the world. This means practicing toward the world in a good way.

One who practices like this practices correctly in relation to oneself and also, having seen the truth, practices in the world in such a way as to be helpful, not harmful, to others. Helping others also helps us to develop good qualities in ourselves. The mind tends toward skillful reactions in its everyday contact. In this way the practitioner sees a relationship between their own personal practice and the practice of relating to the world. One sees that all beings are related and so deals with them with goodwill and compassion, helping them in their need. Furthermore, we understand that all other beings are afflicted with the same illness as we are, they are bound by the three characteristics just as we are. Therefore, it is proper that we learn to help each other as fellow travelers on the path of practice.

Dhamma practitioners should thus not only consider the right way to relate to the various experiences they encounter in the course of their lives, but should also help others. This type of practice was recommended by the Buddha, even up to the level of those who have experienced insight. At one time the Buddha compared the stream enterer (*sotāpanna*)⁴ to a cow with a calf. The cow eats grass to feed itself and also to feed the calf, which follows her around. "Eating the grass" can be compared to one's own personal practice of the Dhamma. Even though she is eating grass, the mother cow does not neglect her calf; she is constantly looking after it and being watchful to keep it from falling into danger. Likewise, one who practices the teaching of Buddhism practices primarily to train oneself in the correct practice, but also gives consideration to one's fellow people and all other beings, so as to help them with goodwill and compassion.

So this fits in with the principle I mentioned at the beginning of this talk: in helping yourself you help others; in helping others you help yourself. All in all, the practice boils down to behaving in the right manner, both to oneself and to others. In this way Dhamma practice leads to progress both for oneself and for others.

Today I have spoken about the general principles of Buddhist practice, beginning by comparing the Buddha to a doctor, one who both administers medicine and also performs operations. To *operate* means to "remove the dart." In the past, one of the most important operations was performed during times of battle, when people were often shot by arrows, sometimes dipped in poison. The victims would experience great agony and even death as a result of their wounds.

The Buddha used the arrow as a simile for sorrow and all human suffering. The Buddha as surgeon cut out the arrowhead. We also must accept the responsibility of removing our own respective arrows by practicing the Dhamma. If we practice the Dhamma correctly, we will realize the real benefit of the Buddha's medicine.

The Buddha has bequeathed to us this well-expounded teaching. It remains up to us to make the most of his kindness by taking up that teaching and practicing accordingly. In this way we can cure the disease that afflicts the five khandhas, remove the arrow, and experience peace, clarity, and purity, which is the goal of Buddhism.

UPĀSIKĀ KEE NANAYON

U nique in this volume, and also a rarity on the Thai Buddhist land-
scape, Upāsikā Kee Nanayon (1901–1978) was a female practitioner who established her own meditation center in Central Thailand.
Eschewing the more formal mode of practice available to women at the
time of becoming an eight-precept *mae chee*,[1] she instead took on the
precepts and practiced as an *upāsikā* (a female lay follower).[2] During
her lifetime she was advised by Ajahn Buddhadāsa and was praised by
well-known meditation teachers such as Luang Ta Maha Boowa.

She was born in Ratchaburi Province. Her mother encouraged her
in Buddhist chanting almost from the time she could speak, and she
showed a strong affinity for practicing the Dhamma from an early age,
using her pocket money to buy flowers to offer to the temple and giving
food to the monks on alms round. She taught herself to read at home
and loved reading poetry and Dhamma books. She began keeping the
eight precepts on observance days in her early twenties. This affinity
developed until she lost all interest in entertainments, preferring to
keep the seventh precept on a regular basis.

Kee often went to various nearby temples on small meditation retreats and developed a strong meditation practice. While her parents
were alive, she helped them with their livelihood of selling things in
the market and also tended to both of them when they became old
and ill, until they passed away—first her mother and then her father.
In 1945 she went to a deserted temple outside a local village, together
with her uncle and aunt, both of whom were also dedicated Dhamma
practitioners. After a time her uncle left, and Upāsikā Kee continued

to practice diligently there alone in what eventually became Khao Suan Luang Dhamma Centre, a place of practice for laywomen and mae chee that is run like a forest monastery, set in a rustic, forested mountain setting, with morning and evening chanting and communal meals. The center is still in operation with about forty mae chee and laywomen practitioners living there at the time of our visit in 2024.

The following talk is from her book *Nae Naew Mong Dan Nai* (Advice on Looking Inward). It is unique in our collection not only in being a teaching by a woman, but also in that it is an exhortation to members of a community practicing under monastic conditions, rather than a teaching to Buddhists in general, as the others are.

SWEEPING AWAY THE DIRT[3]

TODAY IS A DAY WHEN Dhamma practitioners have an opportunity to reflect on their practice. Practice is a personal matter and the most important thing in all our lives. If you don't practice the Dhamma, there is only relentless suffering; it's suffocating.

It is really useful to come to practice in a location like this that is remote from disturbing sense impressions. You should try to examine yourself in deep detail, and then you will obtain the greatest benefit, because it is through not examining yourself properly that you go and do or say the wrong thing. If you regularly examine yourself, mistakes, faults, or forgetfulness will gradually become less.

Dhamma practitioners should be aware of themselves, reflecting, "From the time I began to practice, how much have my attachments to myself and my belongings diminished? Or are they still as great as they were before?" If they are still as thick as they always were, you can say you haven't been practicing properly and you should take another look at yourself. What can you do to get back on the right path as pointed out by the Buddha?

We should try to walk the right path. If there is still some going astray in any way, you should look afresh and try to get back, to give up, to let go or whatever else is required to get yourself back on the right track along the path that relieves and dispels attachment to self and belonging to self. That is the right path, the correct way to extinguish suffering and defilements. If there is any involvement with external matters, it should be in a way that is useful to other people, because if you stray from the right path, it will just create confusion, squandering your own benefit and the benefit of others at the same time.

Therefore, you should guard yourselves well. Control your mind well in the first instance. Don't go putting too much attention on externals, because that will cause you to waste the time of your everyday lives. That is why we must practice with care and with heedfulness as much as we can. That is definitely better than any other way. We should examine ourselves more deeply to see whether there is anything poking out from the depths of our character, in what is known as "myself," or to put it more crudely, "me and mine." We should examine, scrutinize, and destroy it from the outer level to the inner.

Externally, we learn how to compromise, how to endure, how to let go, how to constantly overcome defilements, desire, and attachments. We must observe our practices in order to be safe; otherwise things become really heavy and like a dangerous disease that constantly increases our suffering. You must be very careful and keep your mind on the right track. And then pick it up for proper consideration. Don't just pick up filthy and vulgar things to put on yourself. Help to clean up and sweep them away. Don't go around picking things up to clutter the mind. It's not at all useful.

Let us invite or encourage each other to sweep out the defilements of desire and clinging, or the sense of self, so that the mind is always tidy. If it becomes cluttered in any way, help each other, talk about getting rid of it. It's like when they till the field for planting rice or clear a forest to make fields. They have to clear out the grass or dig up the stumps that they don't want, to clear them all out before they can replace them with their valuable crops. The practices are like this. The bad and vulgar ways of defilements, desire, and clinging are rife in every single person. Since we all have these things in common, we should be considerate of each other. Look at how we should discuss and collaborate and how can we clear things out and not be too cluttered, not too heated or dirty.

Dhamma practitioners should turn around and talk to each other about this matter a lot, more than anything else. Don't talk about how to get the better of each other or compete for bragging rights. It's a waste of time and stirs up the mind. You only get clutter and agitation, nothing else. There is only loss of mental clarity. We should try to invite and encourage each other in the proper way, because coming to practice makes us all sisters, friends in suffering. Please talk with each other and take a good and proper look at it. Don't approach each other with pride and views. It will only bring trouble and confusion.

Examining yourself is the most important of all our duties. Living together, we must have order, such as the various regulations and practices. In all communities there are regulations so that we can live together in an orderly way. We don't follow our own desires, with everyone just doing what they want. We couldn't live together like that. It would be a mess, not peaceful. We must respect the regulations, which are like an outer fence that surrounds us.

Morality and Dhamma are like inner fences. Morality is like a second fence, and Dhamma is the real internal matter. There must be a lot of care, from the most external level to the most internal level. We must carefully examine so that it is appropriate to our station as Dhamma practitioners who have seen the suffering and the harm of the defilements, desire, and attachment.

We should talk about this a lot: How much attachment (*upādāna*) do we still have? Do we still attach to ourselves? We can't bear anything clashing with us because we still have attachment. Even if we have practiced and seen the truth to some extent, our insight fades away, and we return to not knowing in various forms, over and over again. We should be really interested in this point, because this stumbling and falling into these things is a sign that we are still not getting it, and there is no guarantee how long we will live to address the matter.

Regardless of whether you are a child or an adult, decay and dissolution of body and mind are already written into us. When we chant *rūpaṁ aniccaṁ, vedanā anicca* ("form is impermanent, feeling is impermanent"),[4] it is all about ourselves. We must seriously examine ourselves to see the truth of these things, and then we will be wearied of them and unravel our love of them. If we don't examine in this way, our sense of self will increase as we age, because the more you have seen and known, the more you attach to. It's as if your clinging and attachment are even greater than before you started to practice, because the more you know, the more you cling. The self becomes ever cleverer and more boastful. We have to be really wary of this. Don't go bragging and competing with each other. This just goes to feed the sense of self, turning it into a giant or demon. Instead of starving it so that it gets thinner and eventually dies, you feed it and care for it. You must know yourself whether these kinds of practices just increase the harm and suffering, increase our defilements of desire and attachment or not. Examine yourself. Seriously examine yourself and you will have a fresh awareness of yourself. You will become a new person. Don't just be the old person who is still clinging to things just as much as before, or even more so.

Let there be careful examination, and then you will benefit in the sense that you are gradually destroying the self. Whatever the self has attached to in the past, we destroy it or let it go; we don't feed it. For instance, if the mind really wants something, stop. Don't give in to it; don't follow it. Patiently endure; resist it first, look at it first. With practice the mind may realize that enduring and going against desires increases the strength of mindfulness and wisdom, which are like protectors or elder siblings or good friends, helping to prevent the mind from falling into the power of the defilements of desire and clinging like they used to do. We can throw them off, let them go, extinguish them.

This is the arising of the practice that helps us to escape from internal suffering. It helps us to change and renew our character so that we become a new person, not the old, ancient person. The body, speech, and mind change. We develop the feeling that we are polishing off the stains that we had once indulged in. Now we see the harm and suffering of those things, so we become fed up with them and see that it is not worth letting them grow. Therefore, we must scrub them off. If there is no scrubbing off, they will only increase, just like rust that grows on iron: it corrodes the iron and wears it away. Our duty, all of us, is to scrub away, to make our minds more immaculate day by day. Then it will be most profitable for our everyday lives.

If we regularly examine in this way, the more we do it, the more we will feel that the things that confront us through eyes and ears—all the sense contact that we experience—are entirely of the nature to arise and cease in accordance with the norms of nature. Don't go and cling to them as being good or bad or as being the self or whatever. Try looking at them and examining them more carefully, and the mind will become free within itself and not be overly pushed into like and dislike.

If we diligently watch over and guard the mind on a regular basis, this is called the practice of scrubbing, not allowing stains to arise and take over and stir up the mind. This is the big task. This is what must be practiced. We must use this method; we must examine in this way. This will be our tool for extinguishing defilements and gaining ever better results as the days go by. Even if we die while we are examining, our examination will allow us to let go easily. Don't wait until you are really suffering and in torment. That's really difficult. It's not easy to do.

Take this opportunity to train and develop your mind, to do the practice, so that it becomes a base, an excellent refuge, before it all falls apart—that is, you die. If you are interested in this matter more than anything else, this means the practitioner is following the path taken by the noble ones. They practiced along this path, because it is the path that the Buddha pointed out. It is the *bahulānasāsanī*, the teaching that the Buddha gave often—that is, impermanence, suffering, and not-self. We don't have to waste time learning much outside of this. We study the body and the mind as they display impermanence, suffering, and not-self at every single moment, and that is enough.

But we aren't able to study even this: we like to have a lot, to study a lot, to remember a lot, to think a lot, and so it overflows. It overflows until the mind has no freedom; it falls slave to mental fabrication, attachment, and self and becomes a confusing mess. Because we practice along the wrong path, not in accordance with the Buddha's teaching, we cannot extinguish suffering, the self that is lording it over us, to make it become smaller and thinner. You should reexamine this. If you've practiced through the rains retreat, when you get to the end of the rains retreat don't let the awareness that you have developed disappear or fade away through delight in external sights, sounds, smells, and tastes that lure the eyes and the mind and cause you to lose that mental benefit. If you have the aspiration to extinguish suffering, then you have to go a little further, a little deeper. Don't just play around, just knowing a little bit and then thinking "I know it now," and then just let yourself go, delighting in things. It's a real waste of time.

If we know how to restrain ourselves and live modestly, then we will be on the correct path. We will be ready to examine, ready to let go easily. If there are things that we still can't let go of, we can reexamine ourselves and see how stupid we are. Why should we hold on to them? Go in and deal with it. That we don't see our foolishness and that we boast how clever we are or brag about our knowledge and want to teach others are because we have not yet delved inward and taught ourselves. We're just looking at externals, taking on so much from the outside and not knowing that we are actually stupid.

Whoever begins to develop this feeling, seeing that they are very stupid—and stupid on many levels—must try to find out how to gain real knowledge and realization. Then they will discover that attachment and clinging arise from none other than ignorance, from not knowing impermanence, suffering, and not-self. Instead we see wrongly that things are permanent, happiness, and self in accordance with our wrong perception, thoughts, and views. If we have right perception, right thoughts, and right views, it will automatically lead to cessation or destruction.

Now this right knowledge that we have trained to regularly arise frees the mind. How empty or peaceful it is, you can look into yourself and see, because this is something specific to yourself. One who examines it with real, refined wisdom and mindfulness will obtain the mind that destroys outflows (*āsava*) and defilements on gradually more refined levels. If someone does not examine within, does not know within, but merely thinks about externals and holds on to externals, or brags about being clever, this will make them utterly stupid. We can say that they will just sink into the realm of rebirth without ever opening their eyes or ears.

As we are Dhamma practitioners, I want to speak plainly. I'm not bragging about any attainments. It's just a caution. Anything about which I have cautioned myself, I inform you about it so that you will benefit, because we must cut through and penetrate our own stupidity and see how it is done. That's what will be useful for extinguishing suffering. Some things we are still blindly holding on to. Even though we brag about being clever and knowing, we still hold on to them. And that makes me wonder, since there is this clinging and attachment out of not knowing the truth, how can we try, how can we put forth effort to our benefit?

According to the teachings, the Buddha instructed to live in a forest, at the foot of a tree, in an empty dwelling, or in a cave: why was that? It was so that we would get the chance to examine our minds more deeply, without the confusion of being hounded by sense impressions such as sights, sounds, and so on. They cause attachment to deceptions, to all kinds of good and bad. We all know this, because in training the mind we may find out all kinds of things about ourselves, about our foolishness and gullibility. When there is correct knowledge, then we will know how many levels of wrong knowledge and wrong views still remain, and we can grasp them. As long as we still do not have right knowledge and right view, we will still be so damn stupid. Even if we teach and explain the principles correctly, the mind will be surrounded by darkness—it still does not know the truth at all; there is only good memory and clever talking.

If we diligently examine, developing awareness in the mind, and really know within our mind with wisdom, we will notice that the mind becomes dispassionate. There is no swelling of the ego in any way. The mind will be wary and cautious. If it is wisdom or true knowledge in the mind, that's what it is like. It sees defilements, desire, and clinging as like a fire that we should not pick up. It makes us gradually more fed up and put off, until whenever someone gives us a word of caution about any mistake we have made, we will see that as something extremely valuable.

Please look into yourselves and try to encourage each other in the practice, in particular with how we can examine deeply, and in our daily lives we will develop the feeling that we are one who has gained a profit within our minds. It is not a profit of material things or of fame or rank or anything like that. It is a profit in that the mind is peaceful; it is clean; it is empty of the disturbance of defilements or is gradually extinguishing the defilements. The self becomes progressively thinner, smaller. An appreciation arises in the mind of seeing the benefit of suppressing and going against the defilements and the rebellious and obstinate self. We feel that the practice of Dhamma is something that is worth developing even more because it addresses suffering at the right spot; that is, it extinguishes the self or progressively extinguishes the strength of defilements, desires, and clinging until there is only still-ness and quietness within. Carefully examine this. Whenever some-thing arises in the mind in any way, awareness arises immediately and it ceases: it is extinguished within itself.

Practicing in the mind must be controlled and not go astray. For-getfulness must be reduced. You may not yet be able to entirely stop forgetfulness, but you can reduce it. This is called having continuous mindfulness. Being one who speaks little is an excellent way of con-trolling the mind with mindfulness. Notice that if there is frivolous speech or indulgence in the pleasure of thinking various things, the right kind of knowledge fades. When we speak out and think out on so many kinds of issues, it causes suffering and harm in many different ways. We should try to examine it properly, and that will be of much benefit. It is not a small matter.

A life of Dhamma practice has its own value. This value, having come to practice correctly in accordance with the teachings and ex-tinguishing the defilements up until your final breath, is the most ex-cellent value. If your breath ceases at a moment when you have correct knowledge and there is no clinging to self or belonging to self, then that will be the end of it. You won't have to spin around in any more births.

Can you see this? Or would you rather be reborn? Examine it and see just how much suffering there will be if you are born again, how much trouble, how much confusion, how much filth. We examine like this and see that the creation of the "us" and "ours" at any given moment is suffering. Look into it. Conversely, when the mind does not create, when the self does not arise, it's peaceful; it's empty; it is at ease at that moment. Examine it for yourself. Listening right now, your mind is empty of self. You are listening with an empty mind. Just this level is of great benefit and value. We don't have to argue; we don't have to get into a fight. Seeing how empty you are at this moment, try to look into it and notice the characteristics of the mind that is free of mental fabrication. It isn't disturbed by confusing thoughts. It's quiet; it is extinguished. It is empty right now; we don't have to go and be empty anywhere else. It is empty right now. So listening with your mind right now bears fruit right now, right before your eyes. Do not doubt it. If you have not yet found the right spot to examine your mind, keep examining it. Don't get discouraged. If you discard the practice, there will be a lot of trouble.

Regarding Dhamma practice, you have to look inward, not outward. If there is looking inward, there will be so much benefit in terms of seeing impermanence, suffering, and not-self. That is the highest thing; that is the best thing, because this mind clings to the idea that this is self or belongs to self. This is where the practice is useful. It's good when there is no clinging to self or belonging to self. There are only natural realities (*sabhāvadhamma*) that are changing in accordance with causes and conditions. We must stand on this point. Our practice or examination is in order to correctly know impermanence, suffering, and not-self within body and mind, the five *khandhas*. If it's proper self-examination, you can see for yourself whether you pass or fail: if you fail to see impermanence, suffering, and not-self, knowing them only by memory, the mind does not have any weariness or dispassion. You can test this for yourselves: if your mind does not yet truly know, it will go along in a very indifferent, apathetic way. There is delight and holding on just as before. But if you know clearly with wisdom and mindfulness, there will arise dispassion and a sense of urgency. When the mind sees the truth, there is dispassion; it becomes fed up with impermanence, suffering, and not-self, with things that are unworthy of love or clinging.

This all must arise from the internal eye. It is not an external matter. If you look at it closely, you can see it clearly. There are no obstacles or obstructions. The more you look at it, the more clearly you see and penetrate impermanence, suffering, and not-self moment by moment. And then the matters of good and evil and so on are all completely done with.

The mind that sees impermanence, suffering, and not-self has a special power within it. It sweeps things clean in a mysterious way. It goes in accordance with nature in the sense that whatever arises ceases, whatever arises ceases. There is no remainder to cling to, not even a single atom. When we look into materiality (*rūpadhamma*), we see the change within materiality; we see the suffering within it; and we see not-self within the change within it. It is suffering within itself; there is no "us" or "them" or "mine" anywhere to be found. This is how it is, all of it—be it a person, an animal, or an inanimate object. It is all preparing to decay and dissolve in the end. No matter how much is built up, it is all preparing to decay and dissolve in the end, repeatedly and without end.

The Buddha therefore summarized it for us as *sabbe saṅkhārā aniccā*: all formations are impermanent. This is what we chant in the final moments of formations.[5] Look at it in terms of the Dhamma, that all dhammas are not-self. This is a total refutation. The mind examines this progressively until it sees the natural reality, that *sabbe dhamma anattā*, all things, including those that are formed and those that are not formed, are not-self: they are all natural realities. They should not be clung to as self. This is what we have to study. Examine this until you understand it fully, so that it is a clear realization of the truth. No matter how refined or profound it is, we must use mindfulness and wisdom to penetrate within so that the mind is always silent, and whatever thoughts arise and cease have no essence. Regardless of what is fabricated in the mind, it all has the same nature. Because we don't know this and don't see this, we are beset by confusion, by all the fabrication. The mind is always ready to fabricate good and bad, going back and forth about everything.

We like to create things; we don't like to be still. And that's why it becomes a problem. It is a circle, and we are spinning around and changing all the time so that we can't find any peace, we can't be empty. Try it out: At this time, why is the mind empty? We are sitting and the mind is listening: it doesn't create anything else. We are listening, which is a specific kind of feeling, the pure mind. We can be aware of it right now: the characteristics of the mind that is naturally not creating anything, but abiding within peace and emptiness. At the very moment that some creation arises, when there is a memory or perception of some kind, it has to cease. We look at it from the perspective of its ceasing, and it ceases. If we know how to look on it by maintaining the emptiness of the mind, and don't accidentally allow confusion to arise, and look around us knowing that whatever arises, of whatever kind, be it a memory, a thought, a feeling, or even the mind itself that does the thinking or feeling, will cease of itself. This is called looking at the pure, feeling mind or consciousness itself.

Now if a perception of form, sound, smell, taste, or bodily feeling arises, we look to see that perception. Whatever is perceived, in whatever manner, it changes; it degenerates. Please try to notice this. That is the practice of looking inward, where you must examine to know the characteristics of form, feeling, perception, mental formations, and consciousness and how they have the characteristics of arising and ceasing. That is examining clearly, not just looking superficially—clearly seeing the changes, the arising and ceasing as they occur, to the extent that whatever is created or perceived in the mind is easy to read. We constantly watch the feeling of the mind, in whatever way it manifests, such as in seeing a form, hearing a sound, and so on, to see that this bare awareness performs the function of being aware and then ceasing, being aware and then ceasing, at every sense door, at every sense impression. It is all practice that must be examined carefully.

The mind must be calm, not distracted, in order to examine in detail. If the mind is not calm, if it's distracted, you won't be able to examine and see clearly; you won't be able to see the truth of anything. That nature of the mind to be distracted, which arises and ceases in front of you, must be noted. See how confusing is that characteristic of distraction, the distracted thinking constantly arising and ceasing. Don't push it away so as to not be distracted. You must examine and see that, too. If you can't deal with it, if that distraction or distracted thinking does not stop, you must try to know it, to focus on it in some way. For instance, practice noting the breath, so that the mind abides with knowing and does not wander around after a whole lot of other stuff.

Meditation is a matter of training the mind to be calm and then constantly examining within oneself. For instance, you concentrate on the breath. The breath demonstrates change within itself. Breath is the wind element, one of the four elements known as earth, water, wind, and fire. When you examine the wind element, it flows in and out in accordance with nature, contingent on all the four elements. Because we don't resolve to examine it clearly, we don't really know the truth of our bodies, that they are changing, because each of the elements performs the function of creating all kinds of change.

Or we can examine mentality (*nāmadhamma*): feeling, perception, volitional formations, and consciousness. We need to single out consciousness for specific examination, to know the characteristics of the bare mind or consciousness, how it arises, stands, and declines. When cognizing sense impressions, for instance, when there is an awareness of materiality and mentality, how does the mind or consciousness element mingle with it? How does it arise and cease with it? We have to single out and examine them to see the characteristics properly and in detail. Even though it is something that is difficult to know, we must make an effort to do so, because if we do not examine this matter, we will not properly know impermanence, suffering, and not-self in accordance with the teaching of the Buddha. We may chant the words and memorize them, and we can talk about it and explain it in accordance with the teachings, but the mind is still dark and cloudy.

This is called lacking the inner eye. You can't see it, because the flesh eye, the external eye, wanders around connecting with confusion. If you get lost in the external eye, it likes to look at things indiscriminately. Then the inner eye is fenced off. Its functions are snatched away by the external eye, creating all kinds of confusion. We are deceived by the external sense doors, getting lost in looking, lost in listening, lost in smelling, lost in tasting, lost in bodily feelings, and lost in mental impressions, meaning we get lost in the impressions that are created in the mind.

When we get lost like this, will we be aware of it, of how we are getting blindly deluded in a pitiable way? Even though we are able to see the outside, let us turn back and look inward. The inside is more interesting than the outside, because if you look deeply inside, it is really amazing. You will see all mentality and materiality changing, that none of it has any true self, that it fares according to the laws of nature or the nature that depends on defilements—that is, ignorance—for its creation. Then there is the change on account of defilements, desire, and attachment. Looking inward like this is better. Don't be fooled by looking too much at the outside. Just by regularly looking inward you will inevitably be entering the correct path within the mind.

The mind that has true knowledge and vision causes dispassion and detachment to arise. There will be no going out and attaching to external forms, sounds, smells, tastes, and physical sensations. The internal feeling that is the ultimate agent is consciousness, the mind still surrounded by ignorance. If realization occurs, it brings about relinquishment or letting go, and then the mind is free. It becomes pure and clear. Think about it. Is it not desirable to practice to attain this? Or do you still want to indulge in external deceptions? It's up to you. It is up to each individual. Look at it and you will see.

If it's correct knowledge and seeing, this is what you must see. Specifically, see the truth of the impermanence, suffering, and not-self of the consciousness element or mind, which is the ultimate agent, the most important. Then delve into it and destroy the germ within the mind. Is it worth destroying? I want Dhamma practitioners to take this and examine it carefully. The roots of sensual desire, desire for becoming, and desire for cessation lie deep within the mind. Knowledge must penetrate and destroy them with the inner eye, which we call mindfulness and wisdom, or *ñāṇadassana*,[6] which knows clearly within. Should we not try to do this in earnest?

Please discuss this frequently. How are we going to fix this wrong knowledge, wrong view, which blinds and destroys us, causing us to carry on being stupid and gullible? How can we fix ourselves? How can we change it to knowing clearly? How must we examine it? This is the activity that is more important than anything else. Whatever we look at, none of it can compare with seeing the truth of impermanence, suffering, and not-self. In particular, if you look inward and penetrate within, you see that the outside is all impermanent, suffering, and not-self. There's nothing that's good or bad, nothing that's beautiful. Regardless of the level, it is all impermanent, suffering, and not-self throughout the three realms of sensuality, form, and formlessness.

At the moment we don't know this; we've closed off our eyes and ears. We are gullible, so we must try to open our eyes and look at this so that we see it everywhere. If you open your eyes to the inner, then you will gain benefit; you will enter the path, the footsteps of the Buddha, known as *Buddho*, meaning "the one who knows, the awakened one, the one who is bright in the Dhamma." If we merely remember the word *Buddho* and recite it, our mind won't know anything; we will still be sleeping, still wandering around. We won't know the real qualities of the Buddha.

Therefore, Dhamma practitioners should take an interest, examine this, and see the truth in true knowledge. May you become "the one who knows, the awakened one, the one who is bright in the Dhamma" in every moment.

AJAHN PRAMOTE (PĀMOJJO)

Venerable Ajahn Pramote was born Pramote Santayakorn in 1952 in Bangkok. His road to monkhood was a little unconventional in that he spent many years pursuing his education and building a successful worldly life before entering the monkhood at the age of forty-eight. Prior to his ordination, he completed a master's degree at Chulalongkorn University, started a family, and carved out a successful career in Thailand's civil service, culminating with a post at the Telephone Organization of Thailand (TOT).

He showed an interest in the Dhamma from a very early age, learning and practicing meditation under the guidance of Than Por Lee (1907–1961), a prominent disciple of Luang Pu Mun, from the age of seven. As an adult he studied the core Buddhist studies program of the Thai saṅgha and took the Dhamma examinations (*nak tham tri*) while also reading the entire Tipiṭaka twice. He continued to develop his meditation practice, and his intense spirit of inquiry led him to visit and study with Ajahn Buddhadāsa, as well as many eminent disciples of Luang Pu Mun, such as Luang Pu Thate (Thesaraṅgsī), Luang Por Phut (Thāniyo), Luang Pu Sim (Buddhācāro), Luang Pu Boonchan (Chandavaro), and Luang Por Suwat (Suvaco). However, his most influential teacher was Luang Pu Dul (Atulo), also a disciple of Luang Pu Mun. His meeting and studying with Luang Pu Dul were pivotal to his Dhamma practice.

While a layperson, his dedication to Dhamma practice did not go unnoticed by the various teachers he visited. Luang Por Phut suggested that he start writing some Dhamma teachings for lay practitioners, and this he duly did by writing regularly for Dhamma magazines and online Dhamma blogs.

He left the householder life and took bhikkhu ordination in 2001, spending his first five years with Ajahn Suchin (Sucinno), after which he established his own monastery at Wat Suan Santidham in Chon Buri Province, where he lives and teaches to this day.

The combination of his extensive worldly experience together with his intense spirit of inquiry into the Buddha's teaching and Buddhist practice, incorporating studying meditation under many illustrious teachers from a young age, have provided him with a rare ability to explain Dhamma practice in a particularly lucid manner. His teachings, given every Saturday and Sunday at Wat Suan Santidham, are wonderful in their breadth of subject matter and depth of meaning. They can be found on YouTube, and some are available in English and Chinese translation.

The three teachings given here are all freshly translated from the Thai. I have put them together in a roughly graded progression, although they are independent teachings. The wealth of Ajahn Pramote's teachings is such that one could easily pick any three at random and still find much food for thought and inspiration.

Introduction to
Dhamma Practice[1]

TODAY THERE ARE ELECTIONS in Bangkok, right? I haven't voted. These days I don't know anything about politics. I don't know who are the important, powerful people. If you look at a lot of stuff, it's messy. I just know my in-breath and out-breath, and my life is happy and peaceful. If you meddle too much with the outside world, things get complicated. The world is chaotic like this. The more information you have, the more you have to think about. If you think a lot, you start worrying, or you experience defilements. The mind bounces around, and then there is suffering.

In the olden days people didn't hear much news day-to-day. It was all about just making a living, finding something to eat. If you had enough to eat, you were happy. You didn't have to think a lot. When I was a child, they worked the rice fields once a year. When the rice season was over, people could still go to the low-lying areas and find fish and vegetables and live off that. In higher, more barren areas they would have more difficulty. There wasn't much water to drink or use.

The hardship that people experienced in those days was a raw kind of hardship. It was all about making a living. They were glad just to have enough to eat, and society wasn't very complicated. Every now and then there would be a temple fair. That was where people would gather together and relax. With the passing of time, society has changed rapidly. In the old days, changes were slow. Now the acceleration of the rate of change is very fast.

I was born in Bangkok, but now if I go to Bangkok I get lost. I don't know where anything is. Everything has changed. Change is something you cannot prevent. People in the past just thought about making a living, how they could make enough to survive. If they got sick, what would they do? Go to see the monks; go see a village doctor; find some medicine.

Nowadays there are so many material things. But they all have to be bought with money. It's not like the old days: someone could work the fields and catch fish, and they could get by without using money. Nowadays you can't survive if you don't have money. So people give money a lot of importance. They want to get as much of it as they can. Even better if they can become rich, to get more than other people.

The things people consume these days are way beyond the minimum standard required for living. Nowadays you have to carry a handbag worth hundreds of thousands of baht. Your nerves are shot. You have to find so much money to buy a handbag with a brand name and a really high price tag. Tens of thousands of baht for a pair of shoes. We are goaded into consuming more than is necessary, and so we have to work hard to make a lot of money. I don't know if this life is happier or more suffering.

If you want something really fast, you have to borrow money for it. And so we live in debt. The Buddha said that being in debt was a form of suffering in this world. People are happy and proud to have good credit. You have to be in debt to be good; it shows that you have credit. They won't lend money to anyone who doesn't have credit. And so the whole country is in debt. It's hard to believe that some professionals are in debt. Teachers have a lot of debt. They have so much debt, they work until they retire and the debt still isn't cleared. Why must they have so much debt? Because they want to consume happiness.

I'm not criticizing teachers, mind you. I'm just talking generally. We want to have high consumption, so we need a lot of money. So your whole life is dedicated to working. Some people have good circumstances, good opportunities, or maybe they have good past kamma: they find it easy to make a living. They find the right groove to make a living and become rich. But before long, society changes, the economy changes. What once made you rich no longer makes you rich. For instance, thirty years ago I worked at the telephone organization. The telephone organization was rich. People came asking for phone numbers, and there wasn't enough to go around. There was a market shortage. They got seventy million baht per day from the public telephone booths. Nowadays it's all changed. No one uses public telephone booths anymore. There's nowhere for Superman to change his pants.

After the landline telephones came the era of the mobile phone. At that time, whoever did mobile business got rich. Nowadays they're beginning to feel like they can't go on. Everything changes so fast. What was once an easy way to make a living becomes something that just doesn't work anymore.

So we have to adjust ourselves very quickly in order to survive. All this adjusting leads to stress. Mental illness comes knocking; depression comes knocking—all kinds of things. Even children are affected. Children are being forced to study a lot, to do special classes and whatever; they have no time to run around and play—not like children in my day. We had time to run around and do other things. Children these days, if they have any spare time, get sent to special classes. I don't know what they're so busy studying. Statistics show that many children these days suffer from depression. Children are showing signs of being troubled. Their minds are not stable because they are so stressed.

We have progressed to the point where people aren't really happy. At first, we thought if we really developed the country, the people would be happy. Field Marshal Sarit once said, "Work is money. Money is work. Happiness ensues." He thought that if we had money, we would be happy. These days we have money, but do you see? Inflation is here again. I don't know how people can be happy. In their hearts there is only stress and exhaustion. This is how the economy is. The technology of production is like this. You can't stop it, but how can we live with it so that the suffering is reduced, so that we live with these things wisely, not so foolishly that we are being dragged around by them all the time?

Our previous king² used to say, "Live in moderation." If we live like that, then we can survive. We may not be so lavish, so stylish as others, but we also won't be as stressed as others. Why is it that we want happiness, but all we get is exhaustion from work and suffering and stress?

It is at this point that the Dhamma can help. Most people don't know about the Dhamma. They think when you go into the temple you have to bow to this and bow to that, bow to the tree spirit (Nang Takhian) and Ganesha. They even bow to that naked child, what's its name? Ta Khai.[3] They'll bow to anything. Why is that? It's because their life has no refuge.

Now we have a chance to come and study the Dhamma, to learn how to train our own minds so that we are able to live in the world with only a little suffering. We haven't reached the level of living in the world with no suffering at all. You have to really practice meditation (*bhāvanā*) and develop the mind to rise above the world in order to really transcend suffering. If we attain the Dhamma in the initial stages, such as *sotāpanna*[4] or *sakidāgāmi*,[5] these levels have not yet escaped the world. The world can still affect them heavily. But most people haven't attained even this.

If you haven't attained sotāpanna, you must try to walk in the footsteps of those who have gone beyond the world. Beyond the world is what we refer to as the transcendent (*lokuttara*). The path is still there, the path taught by the Buddha for developing mindfulness and wisdom.

We are blessed to have studied the Dhamma that will develop our minds. For instance, among our siblings and our close friends, those we have grown up with, gone to school with, and worked with, where one person does not practice meditation and one person does, at first you can't see much difference. But after many years, the differences will become more apparent. One of them will still be unclean and scruffy, soiled with the dust of the world. *Dust* refers to the defilements (*kilesa*). Each person fares according to their kamma. They have the kamma of being deluded by the world. They sink into the filth of the world with no end in sight. When you come to practice meditation, develop mindfulness, keep the precepts, create *samādhi* (concentration), and develop wisdom, as time goes on you will experience a period where you notice the difference. You will see the difference; you will feel that people in the world are worthy of pity. People in the world are enveloped in blindness. We do not disparage them. Instead, the heart feels compassion. We think, "Before I used to be like that. It's good that I have encountered the Dhamma of the Buddha's teaching and started to practice. I am getting cleaner and purer, reducing the suffering." This we will know for ourselves. Where we used to suffer for long periods of time, we now suffer for shorter periods. Where we used to suffer intensely, now the suffering is milder, only a little. The mind changes. This is something we can know for ourselves and see for ourselves.

Therefore, do not let the time pass by in vain. Don't spend your days messing around with the world all the time, with this news and that news. One moment it's politics, then the economy, then war, then social issues such as scandals with monks and so on. It's just chaos. In the world there isn't anything more, only suffering. It's no use hating it because we have to live with it. But now that we live with it, train and develop your mind well. Try to develop mindfulness.

The simple way to develop mindfulness is to train to be able to read your own mind. When our mind is happy, know that as it happens. When the mind is suffering, be aware of it as it happens. When the mind is indifferent, neither happy nor sad, be aware of it as it happens. When our mind is meritorious and skillful, such as when faith arises and we want to listen to a Dhamma teaching, do some chanting, or on some days when our mind is filled with energy for the practice and we have mindfulness, we note it. If our mind has faith, we know it.

Some days our faith may fall low, because for ordinary people (*puthujjana*) faith pops up and down. The ancients said that the faith of unenlightened people is "tortoise-head faith"—do you know how a tortoise moves its head? It stretches its head out, then it pulls it back in again. It pops in and out like that. That's the faith of unenlightened beings. One minute there's faith; the next there isn't. When the object of our faith serves our interests, we have faith. Whenever it conflicts with our interests, we no longer have faith.

When the mind has faith, we know it. When we want to listen to the Dhamma, we know it immediately. If the mind is fed up and can't be bothered listening to a teaching, we want to go to sleep or go to a pub or a bar, the mind knows immediately. Know your own mind. If the mind has greed, we know it; if it's angry, we know it; if our mind is deluded and wanders off, we know it. When our mind is distracted, we know it; when it's depressed, we know it. When the mind is calm, we know it. However the mind is, we know it. If our mind experiences goodwill (*mettā*), we know it. When goodwill disappears and anger arises, we know it. If our mind experiences compassion—as when seeing others falling into hardships and seeing other beings in difficulty, compassion arises and we want to help free them from their suffering—we know that our mind has compassion. Then, when we have compassion but we don't get what we want, aversion arises in its place. Compassion and anger are opposing conditions. You can get annoyed over it, like when you want to help others and you advise them not to play with this strange money they have nowadays. We say, "Don't play with it; you'll go broke." If they don't believe us and go on to deal with it, then we get annoyed. We get even more annoyed if they play with it and get rich. This is called envy. If the mind experiences envy, we know it.

So train to know your mind. It changes all the time. When you hear one thing, the mind changes in such a way; when you see something else, it changes in another way. When you think of something that makes you happy, it changes in that way. Keep knowing and being aware of these changes in the mind. As you know it, in time you will know that everything that arises in our mind is temporary. Happiness is temporary; suffering is temporary; neutral feeling is temporary. Skillful mental states (*kusala*) are temporary: one minute we have faith, then we don't. Sometimes we are diligent; sometimes we are lazy. Sometimes we have mindfulness; sometimes we lack mindfulness. Sometimes we have wisdom, and see the world as it is; sometimes we get lost in the world and don't have wisdom. Our mind is sometimes skillful, sometimes unskillful. Keep watching and observing it. We will see that, be it skillful or unskillful, it all invariably arises, is established, and ceases.

When you keep watching like this, then when happiness or skillfulness arise in the mind, our mind does not float upward. When our mind has suffering or is unskillful, our mind does not sink down. It doesn't swing upward or downward; it doesn't waver upward or downward. We keep developing mindfulness until we reach a point where the mind is neutral toward all things.

To be centered doesn't mean that the mind doesn't move at all, but whatever arises in our life—even the start of a world war—our mind is undisturbed. If we were to be killed right now, our mind is undisturbed. The body belongs to the world. If it gets destroyed or breaks up, that is natural, it's normal. The mind is neutral.

When our mind is neutral, it will not be so hungry. When the mind is hungry, it isn't neutral. It likes this and hates that: it is hungry for mental objects (*ārammaṇa*). It is hungry for good mental objects and hates bad mental objects. It is hungry for pleasing sights, hungry for sounds, hungry for smells, hungry for tastes, hungry for tactile impressions, hungry for mental impressions. The mind wants this and doesn't want that.

When desire arises in our mind, the mind jumps around. This desire is called *taṇhā*. Taṇhā is the wanting in the mind. The aspect of it jumping around is called *bhava* (becoming). Taṇhā is what creates bhava. For so long as our mind has wanting, our mind is still jumping around; where there is becoming, there is always suffering.

So now we come to develop mindfulness and wisdom to the point where our mind becomes neutral. When our mind is neutral, it doesn't swing upward or downward; it doesn't want this or hate that. It is neutral toward all things. Taṇhā cannot function. Bhava does not arise. There is no suffering. Taṇhā is what creates bhava. Where there is bhava, there is always suffering.

The Buddha taught that no matter how great and special the bhava may be, it is all suffering. For instance, suppose that you are in the bhava of a rich person. You are so proud of being a rich person. But a rich person has a rich person's suffering. A poor person has a poor person's suffering. No matter what bhava you have, it is all suffering. If you're a child, you have the suffering of a child. If you're a parent, you have the suffering of a parent. If you're a husband, you have the suffering of a husband. If you're a wife, you have the suffering of a wife. No matter what you are, it is always suffering.

So what there is in existence is nothing other than suffering. When you say you are this or that, in fact you are suffering, nothing else. Keep looking at it; notice the truth. It's not difficult. When our mind is happy, we know; when our mind is suffering, we know; when our mind is indifferent, we know; when our mind is good, we know; when our mind is bad—angry, greedy, deluded, distracted, depressed—we know. Keep on knowing and observing this, and you will see that all things are equal in that they are subject to the three characteristics. Happiness is not lasting; suffering is not lasting; indifference is not lasting.

When you see this, you will be done with hunger for happiness, because it is not lasting. Why should we struggle so much to seek it? It is impermanent. These days people are struggling to find happiness but making all kinds of suffering for themselves. They think that if they get rich, they'll be happy; that if they have lots of wealth and belongings, if they have handbags worth hundreds of thousands of baht, if they have a car worth tens of millions of baht, that they will be happy. In truth, they don't have happiness. No matter what you have, you will suffer because of it. The Buddha said that if you have fields, you suffer over the fields; if you have cattle, you suffer over the cattle. Whatever you have, you will suffer over that. Just keep watching and looking. Our mind will gradually become neutral.

That happiness that we are struggling for, in truth it is just creating suffering for ourselves, beginning with the struggle to find happiness. Once happiness arises, there is the concern over it, the worry that it will disappear. The mind is like this. It doesn't have any real peace or happiness.

From an ethical perspective, skillful and unskillful are not equal. The skillful brings happiness, while the unskillful brings suffering. But in terms of ultimate reality (*paramattha*), both skillful and unskillful are equal as natural realities (*sabhāvadhamma*). They are realities that equally arise, exist, and cease. The skillful mind arises, stands, and ceases. Unskillful conditions arise, stand, and cease. For instance, when we are meditating, sometimes our mind is peaceful and happy. There is rapture, pleasure, and brightness. Our mind is firm in the Buddha, the Dhamma, and the Saṅgha. This state passes. In a while there is agitation, annoyance, irritation. If we haven't meditated, once our mind becomes irritated we struggle even more to fix the suffering that has arisen. But if we are a real practitioner on the level of insight, when our mind is troubled and suffers, when our mind is gloomy or defilements arise, we don't have to be frightened. We just look into it. If anger arises, just look into it. How long will the anger last?

Don't look at the anger in order to get rid of it. When anger arises in the mind, mostly people look at it thinking, "When will it go away; when will it pass?" The mind is not neutral; the mind has a desire for this state to go away. This is called *vibhavataṇhā*. Once there is vibhavataṇhā, the mind struggles: "How can I make it go away?" The more you struggle, the more suffering there is. But if our mind is clever, we see anger arise, and our mind is just the observer, the watcher. We will see anger arise, endure, and cease.

If we haven't seen this, the mind will struggle. Teach the mind a little. For instance, when we are angry, instead of thinking, "Why won't it go away?" try thinking in a new way: "Let's see. How long will this anger last?" Look at yourself. And talk to it. "How long are you going to be angry?" Look at it like this. I guarantee that anger will scatter and flee. To put it in normal parlance, it will run away like a dog with its tail between its legs. The defilements will run away; they cannot stay. They can't resist mindfulness and wisdom.

So when your mind is gloomy, don't go thinking, "Why won't this gloom go away?" Just look into it. Make your mind comfortable and look into it. "Let's take a look. How long will this gloom last? How long will the mind feel gloomy?" Look right at this point. Train yourself with something that is straight and direct and you will see the truth. Things that are not good, the suffering in the mind, the defilements in the mind, if we know them directly and know them with a neutral mind, not hating them—they will immediately disappear. The mind that can have suffering is a particular kind of mind. It is called *dosa mūla citta*, the mind that has aversion at its root or base. The mind that has greed can experience happiness, but when the mind is gloomy and depressed, just know that the mind contains *dosa*. If the mind has dosa, is gloomy, and suffers, just know this directly.

The Buddha taught that when there is happiness, to know it; when there is suffering, to know it; when the mind is neutral, to know it. This is in the four foundations of mindfulness—the "feeling" foundation of mindfulness (*vedanānupassanā satipaṭṭhāna*). When our mind has dosa—irritation, annoyance, aversion, sorrow, and sadness: these are in the dosa group—the Buddha said, "Bhikkhus, when the mind has dosa, know it as the mind with dosa." He did not say to give it up: he said to know it. So when our mind becomes gloomy, we don't look at it to get rid of it. The Buddha did not teach like that. He said, "When the mind has dosa, know that the mind has dosa." He did not say, "See here bhikkhus, when the mind has dosa, give it up." This is not what he taught. He taught, "See here bhikkhus, when the mind has dosa, know that the mind has dosa. When the mind has greed, know that it has greed." When we know that there is greed, the greed ceases. Then the mind has no greed. We continue to observe, noting that the mind is without greed. It is only for a while, and then that ceases. When the mind is quick to anger, we can see it, right? The mind has dosa.

We know straight and direct like this; we don't go and interfere with it. It ceases under our observation, and we see that. When the mind has dosa, we know that the mind has dosa. It becomes the mind without dosa. When the mind is without dosa, we know that also. The Buddha taught further, "Bhikkhus, when the mind has dosa, know that it has dosa. When the mind is without dosa, then know that the mind is without dosa."

As we continue to observe, we see the mind has no dosa: so what do we do next? There is no "what do I do next?" Just know that there is no dosa: that's all. Deep in our minds we tend to think, "What should I do? What should I do next?" We're always thinking of doing this and that. Doing this is right; doing that is wrong.

If we're practicing insight meditation, there is only one verb that applies, and that is *see*. *See* the body as the body is; *see* feeling as feeling is; *see* volitional activities as they are. Greed, hatred, and delusion are within the volitional activities group. They are part of the *saṅkhāra khandha*.[6] They are in the *cittānupassanā satipaṭṭhāna* (the "mind" foundation of mindfulness).[7] So keep watching, keep observing. You will see that everything equally arises, stands, and ceases. As we meditate more and more, we will see everything arising and ceasing, arising and ceasing repeatedly, and our mind will become more and more neutral. Before, we were hungry for happiness. As we continue to meditate, we see happiness arising, standing, then ceasing, and that hunger for happiness decreases. We can no longer see what it is that we should be struggling so much to find. We are exhausted almost to death, like most people in the world, all struggling to find happiness. They even go so far as to make trouble for the monks, because they're looking for happiness, they don't want suffering. When we look deeper inward, we see that this search for happiness is in fact a search for suffering. Any happiness we do find is only short-lived. The mind sees in this way.

The mind will gradually incline toward neutrality. It does so by itself. You don't have to make it neutral. If you try to force it to be neutral, that goes beyond just seeing. See the mind happy; see the mind suffering: just see. Eventually wisdom will arise. Happiness and suffering are equal in that they are subject to the three characteristics. They are equally impermanent; they are equally unable to endure; and they are equally not able to be controlled in accordance with our likes. When the mind enters neutrality, it ceases to struggle. When it becomes neutral, it no longer wants. That we have desire is because the mind refuses to be neutral. If it's neutral, it doesn't need to want. When it is neutral toward happiness and neutral toward suffering, it doesn't want to run after happiness or run away from suffering. When there is no wanting, struggling does not arise in the mind. The mind attains peace and happiness.

If your powers are strong enough, if morality, concentration, and wisdom are sufficiently strong, the noble path and noble fruit will arise. They will arise on their own. No one can order them to arise.

So as we train to know and observe things as they arise, stand, and cease in the present moment, watching until our mind becomes neutral toward all things, the mind will cease to struggle and cease to be hungry, as our mindfulness, concentration, and wisdom become fully developed. Training to watch and observe, from one who has no morality, we become one who has morality; from one who has no right concentration, we become one who has right concentration; from one who has never seen the three characteristics, we become one who sees the three characteristics. Eventually the mind becomes neutral. Morality, concentration, and wisdom will be developed from using mindfulness to read our own minds. When morality, concentration, and wisdom are developed, the noble path arises on its own. We don't have to order it. When we reach that point, it arises of itself. You can't stop it; it arises automatically.

Our task is not to *make* the path and fruit arise, because, as I said, no one can make that happen. Our task is to develop mindfulness. Be mindful, knowing the body as it is, having mindfulness, knowing feeling as it is. The feeling that is easy to observe is mental feeling. Physical feeling is difficult to work with. If your mind has not really developed the *jhānas*,[8] it's very difficult to watch physical feeling. As feeling gets more and more intense, mindfulness falls apart. So I recommend observing mental feeling: happiness, suffering, and neither pleasant nor unpleasant feeling in the mind. Just keep observing; there isn't anything difficult about it. Right now, if our mind is feeling happy, we know it; if it is feeling unhappy, we know it; if our mind is feeling neutral, we know it. If our mind is skillful, we know it; if our mind is unskillful, we know it. Train in this way.

As we know repeatedly like this, our mind will gradually become cleverer. It will know that all dhammas (phenomena) that are pairs— happiness and suffering, good and evil—these pairs are all equal in that they are subject to the three characteristics. Happiness and suffering are equal in terms of the three characteristics. They are equally impermanent; they are equally oppressed into dissolution; and they are equally uncontrollable. Good and evil are equal in terms of the three characteristics; they are equally impermanent. When good or evil arise in the mind, both are equally oppressed into dissolution and cease. And whether the mind is good or evil we cannot force it. That is, those conditions are not-self. When you see this, when you see the three characteristics repeatedly, the mind will of itself become neutral. This term *of itself* is key. It becomes neutral *of itself*. If you try to force it to become neutral, it won't be *of itself*. So try to observe over and over. There isn't much to meditation. See the body as it is. See feeling as it is. See the mind that is skillful and unskillful as it is.

As the mind becomes subtler, you will see that the very mind itself, this mind that is the observer, the watcher, falls into the three characteristics. At first we have the mind that is the observer, the watcher of the body, and it sees the body falling within the three characteristics. Then we have the mind that is the observer, the watcher of feeling, and it sees feeling falling within the three characteristics. We have the mind that is the observer, the watcher, mindfully recollecting and knowing the skillful and unskillful that arise, and we see that they fall within the three characteristics. And the mind itself falls within the three characteristics too. The mind is one moment the knower, the observer, then it is the thinker, the creator, the fabricator.

Observe this. Train like this. Eventually the mind will enter neutrality. It will be done with hunger. Leave the world with the world. The world ripples up and down, but our mind does not ripple up and down with it, because we understand the world. The world is physicality and mentality. Study your own physicality and mentality; look at your body and mind. If you understand this, you will understand the entire world. It's the same. It ripples up and down all the time; it's never still. Keep training and you will attain something special. Most people are still going to be running around for a long time. They have to continue to accumulate good kamma, traveling through the world of rebirth (*saṃsāravaṭṭa*) for a very long time, running around from birth to death. Sometimes desire, pride, and views drag us down into the ocean. They can drag us down into hell. Keep looking into it. One day you will escape it.

In this world there is nothing. This world contains only suffering. When you see this, you will feel disheartened, disenchanted, and disenamored. There really isn't anything. Foolishness—that is *avijjā*, ignorance—causes us to desire, to want this and that. But once you study the truth, you see that everything arises and passes away, that this world has only rippling. Our bodies and minds consist of only rippling. There is nothing substantial in it, nothing lasting. Our mind will gradually detach from the world step-by-step.

Practice. There is no alternative other than the cultivation of the foundations of mindfulness. With mindfulness, note the body, the feelings, the mind, and dhammas. There is no other way. There is no second path. The Buddha therefore said that the foundations of mindfulness—knowing the body, knowing feelings, knowing the skillful and unskillful mind, and knowing all material dhammas and mental dhammas with mindfulness—that is the one way, the only way, to attain purity and liberation.

We must see this. If we study just by reading, by listening, or by thinking, the defilements are not moved at all. Sometimes the more we study the scriptures, the more selfish we get. We can easily become deluded. We can interpret the Dhamma falsely. Why is that? Because we have defilements. But if you train to know your own mind, you will not misinterpret the Dhamma, because you can see for yourself. If you haven't seen it, you have to rely on thinking, interpreting, sometimes right and sometimes wrong. There is no second way to purity and liberation other than the development of the foundations of mindfulness. Try to study it. At the very least we should know what it is that we have to learn. Physicality and mentality, the five *khandhas*, the six sense bases: these things. Study them. The three characteristics, the four foundations of mindfulness. Go and read about them in the Tipiṭaka. Read it and understand, and you will be able to feel out the path.

When I started out, I began reading the Tipiṭaka. When people spoke of the Dhamma, I understood; it wasn't that I didn't understand. When I heard people talking about the Dhamma, I understood it all because I had already read it all. But I only knew through memory. I didn't really know it clearly. You have to practice Dhamma in order to really know it. I once went and asked Ajahn Buddhadāsa. In those days Ajahn Buddhadāsa was the most famous monk in Thailand in terms of possessing knowledge and skills. In those days there were two: Ajahn Buddhadāsa and Venerable Prayudh. These two had very deep learning. I saw that Ajahn Buddhadāsa had written lots of books. I read his books, and I developed a wrong view that everything is empty. One day I went to a religious conference at government house. I met Ajahn Sucheep Punyanupab.[9] I talked about this being empty, that being empty, and he kindly asked me to approach. I sat on the floor in the "sideways" posture.[10] He was a teacher. He was a layperson, but his learning was immense. He wrote the *People's Tipiṭaka*. He told me that my understanding was not yet correct, that the Buddha did not teach like that. He didn't teach that after death there was nothing. He didn't teach to just let go of everything, that it was all empty. That is all wrong view. He said this to me, and I was stunned. After all my reading of scriptures I had misinterpreted it all. I had read the Tipiṭaka and Ajahn Buddhadāsa's books and misinterpreted them. Ajahn Sucheep corrected me on this.

It so happened I went for a meeting down in Surat Thani, in Chaiya, and I went to pay my respects to Ajahn Buddhadāsa. When I got there, I asked him, "Tan Ajahn. Do you teach that after death there is nothing?" Do you know what he said? "Do you think I have wrong view?" With just this much, I knew straightaway that I had misunderstood his books. I had misinterpreted them and developed wrong view. Thinking that after death there is nothing is wrong view. To think that after death one is reborn is also wrong view. And just making your mind empty, that is also wrong view. So then I asked him, "Tan Ajahn. If I read every single one of your books, will I become a stream enterer?" He answered, "No, you won't. You have to practice." He was adamant. Read all of it, what he had written, cupboards full of books, and you won't get it. You have to practice.

I listened to that and it struck a chord in me, because that was how I already understood it. I had read the Tipiṭaka, the whole cupboard full, and didn't attain anything other than a lot of memory, and then went and ridiculed other people who said the wrong thing. It was just defilements. Later when I met Luang Pu Dul, he taught me to watch the mind, and so I watched that, just like I teach you these days. Watching and observing, the mind gradually becomes neutral. When the mind is neutral, it doesn't struggle, and it gradually enters peace and happiness. Practice it. There is no way other than developing the four foundations of mindfulness.

SEPARATING THE KHANDHAS[11]

BE AWARE WHEN YOUR MIND wanders around, when the mind is not concentrated. Don't force it. If you're afraid of it wandering around and you try to force it, that becomes wrong concentration (*micchāsamādhi*). It's not good. You'll feel oppressed. In meditation, just be aware of yourself comfortably. Just be aware. The body breathes out, the body breathes in. Be aware of it. The body stands, walks, sits, and reclines—be aware of it. The body moves and the body is still—be aware of it. Be aware of it often. At first, it seems impossible to just look at the mind. When the mind is really scattered, you can't see it. The mind just goes touring around all the time. If you can't watch the mind, watch the body. If you look at the body, one day you'll see the mind.

To be aware of the body breathing out and breathing in, we must know it with the normal mind. We don't know it with a mind that is stressed or that is forced, that is pressed into stillness. We know it with the mind that is normal and natural. We see the body breathing out and breathing in. Don't focus on the breath. If you focus on the breath, the mind will become too still and sometimes it gets uncomfortable. If you focus too strongly, you'll get uncomfortable. Just be aware that the body is breathing.

Yesterday someone said to me that while they were watching the breath, the mind became calm and then it let go of the breath. The breath became shallower and shallower until it just seemed to stay at the nose tip, and it became like a light. Rapture and happiness arose. That is the attainment of samādhi, of peace. It's *samatha* (calm) meditation.

The samādhi that is important for us to train in is the samādhi that entails self-awareness, where the mind is knowing, awakened, and bright. Once we see the body, the breath, we continue to observe it. We see the body standing, walking, sitting, and reclining. The mind is the watcher. We see the body moving about and staying still, and the mind is the watcher. We keep watching, but the mind wanders off and neglects its work. For instance, we know the body breathing in and breathing out for a moment, and then it wanders off thinking of something else. We know the body standing, walking, sitting, or reclining, the body moving about and being still, but in a moment the mind wanders off again and forgets about the body. We must know this often: the mind wanders off and we know it; it wanders off again and we know it. Eventually, the mind, the knower, becomes bright and clear. We attain the highest level of samādhi: the samādhi where the mind is firm, knowing, awake, and bright. It is the watcher.

For instance, notice right now we are sitting. Are you aware of your body sitting? Is it difficult to know that you are sitting? It's not hard, is it? Now try moving: you know that you are moving. Is that difficult? There's nothing difficult about it. Meditation is just a very normal thing like this. When the body moves, we are aware of it. We are aware of it with the normal mind. It is not a mind that is stressed, dull, or ignorant. Do this often. When the mind is firmly established, it becomes the watcher. When the body breathes, the mind is the watcher. The body stands, walks, sits, and reclines: the mind is the watcher. When the body moves or is still, the mind watches.

Once we have the mind that is the watcher, we can develop wisdom. Then we can begin to separate the elements, to separate the khandhas. In practicing to develop wisdom, the first thing we need to do is to obtain the samādhi where the mind is firm and is the knower, the watcher. Then we put this samādhi to work. When we look at the body, we see that the body is that which is known and watched. That is not the mind. The mind is the one who knows and watches. When we look at feelings of pleasure and pain, we will see that those feelings of pleasure and pain are what is known and observed. The mind is the one that knows and observes. Now we are beginning to separate them.

We are separating the body from the mind, separating the feelings from the mind.

Sometimes we can separate the feelings from the body. For instance, when we're sitting and there's pain and discomfort, the mind observes it, and we see that at first there is the body sitting, then after a while we see pain and discomfort arising in the body. That pain and discomfort are not the body. That pain and discomfort are not the mind. They are another khandha, another part.

There's no need to be afraid of this Pali word *khandha*. In regular parlance we would just say "parts." We are separating the parts: the part that is the body, the part that is feelings of happiness and suffering, the part that is memory, the part that is the creation of good and bad thoughts, such as greed, anger, and delusion—this is another part—and the mind is another part. Altogether there are five parts, called the five khandhas. You hear the words *five khandhas* and it sounds scary, but in fact it is just separating that which we call ourselves into different parts. The Buddha separated it out into five parts, and we separate accordingly. He has separated it well enough; we don't need to divide it up any further, otherwise it'll just get confusing.

So once the mind is firmly established in watching, the body and the mind will divide into separate parts. We see the body standing, walking, sitting, and reclining, the body breathing in and breathing out, the body moving and the body staying still, as objects of knowing or observation. Pain and discomfort that arise in the body, pleasure and comfort that arise in the body, are not the body. When we first start sitting, we feel comfortable and there is no pain or discomfort, but as we continue to sit, pain and discomfort arise. We see this. The mind is the one who watches, and we see this. The body is one part; the pain and discomfort are another. They are different things. This is called being able to separate the khandhas. We separate the body and separate the feeling.

At first, we separate the mind from the body. The body standing, walking, sitting, and reclining, the body breathing, the body moving and keeping still are all known and observed. This is called separating the body from the mind. When we sit for a long time or walk for a long time, we feel pain and discomfort. We see that previously the body was not in pain or discomfort, but now the pain and discomfort have arisen. The pain and discomfort have arisen afterward, as intruders. They are not the body. They are foreign intruders. So we separate out another part, the part that is feeling. Feeling is not the body. And this feeling, this pleasure and pain, is a thing that is known and observed, the mind being that which knows and observes. So feelings are not the body, and they are not the mind. Now the khandhas are beginning to separate. The thing that we call ourselves is beginning to break up into parts.

The Buddha taught to cultivate wisdom. The Buddha's method of cultivating wisdom is to separate out the things that we think of as real entities into different parts, and we will then see that in reality they do not exist. Finally, after separating them we see that there is only emptiness.

This method of seeing the truth through analysis is called in Pali *vibhajjavidhī*, the method of analysis. For instance, when we see a car, we think that it really exists, but what if we dismantle the parts of that car? We remove the wheels. Are the wheels the car? The wheels are not the car. We remove the light bulbs, remove the wiring and remove the motor, remove the steering wheel, the fenders, all the seats. None of those parts is a car. But when we bring them all together, we suppose it to be a car.

In reality there is no "us." The Buddha taught us to separate what we feel to be ourselves into separate parts, like dismantling a car into parts. When the parts are all disassembled, the car disappears. All that's left is the car body, the steering wheel, the tires, all the different parts. It's not called a car anymore. It's the same for that which we call ourselves. When we separate the different parts, the "us" disappears.

The Buddha taught to separate into five parts. *Rūpa* is the part that is the body. *Vedanā* is the feelings of happiness, suffering, and indifference. In the mind, vedanā includes indifferent feeling. *Saññā* is the part that is memory and perception. Memory is like remembering that this person has this name, that person has that name, this person is our father, this person is our mother, that person is our enemy, and so on. This is memory. Perception is comparing. When we see something new, we don't know what it is, so we must compare it to previous memories. For instance, we know cats. We've seen cats catch mice. If we see a tiger, it's bigger than a cat, but its facial features and stance are similar. It probably doesn't catch only mice; it could catch us to eat as well. And so we perceive that this animal could be dangerous.

Perception on a more profound level is the perception that is necessary in the development of insight, knowing how to see things correctly—that is, seeing that which is impermanent as impermanent, that which is suffering as suffering, and that which is not-self as not-self. We are always perceiving things wrongly. The body and mind are not us or our belongings, but we perceive them to be us and belonging to us. We love and cherish them. If anything happens to them, we suffer over it and become distressed and depressed. When we get old, we get depressed; when we get sick, we get depressed; and if we're going to die, we get depressed. This suffering arises from wrong perceptions. When we perceive wrongly, we think wrongly. When we think wrongly, we believe wrongly, believing that our self really does exist.

That is why we are taught to separate the khandhas so that we can perceive correctly. We can perceive that deep down, that which we call the self is only the five khandhas. Each of the khandhas is impermanent and is suffering. It is suffering in that it is constantly oppressed into dissolution. And it can't be controlled; it fares according to causes and determinants, not according to our commands or our preferences. We are told to study the truth like this.

In order to see these three characteristics, we must first separate the khandhas. In order to be able to separate the khandhas, we must first have a mind that is firmly established, that knows and watches. The mind that is firm, knowing and watching, arises from having mindfulness, being aware of the mind that wanders off. Here we are with the body; we see the body standing, walking, sitting, and reclining; but momentarily the mind wanders off and we forget ourselves. Our mindfulness is aware of this. Just now we were watching the body breathing, the body standing, walking, sitting, or reclining, but then in a moment the mind has wandered off somewhere else. When we have mindfulness, we become aware that the mind has wandered off. We know like this often. After a while, the minute the mind wanders off, we know it; it wanders off and we know it straightaway. Then the knowing mind arises of itself. As soon as you know the mind has wandered off, the deluded mind ceases and the knowing mind arises. It arises automatically.

So when I say to make the mind the knower, it doesn't mean to create some knower to arise but to have mindfulness that is fully aware of the deluded mind. The mind wanders off after a thought, and we know it; it wanders off to look at something or listen to something, we know it. As soon as you know, delusion ceases, and the knowing mind arises. Train yourself like this often, and eventually the knowing mind arises frequently and becomes stronger. Then we can begin to separate the khandhas using wisdom. When the body breathes, the body stands, walks, sits, and reclines, moves and remains still, the mind is merely the knower, the watcher, and it can discern that the body and mind are two different things. Then we can separate things in more detail. Pleasure and pain in the body and pleasure, pain, and indifference in the mind are not the body. They are intruders that arise in the body. They are not the mind; they are intruders into the mind. The mind is the one who knows. Now we are beginning to separate things. The body is one thing; the feelings of happiness and suffering are another; and the mind that is the watcher is another. We have separated things into three parts.

Perception/memory (*saññā*) is difficult to watch. Let's put that aside for now. I explained it a little just now. When we practice insight (*vipassanā*), we must use perception. Without correct perception, there cannot be wisdom. Correct perception is perceiving the body, perceiving feelings, perceiving perception itself, perceiving volitional activities—that is, the creation of skillful and unskillful mental states—and perceiving consciousness that arises through the eyes, ears, nose, tongue, body, and the mind, as impermanent, as stressful, and as not-self. Without this kind of perception, insight cannot arise. Perception is necessary, but we must understand it.

Most of us have distorted perception (*saññā vipallāsa*). This impermanent body we feel to be permanent. We think we have lived for many years so we will probably stay like this. The body is oppressed by suffering, but we think that it is sometimes happy, sometimes suffering. This is wrong perception. In reality, it is much suffering and little suffering, not suffering and happiness. This body is something that we can't really control; we can't order it not to age, not to sicken, or not to die, but we feel that we can control it.

Once when I was practicing, I lay down for a rest, and when I woke up, I experienced a moment where I couldn't move the body. I clearly saw that the body was not me, that the body was something I couldn't control. When perception is correct, then our thinking will be correct, and our belief, our view will be correct. Right view arises. Perception itself is not an enemy of wisdom. Distorted perception—seeing that which is impermanent as permanent, seeing that which is suffering as happiness, seeing that which is not self as self—that kind of perception is an enemy to insight. It is an obstacle to wisdom, because it is stupid from the outset.

Through listening to the Dhamma, learning the Buddha's teachings, we begin to separate the khandhas. We consider each of the khandhas, whether it is permanent or impermanent. Is the body permanent or impermanent? Are happiness and suffering permanent or impermanent? Are good thoughts and bad thoughts that arise in the mind permanent or impermanent? Is the mind permanent or impermanent? Observe the reality. The mind is not permanent. One moment it is the knower; the next it is the thinker; then it is the knower; then it is that which sees visual forms, which hears sounds, which smells odors, which tastes flavors, which is aware of bodily sensations, which generates thinking in the mind. You see? It is not stable; it's always changing. Now it arises at the eyes, then at the ears, then at the nose, then at the tongue, then at the body, then in the mind. The mind itself is impermanent.

Our separating the khandhas is in order to see that each of the khandhas is impermanent, is oppressed, and cannot be controlled. *Impermanent* means that which was once there is no longer there. *Suffering (dukkha)* means that which is there is being oppressed into dissolution. For instance, if a happy feeling arises—have you noticed?

When we note it with mindfulness, we will see that that happy feeling is gradually oppressed into dissolution. Eventually the happy feeling disappears, and then there's a feeling of indifference. Have you ever been really glad? Have you ever been really happy, like when winning a big prize in the lottery? Does the happy feeling last for a long time? It doesn't stay long. You may win the first prize in the lottery, all of it yourself, many millions. At first you will be glad. Then after that you may start to feel depressed. What if thieves come to steal it? What if people come to ask for loans? What will I do? I have a lot of debt, now all my creditors will come asking for their money. The happy feeling is only momentary. Then it is pressed into fading away.

The state of things existing and then not is called impermanence (*anicca*). The state of things existing but being oppressed into dissolution is called suffering (*dukkha*). That things exist because they arise, stand, and dissolve only due to determinants, not under our control, is called not-self (*anattā*).

In order to see impermanence, suffering, and not-self of the mind and body, or the five khandhas, the mind must be firm; it must be the knower and the watcher. When the mind is firm, is the knower and the watcher, then we can separate the khandhas. We see the body sitting. The mind is the one that watches and knows this. After a while, as we sit, pain and discomfort arise. When pain and discomfort arise, the mind becomes agitated, annoyed, and restless. We want to get up and go outside, but we can't get up because we don't want to embarrass ourselves in front of the monks. And so we get annoyed. This is mental formations (*saṅkhāra*), which is another khandha. The irritation and the pain are two different things. Is it possible to be in pain but not annoyed? Yes, it is, if our mind is well trained. But if we haven't practiced, the pain will cause us to get irritated. This pain and the irritation are not the same thing. They are two different things, different parts, different khandhas. And the mind that knows that is another part, another khandha.

When we can separate things like this, we will see that each of the khandhas displays the three characteristics. The body displays impermanence: one moment there is an in-breath, the next an out-breath;

one moment it stands, the next it walks, sits, or lies down. The body is oppressed by suffering all the time. Just in sitting here there is pain and discomfort. When you are hungry, that is suffering; being full is suffering; wanting to go to the toilet is suffering; illness and injuries are suffering. The body is not a good thing at all. The body is oppressed, which leads it eventually to dissolution. No one can prevent this oppression and dissolution. If it's too hot, we die. If it's too cold, we die. If we're too hungry, we die; and if we're too full, we die, like Jujaka[12] who ate until his stomach burst.

The body is being oppressed and moving closer to death every day. Most people have never seen this and don't want to see it. As a practitioner, we separate the body and mind, and we see that the body contains only things that are impermanent and are oppressed into dissolution, and we can't prevent it. The fact that we can't control it or prevent it means that it is not-self. Keep observing and knowing this and wisdom will arise. It's the same with watching feeling: pleasant feeling is impermanent; unpleasant feeling is impermanent; it's all impermanent. All feelings are impermanent. Keep observing like this and you will see it.

For instance, when we're sitting in the sideways posture or sitting meditation for a long time, at first we may feel numb in the legs; there may be pain and numbness. If we bear with it and keep sitting, that feeling disappears. The feeling of numbness in the legs can go away. The pain can go away. When we get up and walk around, we feel normal. Even the feeling of numbness in the legs is impermanent. We can't prevent numbness from arising. If the body is going to be painful or uncomfortable, or be hungry, cold, or hot, we cannot prevent any of it. That we can't forbid it means it is anattā. We observe everything and know what we refer to as our self with a mind that is knowing, firm, and neutral. We see that each of the khandhas is impermanent, oppressed, and uncontrollable. They don't fare according to our desires.

As we see this over and over again, we come to know that the body is not a good thing. How can it be good since it's impermanent? How can it be good since it's oppressed? How can it be good since it does not belong to us? In the end the body passes away, and then it is cremated.

I never see anyone complaining about being cremated. When you go to a funeral, have you ever seen the body cry out? No, there is no crying out. The body has been discarded.

Keep on observing like this and you will see. The body is impermanent, suffering, and not-self. Feelings that are pleasant, unpleasant, and neutral are impermanent, suffering, and not-self. Volitional formations, the creation of good and bad thoughts, are impermanent, suffering, and not-self: sometimes we feel faith and want to listen to the Dhamma. As soon as bookings for the Dhamma talks become available, we reserve a spot straightaway. The mind is eager to hear the Dhamma. But when the time comes to listen to the talk, we don't want to get out of bed. It's a cold morning; we want to sleep in. Those skillful mental states are impermanent; they turn into laziness, which is an unskillful state. We almost kill ourselves fighting for a spot to get into the Dhamma hall, but if I keep on talking without stopping, you won't want to stay. You'll want to go somewhere else. It's something that you have struggled to obtain with great difficulty, but after a while you don't want it. Our mind has changed. It becomes jaded.

When we get married, before the wedding day we court our partner for a long time. This is in the old days. These days there isn't any courting. They just give a wink and send an emoji and they're off. In my day you couldn't do that. You had to go and see the parents, too. Once you had conquered the young lady's heart, then you had to go and conquer the parents. It was really complicated. It took a lot of effort, but then once you had obtained a partner and were married, then you became indifferent. The wife who was once so cherished becomes like a bit of the furniture that's been in the house for a long time. There's no need to be alarmed. It's just natural. We see it a lot.

The exception is those who have accumulated perfections (*paramita*) together, who have created good kamma together in the past, who have made offerings, kept the precepts, practiced meditation together, and their minds have progressed together. These people are hard to find, the ones who have created good kamma together in the past. Nowadays there are more kammic-debt partners. Their meeting is like coming together to claim their respective kammic debts. The external bad kammic debtors from the past are those who, even though they are our friends, try to tease us and harass us to stop us from meditating. The most important kammic debtor is our own body. It is born out of old kamma. We might be in the middle of our practice but die first, and our practice is terminated.

Look and see within the body, at the pleasant and unpleasant feelings within the body, at the pleasant and unpleasant feelings within the mind, the good and bad thoughts in the mind, the awareness of mental objects through the eyes, ears, nose, tongue, body, and mind. When we see and know them, we see that they are impermanent, suffering, and not-self. Once we see this, we know that the body is not a good thing, that feeling is not a good thing, that volitional formations, good and bad thoughts, are not a good thing, that the mind is not a good thing, nothing special. All of them fall within the three characteristics. They can't be held on to as a real refuge. When we see this, we will become disenchanted. We see the truth. We see the body and all the thoughts in the mind, as impermanent, suffering, and not-self. When we see them as they are, we become disenchanted with them. Being disenchanted, we lose our attachment. When attachment is lost, then there is liberation.

Once there is liberation, we know that we are liberated. It is easy to see it. Once we are liberated, we look within ourselves and see that our mind no longer picks things up. It doesn't hold on to things because there is no desire that could make it do so. There is no clinging. One does not hold on to anything anymore. Then there is nowhere to be born.

We will see this for ourselves. We will see it within ourselves. This is what the teachers have taught me. Don't get the idea that I'm bragging about superhuman attainments. This is what my teachers have taught me. I'm just passing it on.

So how do we practice? We keep the five precepts. And train with a meditation object. When the mind wanders off from the meditation object, we know it; it wanders off and we know. What we will obtain is a mind that has samādhi, in which the mind is the stable observer. Once we have samādhi in which the mind is the stable observer, we look into the body, the feelings of happiness and suffering, and volitional formations, good and bad thoughts. And finally we look at the mind itself. One moment it's the knower; the next moment it's the thinker; then it's the knower; then it's the seer of forms, the hearer of sounds; then it's the knower. It's like this and that. Sometimes it's the focuser.

Eventually we will see that everything is impermanent, suffering, and not-self. In the end we will see that it is wearisome. The five khandhas, which go into making what we call our self, are wearisome. You can't rely on them. They don't give us real happiness as we may believe. Our mind will release its clinging to the body and mind. Once it no longer clings, when the body gets old, gets sick, or dies, the mind is unperturbed. Whether feelings are good, bad, or indifferent, the mind is unperturbed. The mind is free of all formations, and it reaches the deathless, purity, and liberation.

Keep training. It begins with the five precepts, following a meditation technique, and being aware of the movements of the mind. When the knower arises, look inward and separate the khandhas, seeing each of the khandhas displaying the three characteristics, and you will know that the khandhas are nothing great, nothing special. The mind releases its clinging. When the mind doesn't attach to the khandhas, it no longer suffers over the khandhas.

It's like when we have a new car. We are really possessive over it. We don't want anything to touch it or scrape it. If a crowd gathers to look at it, we're afraid it will get damaged. After driving it for twenty years, you can't find anything beautiful about it. You drive it, and it bumps into cats and dogs and you don't take any interest. One isn't so enamored of it. When we look at the khandhas, they are like a mangy dog or an old piece of junk. There's nothing special about them. If they have to break apart, the mind is unperturbed. Keep practicing and one day you won't suffer.

The Task in Relation
to Suffering[13]

KEEP PRACTICING. Don't be discouraged. The reward of meditation practice awaits us if we keep up the practice. People are searching for happiness in the world, but it's never full or satiated, this worldly happiness. It's always lacking and imperfect. I can say this with confidence, because I was a layperson for a long time. I could be considered to have attained success in my household life. The happiness that householders have, I know about that. But that's all it is. It's like a drug. You take it, inject it or inhale it, and you feel good momentarily. Then suffering arises again. Then you get hungry. The heart has no happiness. There is no real happiness in the world.

When we come to practice meditation, we aren't aiming for happiness. We are aiming to learn suffering. Make sure you have the right objective. If you're practicing for happiness, you won't find it. Happiness is an illusion. When suffering is reduced, you feel happy. When suffering increases, then you feel suffering. But if we have the proper aim in practicing meditation, we will be practicing to learn suffering. When we learn suffering, then our mind lets go of suffering. The mind transcends suffering. When the mind has transcended suffering, we don't have to talk about happiness. That's just a freebie. Simply not having suffering—that's happiness.

But if you aim for happiness, you will have even more wanting. When there is no happiness, you want it, and when there is happiness, you want it to last forever. But in reality, there will soon be suffering. You can't have happiness all the time. When the mind has desire, wanting arises. The mind struggles, and suffering arises again. The worldly way is to feed desire all the time. We want, and we try to constantly feed our wants. We hope that by feeding our wants we will be happy, but the happiness only arises momentarily. Then you want something else. There is no fulfillment or satisfaction with worldly happiness.

When you come to study suffering, any day that there is no suffering, that is the perfect happiness. The way to know suffering is to know that what we refer to as suffering is just mentality and physicality, the body and mind. Don't translate it wrongly. The suffering that we are to learn about is body and mind. The Buddha said *saṅkhittena pañcupādānakkhandhā dukkhā*: "In short, the five khandhas of clinging are suffering." The khandhas that are the base for clinging, the khandhas that we all have, are called the *pañcupādānakkhandhā*.

There are two parts to the khandhas. There are the khandhas of clinging and the khandhas that are not khandhas of clinging. The khandhas of clinging are the khandhas that we all have. There is *rūpa*, form; *vedanā*, feeling; *saññā*, memory and perception; *saṅkhārā*, creation of good, bad, and neutral thoughts; and *viññāṇa*, awareness through eyes, ears, nose, tongue, body, and mind, the various kinds of *citta*. These are the khandhas of clinging, the khandhas that are clung to.

That which is not the khandhas of clinging is the group of transcendent cittas (*lokuttara citta*) and the mental concomitants (*cetasika*) that arise in conjunction with the transcendent citta. These are not khandhas of clinging. They are not bases of clinging. All the other khandhas are things that can be clung to. That which can be held on to is the khandhas of clinging, which are suffering. As it is said, *saṅkhittena pañcupādānakkhandhā dukkhā*: in brief, the five khandhas of clinging are suffering.

If we know suffering, we know that the task in relation to suffering is not to get rid of it. People in the world are all focused on getting rid of suffering. The Buddha did not teach us to get rid of suffering. He taught us to *know* suffering. First he defined it: what we call suffering is the body and mind, the five khandhas. The task in relation to suffering is not to get rid of it, but to know it.

Once we know suffering as it is, seeing the truth as it really is, we see that this body is itself suffering and the mind is itself suffering. When you see suffering clearly, the mind will unwind its attachment. To see suffering is to see things as they are. The Buddha said that, through seeing the truth, seeing the body and mind, seeing physicality and mentality as they really are, there will arise disenchantment. With disenchantment, clinging is released; with the release of clinging, there is liberation. When there is liberation, there is the knowledge that one is liberated. Birth—the action of the mind clinging to eyes, ears, nose, tongue, body, and mind—is ended. The holy life—that is, the practice of the Dhamma—has been completed. There is no further task to be done for purity and liberation.

Worldly work is never completed. For instance, today you cook a meal to eat; tomorrow you have to find something to eat again. There's no end to it. Today you have a shower; tomorrow you have to shower again. You buy a house, then you have to repair it. There's no end to worldly tasks. But knowing suffering, knowing the body and the mind as they really are, leads to the end of the tasks of our mind.

What do you get if you know suffering? When you know suffering, you will know the truth that the body is itself suffering and the mind is itself suffering. If the body is suffering and the mind is suffering, in this whole world you won't be able to find any happiness. If we see that the mind is itself suffering, whatever realm or world the mind arises in, it is all suffering. There is nowhere that you can place your foot and find happiness. If we see that the body is itself suffering, no matter where you live, whatever country, it is all suffering. If you see that the mind is itself suffering, even if you go and live in the brahma worlds—the brahmas don't have physical bodies—it's still suffering.

Once we see the truth that this body is entirely suffering and the mind is entirely suffering, desire (taṇhā) will cease. Desire is all kinds of wanting: wanting to have sights, wanting to have sounds, wanting to have smells, wanting to have tastes, wanting to have bodily sensations, and wanting to have mental sensations that are pleasant.

If we look really closely, we will see that the desire for all these impressions is based on thinking that by obtaining them we will be happy, that we won't have suffering. In truth, in struggling to find these sensations we are all aiming for happiness. We want to go out and find some delicious food, thinking it will bring us happiness. We want to listen to beautiful music, thinking it will bring us happiness. We want to have a beautiful wife, thinking this will bring us happiness. We want to have genius, clever children, thinking this will bring us happiness. If your children are stupid, you get depressed. We want to be rich because we want to be happy. You see? The core of our desires is that we want to have happiness. We want to not have suffering. Our mind is hungry for happiness, constantly struggling.

No matter how much it struggles it is never satiated. Once you get so much, you want more. You want more and more. At first, just getting enough to live on day by day is good enough. Once you have enough to live on, then you want to be rich. If you have one million, you want ten million, one hundred million, ten billion. If you get ten billion, then you want to be the prime minister or the president. If you become the president, then you want to be the king of the world. Like the big nations—there is no end to their wanting, their hunger. There is no way they will be liberated from suffering.

The Buddha taught us to come back and look at our own bodies, to look at our own minds. If we see the truth—that this body is itself suffering—we see that there is only great suffering or mild suffering, not suffering and happiness. These days we think that the body has some suffering and some happiness. This is wrong view. What we call happiness is "mild suffering." When suffering is reduced, we feel happy. For instance, if from the time of our birth we were whipped ten times a day, on any day we are whipped eleven times we would feel more suffering, but if we were whipped nine times, we would feel happy. Suffering and happiness as we know them are all relative. They arise from comparative feelings. In reality the body is purely suffering. It is just that there is sometimes more suffering and sometimes less.

If we have mindfulness of the body, we will see this. For instance, just sitting here, do you think you are comfortable? Some people buy chairs worth hundreds of thousands. They think they will be comfortable. It's not comfortable. They sit for a while, and soon it's suffering. You buy a quality bed to lie on. You lie there for a while, and you start to feel stiff; you toss and turn left and right. Suffering is constantly hounding us. Standing, walking, sitting, or reclining: why do you have to constantly change your positions? That changing of positions is to escape suffering. If you sit for a really long time, it's suffering; you have to lie down or get up and stand or walk around. If you walk for a long time, it's suffering, isn't it? So you change to sitting or lying down. If you stand for a really long time, it's suffering. In reality the body suffers in every position (*iriyāpatha*). But we don't pay attention and don't really know it. We're not interested in learning this. We don't want to know suffering and we don't want to know our own bodies and minds, and so we don't know that the body is itself suffering.

If we watch the mind, we will see that the mind, too, is itself suffering. For instance, when we think of the mind, we think that it is sometimes suffering, sometimes happy. Because of this wrong view, we see two options: happiness and suffering. And this leads to the struggle to search for happiness, the struggle to flee suffering. But if our mindfulness and wisdom are truly developed, we will see the truth that the body is purely suffering—sometimes a little, sometimes a lot—and the mind is purely suffering—sometimes a little, sometimes a lot.

When we see this truth, we will feel that the body is wearisome; it isn't something that should be loved or cherished. The mind is wearisome, not something that should be loved or cherished. They are themselves suffering. When we see this, our mind will gradually release its clinging. When the body gets old, it is suffering that gets old; why should we be troubled about it? When the body gets sick, it is suffering that is getting sick; why should we be troubled by it? When the body dies, it is suffering that dies; why should we be troubled by it? The mind becomes resilient. The body suffers, but the mind does not suffer along with it.

When we come to meditate, we see that happiness is impermanent and suffering is impermanent. We see that running around struggling to find happiness and flee suffering is truly foolish. Happiness is impermanent; why should you go looking for it? Suffering is impermanent; why should you hate it? Every time you love, every time you hate, the mind struggles. When the mind struggles, it immediately has suffering.

Knowing suffering is to know the truth of the body, to know the truth of the mind. Finally we will be done with desire, done with wanting, done with struggling in the mind. The struggle in the mind is what we call *becoming* (*bhava*). Have you heard the expression, "birth and becoming have ended"? People just say the words, but they don't know what birth and becoming are. *Birth* is obtaining eyes, ears, nose, tongue, body, and mind. The mind "picks up" eyes, ears, nose, tongue, body, and mind one at a time. It doesn't pick up many at any one time. *Becoming* is this very struggle of the mind, the mental fabrication and struggle, fabricating some good, some bad, creating emptiness. It fabricates in the sensual realm, in the realm of form, and in the formless realm. This struggle is what we call *becoming*, the mind's struggle.

If the mind sees the truth—that this body is itself suffering, the mind is itself suffering—the desire for the body and mind not to suffer does not arise. The desire for the body and mind to be happy does not arise. In this way we reach the cessation of desire by knowing suffering.

The science of the Buddha is an amazing science. Others searched for ways to resolve suffering. Some of them could see that if you had wanting, you would have suffering. They were clever. They searched for ways to destroy wanting by tormenting it: if you want to eat, don't eat; if you want to lie down, don't lie down. But they were only half clever. They knew that wanting was the cause of suffering, but they did not know how to deal with things in order to get rid of wanting. They used the method of denying it.

Another group sought to get rid of suffering by satisfying desires. If you want to eat, eat. If you want to lie down, lie down. If you want to travel around, then travel around. Whatever you desire, satisfy it. Whenever you satisfy a desire, the desire goes away and you feel comfortable. But in no long time suffering arises again. There is no end to it.

The Buddha taught us to *know* suffering. Then we will automatically give up wanting by knowing the truth of the body and the mind— that the body is itself suffering and the mind is itself suffering. They are not a mixture of suffering and happiness. The body is itself suffering; the mind is itself suffering: wanting them not to have suffering is stupid. It's like wanting fire not to be hot. You see fire in an oven: you want it to not be hot; it looks beautiful, so you want to pick it up. That's stupid.

When you see the truth of the body and the mind, wanting will not arise. All the different kinds of wanting can be boiled down to just wanting the body and the mind to have happiness, wanting the body and the mind to not suffer, aiming for happiness, aiming for the denial of suffering. All the different kinds of suffering—the 1,500 kinds of defilements, the 108 kinds of wanting—can all be boiled down to wanting the body and the mind to be happy, wanting the body and the mind to not suffer. If you have the wisdom that sees the truth that the body is itself suffering and mind is itself suffering, wanting will no longer arise.

The arahants are not particularly brilliant, but the arahants are people who clearly realize suffering. They know the world, what we know as the world, as body and mind (*rūpa* and *nāma*). It is simply suffering. They know the world; that is, they know body and mind clearly as they are—that body is suffering, mind is suffering—and so wanting no longer arises.

As soon as you know suffering clearly as it is, then *samudaya*, the cause of suffering, will be automatically abandoned. As soon as the cause is given up, cessation (*nirodha*)—that is, nibbāna—will automatically appear. You don't have to go searching for nibbāna anywhere else. Nibbāna isn't in the temples; it isn't at Wat Suan Santidham; it's not with me; it isn't with the Buddha. Nibbāna lies in front of us, but wanting (*taṇhā*) obscures it. Our eye, our Dhamma eye, is closed off by wanting. So we don't see nibbāna, even though it is right in front of us.

You must learn suffering, learn the truth of the body, learn the truth of the mind, keep on with it. If you have a lot of good accumulated perfections, you could attain arahantship in only one day, seeing the truth of the body and mind in full. If your merit is a little less than that, it might be three days or seven days, seven months or seven years. If your merit is less than that, it might be seven lifetimes. Keep on practicing.

The practice is fair: whoever does a lot of practice, and does it correctly, will obtain results quickly and obtain excellent results. If you're lazy and don't practice, you won't get results. If you don't create the cause, you don't get the result; if you create the cause, you get the result. The cause that will give us results is knowing right here, knowing this body and mind. That is wisdom.

The Buddha taught that we attain purity through wisdom. This wisdom is not worldly cleverness, knowing how to cheat people. That's stupid. If you can cheat others, other people suffer, and you will suffer. The defilements just get stronger and stronger. True wisdom is knowing the truth of suffering (*dukkha*). When you clearly know suffering, you give up the cause (*samudaya*), and you realize and attain cessation (*nirodha*), which is nibbāna. And at that moment when you touch nibbāna, the noble path (*magga*) arises.

Suffering—know it; the cause—relinquish it; cessation, nibbāna—realize it; the path—develop it. All these four tasks are performed at once. We complete them all at once, in the one moment. When we see suffering, we relinquish the cause; when we relinquish the cause, we realize cessation; when we realize cessation, then we have developed the path. These four tasks are completed at the one place in the one moment. At the one place: that is at this very mind, in only one mind moment.

Our task is to know suffering. Get it done, know suffering: know the body as it is, know the mind as it is. This is the science of the Buddha. What do you get from it? First, the end of desire. This is called *virāga*. The end of suffering, liberation from suffering: this is called *vimutti*. There are vimutti and virāga and the end of mental struggle, which is called *visaṅkhāra*. When you reach nibbāna, it's *santi*, peace. There are many words that reflect aspects of what we call nibbāna, e.g., *vimutti, virāga, visaṅkhāra, santi*. They are all names for nibbāna. We can experience nibbāna, see nibbāna, when we clearly see suffering. There is no other option. You must know suffering, keep knowing the body and the mind. Know them as they are.

How can we know the body and the mind as they are? The important tools are right mindfulness and right concentration. These are what will enable us to know suffering. Mindfulness is not just the worldly kind of mindfulness. All skillful mental states contain mindfulness, but the mindfulness that enables us to attain the path and fruit is the four foundations of mindfulness: *kāyānupassanā* or mindfulness of the body; *vedanānupassanā* or mindfulness of the feelings, which is mindfulness of mentality; *cittānupassanā* or mindfulness of the mind (*citta*), which is mindfulness of mental volitional activities (*saṅkhārā*); and *dhammānupassanā* or mindfulness of dhammas, which includes both physicality and mentality, both skillful (*kusala*) conditions and unskillful (*akusala*) conditions, and both causal and resultant conditions. This is called *dhammānupassanā*. Once again, it's just physicality and mentality.

Try to learn your own body and mind. They have many, many forms. You don't have to learn them all. Just do what you can do. For instance, if you are watching and being mindful of the body with outbreaths and in-breaths, if you do this a lot, you can use this breathing body to practice meditation. It's not using the breath to develop meditation, it's using the body to develop meditation. We observe the changes within the body. We observe change through the breathing. The body that breathes out is one thing; the body that breathes in is another. The body that breathes out is impermanent; the body that breathes in is impermanent. The body that breathes out is merely a physical element; it is not our self. The body that breathes in is merely a physical element; it is not our self. We are observing the body, and this is called kāyānupassanā, but we are observing only some aspects, such as the body breathing.

Observing some aspects of the body is referred to as seeing "the body in the body."[14] When they say, "the body in the body," "feeling in feeling," they mean looking at some aspects of feeling, for instance. Seeing mind in mind is seeing some aspects of the mind. When we see the body in the body, we see the body breathing in and breathing out. It is not "us" who are breathing in and out. All the remaining aspects of the body are not us. It is no longer the body that is our self.

If you don't like watching the breath, you could observe the bodily positions: standing, walking, sitting, and reclining. This is another kind of kāyānupassanā. The body standing is impermanent. The body that walks, sits, and reclines is impermanent. The body that stands, walks, sits, and reclines is merely a material object. This material objects stands, walks, sits, and reclines. It is not our self that stands, walks, sits, and reclines. The body that stands is impermanent; the body that walks is impermanent; the body that sits is impermanent; the body that reclines is impermanent. Observe like this, and you will see that all physicality is impermanent.

The body that stands, walks, sits, and reclines is merely a physical object, like a robot. It is a worldly object. There are worldly elements entering and leaving it, beginning with the sperm cell and egg from the parents. These are material elements. They arise from the world. They combine; they receive water, nutriment, and air. These all belong to the world. And we grow bigger.

The body is a physical element. There are elements entering and leaving it all the time, such as when we breathe in and out, eat food, and defecate. If you eat and do not defecate, what happens? You die. If you defecate but don't eat, what happens? You also die, right? In the end, the body cannot endure. It is oppressed by suffering until the point where it has to break apart. Some people break apart on account of an accident, some on account of illness, some on account of old age. There are many different reasons, but in the end the body must break apart.

So we know the body standing, walking, sitting, and reclining, the body breathing out and breathing in, full of impermanence, full of suffering, being oppressed, full of not-self, just a material object. It is a lump of elements. It is not ours; it belongs to the world. When you see this, you will be done with clinging to the body.

And then you observe the mind. You can start at the mind if you want or you can start at the body—whatever is more convenient or easier for you. The old teachers mostly began with the body. Myself and Luang Pu Dul do not teach at the body. Luang Pu Dul taught to observe the mind. You can do it that way too. You can start at the body or start at feeling or start at mental activities (*cittānupassanā*) or start at contemplation of dhammas (*dhammānupassanā*). It all comes down to the same place, which is seeing the truth of physicality and mentality, the body and the mind.

If you see the truth of physicality and mentality, you don't cling. When you don't cling, you don't want. The mind does not delight in or despise happiness and suffering. It stops struggling. There is no wanting, no mental hunger. The mind is free of defilements and desire. It experiences a unique kind of happiness. When you want happiness, you struggle almost to death and don't obtain it. You get it only for an instant, then it is lost. When you no longer desire happiness, when you just observe suffering, [seeing that] the body is suffering, the mind is suffering, when you let go of the body and mind, you obtain an incomparable kind of happiness. That's the happiness of nibbāna. It is a happiness that will cause the tears to flow. "Oh, there is such a happiness like this?" It is a really powerful kind of happiness.

Observe suffering; look at the body and the mind. This is the reason that we must watch our body and our mind. If you know the body and mind as they really are, you see the three characteristics of body and mind. When you see the truth of them, you become disillusioned with them and release your clinging. When wanting and clinging are gone, the struggle is gone, and you are liberated from suffering. When you are liberated from suffering, you have an incomparable kind of happiness. It is a happiness that doesn't change in response to sights, sounds, smells, tastes, bodily feelings, and thoughts. It is a happiness that is independent of sights, sounds, smells, tastes, bodily feelings, and thoughts. It is independent of things that are uncertain. Sights are uncertain; sounds, smells, tastes, bodily feelings, and thoughts are uncertain. As long as you are dependent on things that are uncertain, then your happiness is uncertain. When you don't rely on things that are uncertain, don't rely on anything in the world, then you attain the true, perfect happiness.

So keep practicing. Today it might be difficult. In the future it will be easy. Just keep watching the body and the mind. Today there are many defilements. In the future there will be fewer. Today there is a lot of suffering, and it lasts a long time. In the future there will be little suffering, and for a shorter amount of time, until eventually suffering comes to an end. Whoever does it will attain it. But you have to do it properly. Don't use the methods that the Buddha didn't teach, such as the method of feeding desires. This doesn't work. The method of denying desires, that doesn't work either. The method of knowing suffering until you automatically relinquish desire: that's the method that works.

AJAHN PAISAL (VISĀLO)

Ajahn Paisal (Visālo) was born Paisal Wongworawitsit on May 10, 1957, in Bangkok. After completing high school he enrolled in tertiary studies at Thammasat University in 1975.

While studying at Thammasat University, he was the editor of the magazine *Pajarayasara*. As a member of the Thammasat Buddhist Society, he participated in a peaceful group fast to protest the deposed despot Thanom Kittikachorn[1] being accepted into the Thai saṅgha as a novice. For his role in the protest he was detained at the Police Academy in Chonburi for three days.

In 1983 he took bhikkhu ordination in Bangkok, following which he went to study meditation with Luang Por Thien Cittasubho at Wat Sanam Nai. Luang Por Thien is well-known for his distinctive approach to meditation, in which practitioners perform stylized movements as a tool to develop meditation, and his emphasis on developing mindfulness in daily life. While staying at Wat Sanam Nai, Phra Paisal developed his meditation practice through the day-to-day monastic activities and also took time for solitary meditation. He received direct instruction from Luang Por Thien, at first on a daily basis and then from time to time as needed. After about four months with Luang Por Thien he went to spend his first rains retreat at Wat Pa Sukato in Chaiyaphum Province, studying meditation with Luang Por Khamkhian (a disciple of Luang Por Thien). He has resided at Wat Pa Sukato since then and has been acting abbot of the temple since Luang Por Khamkhian passed away in 2014. Since then he has shared his time between Wat Pa Sukato and Wat Pa Mahawan in Chaiyaphum Province.

Phra Ajahn Paisal has been an active teacher on many fronts. He is a prolific writer, having authored hundreds of booklets on Buddhism and Buddhist-related themes such as "Buddhism and modern values" and "humanity in the computer age," but mostly focused on techniques and reflections for dealing with suffering and finding happiness in life. He was active in the Coordinating Group for Religion in Society from 1977 to 1983 and is a cofounder of Sekhiyadhamma, a network of Saṅgha members promoting a socially and environmentally active brand of Buddhism, as well as a consultant for the International Network of Engaged Buddhists.

His talks are freely available on YouTube for those who are fluent in Thai. One thing that does not come through in these written translations is the utterly calm and measured delivery of the talks, given by Ajahn Paisal in the rustic wooden hall of Wat Pa Sukato. The calming delivery is itself an integral part of the teachings, which hopefully is illustrated in the following translations.

MANAGING EXPECTATIONS[2]

WHEN WE WERE STUDENTS, the teachers would often advise us, when we were doing exams, to do the easy questions first and leave the hard ones till later. The reasoning was that if we did the hard questions first, it would take a long time. By the time we'd finished them, there might not be enough time left to complete all the easy questions, even though the questions were worth equal marks. Also, with the hard questions, if they were really hard, we might become confused, lose concentration, and get stressed, and that might cause us to be unable to figure out even the easy questions. If our mind were clear, the easy questions would be really easy, but if our mind were not clear, we would be stressed, and we might not be able to do even those easy ones. As a result, we would get a poor result.

This is a principle we can use in our own lives. In doing good actions we should start with what is easy. This is something that we can observe. Good actions, in the teachings of Buddhism, begin with generosity (*dāna*). Generosity is something that's relatively easy to do. This is followed by morality (*sīla*). Morality is harder to practice than generosity. And the most difficult level is meditation (*bhāvanā*). If we're going to develop goodness, we begin with generosity, with giving up material or external things. Then we start to train in giving up in speech and actions, which is morality, and then training the mind, which is meditation.

We can see that for Thai people, making offerings (*tham boon*) is really easy, but many people, having given offerings, don't take the next step, which is practicing morality, because it is more difficult. Even more so with meditation, which is largely neglected. But in fact, if we begin with what is easy, that will help us to be able to do that which is more difficult.

This principle also applies to practicing meditation. In meditation, start with what is easy—for example, beginning with doing just a small amount, maybe just five or ten minutes every day—and this will be a foundation for doing longer periods. If we do it every day, even just a little bit, it will give us the drive to do longer periods, from five minutes to ten minutes, from ten minutes to fifteen minutes to twenty minutes. It's like exercising. If we were to start exercising by trying to do too much, running for one hour for example, most people would not be able to keep it up. They could only do it for a couple of days and then give up. But if you start with what is easier—a small amount, for example running ten minutes a day—and do this every day, then you can stretch it out to twenty minutes and eventually you can do one hour easily. You do it regularly so that it becomes a habit, and if you skip a day, you feel like you're missing something.

In practicing meditation and developing mindfulness, this principle of starting from a little and going to a lot, or starting from easy and progressing to the more difficult, includes at first not focusing too much on quality. Go for quantity first. In going for quantity, aim to do what you set as your goal; do a lot. The quality is a different matter: don't worry about that for now. Some people, as soon as they start, just aim for quality. For instance, they think their mind must be calm as soon as they start. They do it once or twice and they expect the mind to be calm or to have mindfulness and awareness, but the mind doesn't play along. The mind floats off. Many people do it only a few times and get discouraged. You ask them why they got discouraged and gave up, and they say, "Oh, my mind was wandering all over the place." Even though they only do it for five minutes, the mind wanders a lot.

Actually, wandering is not the problem. The problem is our expectation that it won't wander or that it will be calm. We want our mind to be quiet, even though we're beginners, just learners. When the mind doesn't behave as we want it to, we get discouraged, annoyed, upset. Instead of being clear and calm, we get stressed, and in the end just give up because we are suffering more in the practice than we did without the practice. Before we practiced meditation, we didn't seem to be suffering very much, but when we start practicing, there's suffering. This is because we have set up the mind wrongly. We aimed for quality, we wanted the mind to be excellent and perfect, even though we're only beginners. But we can set up our mind correctly: go for quantity first—for example do a full hour—regardless of how much the mind wanders. We might wander for 90 percent of the time, but that's OK.

Many people can't do this, especially the high achievers, the perfectionists; and this might include the good students, the top of the class: when these people start to practice meditation, in no time at all they're stressed—because they want to do it well, they want the mind to be calm. They want the mind to have continuous awareness for 80 or 90 percent of the time. With an expectation like this, they struggle. This is because they're starting out with the difficult. Just start with the easy way; that is, just go for quantity, and leave the quality to later.

Even just going for quantity is not an easy thing, because the mind doesn't like it, it's not used to it. For beginners, even ten minutes seems like a long time. Even five minutes of lifting the arms[3] and they get sleepy. One hour is really difficult. But as I said, start from the easy and progress to the more difficult, from a little to a lot; by going for quantity first, the quality will come later.

Actually, the meditation system of Luang Por Thien is easy. He taught to start from the easy. When Luang Por Thien was teaching me, the very first thing he said to me was, "Just do it for fun. Don't do it for real." Start by doing it for fun, meaning don't have too much expectation. It doesn't matter if the mind wanders or forgets, just do it "for fun." But really do it, do it all day, from the moment you wake up till the time you go to sleep. Many people don't know how to do it for fun. They just want to achieve, to attain the goal. They want to overcome defilements and overcome the wandering mind. Thinking in this way, from easy it becomes difficult. And as it gets more difficult, they just get discouraged and give up.

Speaking about our lives, starting from the easy and going to the difficult is a really good way to get our lives to progress. But this is in regard to doing good things. It doesn't apply to doing bad things, because sometimes bad actions are easier to do than good actions. For instance, for some people, dishonesty or cheating is easier than being industrious and making an honest living. If someone is dishonest, if they find that easy, they can make hundreds of thousands or millions in only a few minutes, while if you relied on mere hard work, it might take years to make a million.

For many people, doing bad actions is easier than doing good actions. Many students find that making their own reports, doing their own homework, is more difficult than copying it from other students or copying and pasting from Google or Wikipedia. For these people, diligent effort is difficult and cheating is easy. This is not related to what I was saying earlier, about doing the easy first before going on to the difficult. That was said in relation to doing good actions. But for bad actions, even though it is easier, it should not be done.

It's human nature that anything that matches our desires is easy to do—or is easier than something that doesn't match our desires, even if it's good. For most people, whatever feeds our desires, even if it creates problems later, if it is easy to do and brings a quick result, we will do that first. This includes when we come upon something that we like. If we see something we like, we just take it.

There is a story by a Chinese Taoist philosopher named Zhang Zhou. He was clever. His stories were very short, as was this one. There was a man who was tending monkeys, who had just started on the job. He was tasked with feeding the monkeys. At first he gave the monkeys three boxes of chestnuts in the morning and four boxes of chestnuts in the evening, making seven boxes. Three boxes in the morning, four boxes in the evening. The monkeys weren't happy and kicked up a fuss. The monkey attendant didn't argue with the monkeys. He just changed from three boxes in the morning to four boxes, and from four boxes in the evening to three boxes. And the monkeys were happy with that.

So that's the story. What was he teaching? He explained that the monkey attendant was clever. He didn't waste his time arguing with the monkeys. If the monkeys didn't like three in the morning and four in the evening, he gave them four in the morning and three in the evening. The result was the same. This story tells us something about the nature of monkeys. And the nature of monkeys is similar to human nature. We want to take the bigger option first. Getting more first and getting less afterward is preferred to getting less first and more afterward.

Whatever we like we want that first. Anything we don't like we want to put off till later. Notice that with some people, when they're eating a bowl of noodles, they eat the parts they like first; they eat the pork balls first and leave the noodles till later. But some people like to save the favored bits to later. They eat what they like less first, the noodles, and save the pork balls till later. But usually for most people what we like first comes first, and we leave what we don't like till later.

About twenty years ago there was a tea called Oishi tea that was popular. They opened a market in Cambodia, and the sellers did a promotion there: if you bought two bottles of Oishi tea for forty baht you would get a free doll. It didn't really sell. However, the manager noticed that when the presenter advertised the tea and showed people the doll, both children and adults alike really liked it. So he changed the promotion. Instead of advertising two bottles with a giveaway of a free doll, he changed it to: if you purchase a doll for forty baht, there was a giveaway of two bottles of Oishi. And then it sold really well. They sold out in only two days, even though it was the same price of forty baht. But why is it that it didn't sell well when it was a promotion of a free doll for every purchase of two bottles, but sold really well when the deal was getting two bottles of Oishi free for every purchase of a doll? It's no different from changing the three in the morning and four in the evening to four in the morning and three in the evening for the monkeys. We're the same as those monkeys. We like four in the morning, three in the evening: that is to say, we want what we like first, and what we don't like we leave till later.

We can see in people that between happiness and suffering, people would tend to choose happiness first and suffering afterward over having suffering first and happiness afterward. You tell students to knuckle down to study, to agree to the initial hardship, giving up pleasures and leisure activities, in order to have happiness, comfort, and a good profession afterward, and some aren't really interested. They tend to choose laziness and comfort first, and leave the suffering to later. Laziness is a certain kind of happiness. It's agreeable to our defilements. Many people would choose the laziness first and not have to be diligent, and just watch movies and listen to music. "Never mind how difficult things will be in the future, I choose this first."

If it's giving up alcohol or giving up cigarettes in order to be happy and healthy in the future, people don't really like this. They tend to choose the comfort and pleasure of the present moment, even if the future will be difficult. "If I were to give up alcohol and cigarettes now, that would be torture." Even though they know that if they agreed to this hardship in the present, today, the future would be better, they do not choose it. They still tend to choose pleasure in the present moment, to keep drinking alcohol and smoking. "I don't care how much difficulty there will be in the future." But when the time comes for them to really suffer, to come down with cancer, emphysema, cirrhosis, or liver cancer, they moan, "Oh no, if I knew this would happen I would have given up ages ago."

It's like the lazy students. The reason they don't apply themselves to their study is because they are attached to momentary pleasures. Even though they know that in the future they will have difficulty, and when that time arrives they really are in difficulty, they complain, "Oh, if I'd known it would be like this, I would have applied myself back then." We tend to only know this after the fact. When we have the time to make a decision, we tend to choose the easy way first and have difficulty later, even though the difficulty is much heavier and more extreme than the tiredness and difficulty of applying ourselves beforehand.

So when I said earlier that we should start at the easy and progress to the more difficult, I want to emphasize that this is in regard to doing good things. When it comes to doing bad actions or anything that is in the service of defilements, even though it is easy we should not do it; we should not choose that way, especially when it comes to taking or indulging.

This is the human problem. People tend to choose happiness first and put suffering off till later, even though if we agreed to have some difficulty or discomfort beforehand we would be better off afterward. It is the same for practicing the Dhamma. Many people think, "Why should I practice? It's too much trouble. You have to go and stay in a temple. Life is very tasteless there." Many people would choose to have a comfortable life, to indulge in pleasures, even though they know that enjoying themselves today they will have difficulty later. When they get old, or when they encounter suffering such as a loss or separation, they won't have any knowledge to help them deal with these things. But they aren't interested, because the happiness in the present time has more appeal. The happiness of today has more appeal than future happiness, even though that future happiness is finer than the happiness today.

For example, when we come to practice the Dhamma, even though we may have some difficulty today, even though life will seem to lack flavor and zest and we have to fight with the defilements, it will result in a better happiness in the future, a peaceful mind, a knowledge that enables us to deal with suffering, to know how to let go. It's better than a happiness for today, indulging in pleasure, and then in the future having great suffering because of the changes in life, because of aging, sickness, and eventually death. But we mostly ask for happiness for today and are not interested in any suffering in the future.

Wise people will be prepared to endure some suffering today in order to be comfortable in the future. They will go without and, as the expression goes, "endure the sour to taste the sweet." This is an old expression, meaning we are prepared to face hardship today in order to taste sweetness in the future. We should take this as a motto. If we can obtain comfort and ease in the future by agreeing to some difficulty in the present, we should do it.

Readying the Mind
for Turmoil[4]

Most people come to the temple for peace of mind, to feel good. But different people have different ways of finding peace of mind and comfort in the temple. Some people come to the temple to get rid of bad luck, or sometimes they use the ceremony known as *kae kam* ("reversing kamma"), which in fact is just lighting candles. And they feel good. Some people are troubled, but when they come to make merit, they become hopeful that they will be relieved of their suffering and sorrow. And they are happy; their troubled minds are calmed. Some people, just by coming to bow to the Buddha image, seeing the Buddha image's face looking radiant, serene and full of kindness, are inspired by it. Where they were in despair or depressed, they are energized and instilled with hope, and they feel better.

But some people have more suffering than that. They've lost a loved one or are contending with a dangerous illness. Sometimes, just making merit or doing the ceremony to get rid of bad luck may not be enough to make their minds calm, peaceful, or at ease. Or these methods may be effective, but it is only short-lived. It's still relying on things outside of ourselves. It would be better if we could know how to rely on ourselves, if we were able to train our minds to find peace. This requires practice: what we call Dhamma practice or practicing meditation.

This is the reason many people come here, which is not an easy place to get to. You have to set aside many days' time to come and practice here and travel long distances. But once you get here, you don't necessarily find the peace you expected. Many people, when they first get here, feel lonely, or they may even feel bored, because the life and atmosphere here is simple and rustic. Sometimes they may feel bleak and confused because their mind is accustomed to focusing on other things that are pleasurable or exciting, such as watching movies or listening to music. Watching movies or listening to music seems to relieve feelings of alienation. It's the same with working: when there is work to do, the mind is focused on that, and it ceases to be distracted for a while.

But when you come here, there is nothing much to attract the mind. There are no movies to watch, no songs to listen to; there is no work to do. With no work to do, the mind sets off on its wanderings, creating all kinds of thoughts. This is normal for people when they first arrive at the temple, regardless of whether they are householders or monks. After staying here for a while, their minds begin to become peaceful. It's like water that has been stirred up so that any sediment floats up into the water: if you leave it still for a while, the sediment sinks to the bottom and the water becomes clear. The environment and lifestyle here can help to make the mind more peaceful without much difficulty. A life that is not hurried and has few duties, and also living with people who have similar ideals or methods of practice, means that there is little conflict through speech or actions. Even more so if there is a clear and correct method of practice, and the mind becomes peaceful. This is on account of the environmental factors, both in terms of physical factors and in terms of people, or social factors, that help to support or train the mind so that it gradually becomes calm. What's more, if there is true and dedicated practice, one will know how to cure the mind of its distraction and confusion.

As one lives here, if one does not neglect the practice, one will find peace and calm in the mind. However, we should not simply hope to find peace in our practice. Our practice should also prepare us for unrest as well. If we practice simply to find peace, we will be disappointed, because when you change your location, change your environment, or when you go back home, you will encounter a lot of things that are not the same as here. You may be in a place that is hurried, where there is a lot of work, and where there are many people with whom to come into conflict. Things don't go according to our wishes. That peace that we found in the temple quickly dissipates and breaks up once we get back home.

This mind of ours is not something that will be calm all the time. Yesterday we practiced meditation, and we felt peaceful. Distraction was hidden. But today, distracted thoughts surge up again. What was peaceful yesterday is no longer peaceful. Practice is good in that it allows us to experience calm in the mind, but it will be even better if it can also show us the way to be ready for unrest in the mind. Even though we desire peace, clarity, and lightness in the mind, don't forget that the mind is not within our power to control, because it is not self (*anattā*). This is one of the characteristics of not-self—that is to say, it is not possible to force things to go in accordance with our desires. Our mind is something that can't be controlled. You may want it to be peaceful, but it isn't; you want it to be cool, but instead it is hot; you want it to be light and clear, but instead it's heavy and muddled. Sometimes it looks like there is no reason to it. Some days you feel clear and fresh, but the next day you feel depressed or befuddled. It's because the mind is not within our power to control. Sometimes it is not peaceful; sometimes it is gloomy; sometimes it is heavy.

We must learn how to deal with these kinds of moods in the proper way. To put it simply, we have to be ready to encounter these kinds of moods, which we can simply call "unrest." The practice that enables us to encounter peace is indeed good. But if it is not capable of teaching us to be ready for unrest, it is not yet a practice that we can really rely on or that can be a refuge for us.

Even if we have already practiced a lot, we must be ready to encounter unrest in our minds, because it is part of the nature of the mind. We can't deny it or run away from it. Distraction, irritation, perplexity: we must encounter these things as long as we are still unenlightened beings (*puthujjana*). Even if we have developed the practice and found some peace in the temple or in a shrine room, that peace that we have found is impermanent. It is the nature of all things to be impermanent. One day they will disappear, and unrest arises in their place. We have to be ready to meet with unrest when it arises in our minds.

How can we be ready to deal with unrest? One thing that can help is for us to have mindfulness. Mindfulness is something that looks after our mind and prevents it from falling into that unrest. Unrest arises because of many causes and factors over which we have no control, but one thing we can do is to have mindfulness to look after the mind and not allow it to fall into that unrest. As Luang Por Khamkhian used to say, "Seeing it is not being it." In part this arises from accepting the truth that "the mind is just this way." It's not that there are only good things, things that we desire. Things that we don't desire can arise too. But once they arise, if we push them away or if we complain about them or kick up a fuss about them, then we are even less peaceful.

Many practitioners who desire peace end up with a mind that is distracted and confused because they don't know the way to deal with distraction. For instance, when distraction arises, they go in and try to suppress it. If they experience irritation, they go in and push it away. They are fighting with what has arisen. In fact, simply knowing can help a lot. We cannot forbid things from arising, but what we can do is to know them—"simply knowing." When it arises, we simply know it. We don't follow after it, and we don't oppose it. Before, we used to follow after these things all the time. We allowed our mind to follow after mental states. But when we start to practice, we might no longer follow them, but instead we oppose them. That's not right either. If we know how to watch them from a distance or "simply know" them, they can't do anything to our mind. This is one method for dealing with unrest or unskillful states that arise.

The practice as taught by Luang Por Thien is a method that prepares us for dealing with unrest, because it is a method that doesn't emphasize controlling the mind. There's no closing the eyes, and it doesn't involve being very still. People who want to get mental peace want to close their eyes; if they could close their ears as well, then all the better. If they can't close their ears, they close the windows and doors so as to avoid loud noises. And they force the mind to not think. When there is no thinking, then it is peaceful. But the mind can't be controlled. Even if you try to control the mind by focusing on the feet, on the breath, or on the belly, it doesn't obey. It fights back and resists. The more you try, the more obstinate the mind becomes.

It turns out that the more you want to be peaceful, the more unrest there is. Even if there is peace, any peace that arises is only temporary.

When you leave the temple, switch on your phone, and see the messages—be they news about the country or news from sick family and relatives or problems with work—as soon as you look at them your mind wavers. Once the mind wavers, you don't know how to deal with it. We don't know the method for dealing with worry and care and irritation. What is the result? The result is more distraction and confusion. It becomes even less peaceful. But if we know how to respond to it, such as in the practice of Luang Por Thien, there is no emphasis on controlling thinking. He didn't teach to forbid thinking. If the mind thinks, that's its business; we don't think along with it.

Some kinds of practice, those that we are familiar with, stress controlling thoughts. They believe that if we can control thoughts, then the mind will be peaceful. But the mind doesn't often stay within our control. It thinks all over the place. In this practice, thinking is allowed, because the important thing is not whether you think a lot or think a little but whether you are aware of that thinking. This is more important. If you think only a little but you are not aware of it, or if your mind is peaceful but you are unaware of that peacefulness or are deluded by that peacefulness, that is not a good thing. If the mind is not calm, but you know that it is not calm, this is better. Whether you think a little or think a lot is not as important as being aware of that thinking.

This is a training to be aware of thinking—and not only thinking, but all mental impressions (*ārammaṇa*) that arise, be they positive or negative. Just by being aware of them, our moods will settle down or lose their power. Just by being aware, we can make the mind calm. This is a peace that is not based on unknowing, not a result of preventing thought, but a peace that is a result of knowing, of being aware—being aware of thoughts and moods and knowing the nature of the mind.

Luang Por Thien used to say, "The more you think, the more you know." *Thinking* here means the wandering mind. Just let it wander. The *know* here means to be aware as it happens. At first your mind wanders all over the place, thinking a hundred different things. You may only be aware of 10 or 20 percent of them as they happen. But as you continue to practice, you will be aware of more of them, 30 or 40 percent. Later on you know 50 or 60 percent of them as they happen. When you are aware, this brings the mind to calm without difficulty.

This is a method that can help us to be ready to deal with or contend with unrest when it arises. When it arises, be aware of it as it happens. Don't allow it to come in and take over the mind. Don't just follow it around. Once we are ready to encounter unrest, we will encounter peace. If you set out with the thought, "I will aim for peace," but you're not ready to deal with unrest, it will be difficult to find peace. Conversely, if you are ready to meet with unrest, eventually you will find peace. It is the peace that arises from being aware of thoughts and moods.

So when you practice, don't go and get annoyed or disappointed when moods or thoughts arise, because the more annoyed you get, the more suffering and unrest you will feel. Allow it to arise. Treat those things as training aids. They have arisen for us to develop our mindfulness. If practitioners want only peace and don't want, or don't want to encounter, unrest, don't want to experience unskillful mental states, this means they don't yet know the nature of the mind and are not yet ready to bring their minds to true peace.

Once we are ready to encounter unrest, unskillful mental states, or undesirable moods that arise in the mind, we will then be ready to encounter sense contact (*phassa*) that we had previously seen as undesirable—that is, forms, sounds, smells, and tastes. At first, when undesirable mental objects arise, we do not push them away; we accept them. We "just know" them. In time, our ability to deal with undesirable things will expand, from mental objects, thoughts in the mind, to external things: loud noises, undesirable images, odors, or bodily sensations such as pain that cause feelings of suffering (*dukkhavedanā*). When sickness arises, we can look at the sickness with a mind that does not suffer. The body suffers, but the mind does not. Unpleasant feeling is restricted to the body, but the mind does not suffer along with it.

This is because we know how to deal with unrest that arises in the mind. When undesirable images, sounds, odors, tastes, and bodily sensations arise, we can deal with them with a mind that is not suffering, or if the mind does waver, we can be aware of it and let it go. We let go of both the mood that arises and also the images, sounds, odors, tastes, and bodily sensations that have touched the mind. In time, when we encounter a dangerous or undesirable event, when we are separated from what we love, or have to encounter something that we do not like (as we chanted this morning), we are able to deal with it. When we encounter illness or loss of possessions, we are able to deal with it because we see these things as normal, as part of nature that cannot be prevented. We know how to look after the mind so that it doesn't suffer over these things. This arises from our knowing the trick to dealing with mental objects that are unpleasant, which is to simply know them, being aware with mindfulness, or knowing how to bring forth self-awareness.

So when you come to practice here, don't just hope to find peace in the mind. Think a bit further, that you must be ready to encounter unrest when it arises in the mind. When it arises, don't make a fuss over it or push it away. Accept it, and allow it to arise. Don't allow your mind to fall into those mental impressions. Simply speaking, we see it, we don't be it—we simply know it.

REFLECTIONS ON DEATH[5]

AT THE MOMENT there is a natural event that a lot of people are taking an interest in. It's a meteor shower, which was at its brightest last night up until dawn this morning. Just now, before I walked here for the morning chanting, I saw a couple of shooting stars. They call it a meteor shower because it is a time when a lot of shooting stars appear, a bit like a shower. It's not really like a rain shower, but it is more than what we normally see. Many people go without sleep so they can see the shooting stars. Some people even go so far as to travel and stay overnight up-country where there isn't any interference from city lights.

People are interested in this because it's unusual. You only get a chance to see it every once in a while. In fact, there are shooting stars every night, but there aren't that many. They don't occur as frequently as during a meteor shower.

Some people see it as not so much strange but beautiful. It looks like someone has drawn a white line across the sky. It's bright, and it flashes, then it goes out. Before it goes out, it flashes brilliantly, but only for an instant. It's a beautiful sight, especially on a moonless night.

We people have a lot of connection with light, be it sunlight, moonlight, or starlight, and, as sometimes happens, a meteor shower. This strangeness or this beauty is something that many people will go without sleep in order to see. Having seen it, they feel that it's been worth their while to have stayed awake. But it is more valuable if we can watch the shooting stars and then look back into ourselves, to see that our lives are no different from the shooting stars. When they flash brightly, it's only for an instant. They light up the sky as if out of nowhere, and then they disappear in less than a second. It is a very brief time. They may be beautiful, but it is only fleeting. They demonstrate impermanence, which is the natural way of all life. If we look at a meteor shower in this way, we can get some perspective that can teach us about the impermanence of our lives. Life is only brief, briefer than dew on a leaf that evaporates in the morning.

If we look at it like this, we can glean many lessons from it. But most people don't want to look at it like this, because looking at things like this makes us think of death. If we think about the impermanence of life, we must go on to think about death, because death is something that comes with all life. And these days, it must be said, people are really afraid of death—to the extent that we don't really use the words *death* or *die*. Notice when someone dies, people try to avoid using the word *die*; they will use other terms and expressions, such as *passed on*, *passed away*, *left the world*, *given up the ghost*, or *gone back to nature*. There are many indirect expressions to use for dying that people in the present time have come up with in order to avoid *die*. This differs from olden days. Back then, *dying* was *dying*. They didn't have to use a lot of other words.

So why are we so afraid of dying? As to this, the reason is that we have attachments. When we have attachments, then we will be afraid of loss. And there is nothing that gives us more loss than death. Your house can burn down, or you can be cheated out of your business: these are great losses, but not as great as when you must die. If your house burns down, you lose just the house and some assets. But you still have life. Your name and reputation are still there. You still have your friends and family. But if you die, there is nothing left at all, even a little, even your breath. Death is the ultimate loss, the mother and father of all loss.

The more you attach to things, be it wealth, loved ones, fame and reputation, or even the self, the more afraid of death you will be. If you want to see how much people are afraid of death, you must look at this point: at how much they are attached. The more attachment you have, the more afraid of death you will be.

Attachment means to hold on to things as "me" and "mine": "my wealth," "my children," "my loved ones," and "my body." The more you attach to me and mine, the more afraid of death you will be.

That is why Ajahn Buddhadāsa taught that we must train to die before we die. We Buddhists should train ourselves to die before we die. The first death is of the "me." It is the dying of "me." Train your "me" to die before your last breath. Actually this me isn't really there from the outset, but he puts it in a way that is easy to understand, to make this "me" die. To put it more correctly, it is to cease the attachment to me and mine before you die, because as long as there is me and mine, there will be fear of death, no matter how brave you are, even if you are a brave soldier or a veteran of many battles. You would think that these people have little fear of death, but as long as they have attachment to me and mine, they will still have fear. To really be free of fear, you must bring this attachment to self to an end, or to put it another way, we must make the "me" die.

People these days are molded and conditioned to have a lot of attachment to me and mine. You might even say that it is more than at any other time in history. It may be hard to understand this at first, but if we take a moment to think about it, we will see that people these days are conditioned to have lots of possessions from the time they are small children. They are conditioned to have a lot because having a lot of possessions is seen as a sign of a successful life. A child who has success in life is one who grows up to have a high wage, a house, a car. Any son or daughter who has a low wage, who has no house, or only a small house, who has only few cars, or no car at all, is seen to be less successful than the child who has many possessions. Parents want their children to have lots of things. Having a lot is seen as a sign of success and a sign of happiness. We are conditioned to think that we have to have a lot of things in order to be happy.

In the past, Thai people didn't have this kind of belief. Of course, we still had greed, but our greed was not prodded and goaded as much as it is for people in this age of capitalism and consumerism. People in the olden days may have had greed and desires (*lobha*), but it wasn't a lot because they were taught and believed in moderation (*santosa*), not to desire many things. Then around fifty to sixty years ago, during the coup by Field Marshal Sarit[6] when the government wanted Thailand to become a developed country, they found that the obstacle that caused

Thai people to lack effort in making a living and creating income was this belief in santosa. As a result, Sarit issued an order or request to the monks all over the country to stop teaching about contentment with little; otherwise the Thai people would be lazy. They had to be prodded with the slogan "Work is money, money is work, leading to happiness." When I was a child, I heard this slogan a lot: "Work is money, money is work, leading to happiness."

Why did we need to have such a slogan? Because in the past Thai people did not really want to amass things or look for wealth. They needed to be urged to be diligent and work hard in order to get money, and told that money would bring them happiness. This slogan was really famous when I was a child. There was also the teaching that people should discard contentment with little, because it prevented the country from progressing. This shows that, in fact, in the past Thai people did not have a lot of desires. Just to have enough to live on was enough. Of course, there were people who wanted to be rich, to have some money, but they were not overly passionate about it.

It's not like these days. These days we are prodded into having a lot of desires, to amass a lot. Not just in clothes—some people have dozens of pairs of shoes. They've got money, but they want more. This heavy stimulation of desires has the effect of bringing on fear of loss when death approaches.

Even the attachment to self is very heavy. Nowadays we are urged to have a very high attachment to self in comparison with the past. In olden days, when people created something special or beautiful, such as a beautiful Buddha image or wall paintings in a temple, they did not sign their works. We do not know who created the Buddhachinaraj Buddha image,[7] which is one of the most beautiful in the country. But nowadays people have to leave their name on everything, not only for artworks such as paintings or sculptures, but even when making offerings of tables or chairs or paying for one pillar in a temple building, they have to put their name on it. Even plates and bowls have the donors' names written on them. Their names are written on the floors and walls and on temple fences. People donate five or ten baht, and they want to have someone record their name. When they make an offering, they take a photo so they can announce it on Facebook so that the world can see that "I have given some money." This is attachment to self. A lot of importance is given to the self.

People in the past were attached to the "me" too, but it wasn't as much as we see these days. They followed their family and their country. The family and the country were important, but now this me is more important than anything else. There has to be something for me, according to my style. One of the major cell phone companies advertised with the slogan "Have your kind of life." A major car brand erected a large billboard along the expressway with a very short slogan in English: "Never follow. Be yourself." This is the me and attachment to me. If you attach to me a lot, what happens? Well, you're afraid of death, because you're afraid that this me will disappear. It's intolerable.

Nowadays we have the word *selfie*, which clearly points to the me. If you're going to photograph someone, no one is as important as this me. That's what we call a selfie. It's become the fashion. We don't realize that it reflects this attachment to me and mine on a level that people in the past did not have. So if we say that attachment leads to an increased fear of death, then we must say that people these days have a great fear of death.

This is because, apart from the increased attachment to things, religion has become less influential and people are more attached to material things, especially to happiness in the present life. "I don't care if there is a next life. I want to have happiness in this life." And people have to amass lots of things, leading to attachment. Once attached, then there is fear. They're afraid of death because death means loss.

Another reason that people these days are so afraid of death is that death has become so far removed from us. People these days think of death as something remote. There is a connection between the thinking that death is fearsome and that death is remote. Once you're afraid of death, then you try to push it away, as far away as you can. There are many things that cause us to think that way, because in present-day life we are conditioned or encouraged to look only at beautiful things. Anything to do with death or that is not beautiful we try to sweep under the carpet or push it out of our lives.

We only want to know about death through entertainment. Action movies have a lot of slaughter. This is death being presented as entertainment. People are OK with this. But real death, the death of someone who is close to us, is pushed away from our lives as far as possible. This becomes clearer when we compare this to the lives of people in the past or people living in the countryside. In the countryside, when someone is approaching death, they bring that person to their home. They don't stay in the hospital. They don't prolong their lives. In the villages around the temple here, when the villagers are approaching death, they ask to be allowed to die in their homes. That way people get to see someone approaching death. The children see it; teenagers see it. After death, they get to see the lifeless body in the home before it is put into a coffin. The funeral ceremony takes place in the home. It doesn't happen in a temple like they do these days in the city. When it's time for the cremation, they carry the coffin to the temple. At the temple they open the coffin to anoint the body. Even small children get to see it. They see death in this way year after year. They see people dying. And it's people that they know, not strangers. It's neighbors, relatives, elders, aunts and uncles. In a life where death is seen many times a year, this makes it easier for people to accept death as a normal part of life, as something that is very close.

It's different from people in the present time, where death is hidden away from real life. When they get sick, they go to the hospital. When they die, they die in the hospital. The body is prepared and laid in state at the temple. At the cremation, the coffin is loaded into the crematorium. Sometimes you don't even get to see the deceased. By the time people get to see someone die, be it a parent or grandparent, it's when they are already forty or fifty years old, because these days it's usually a long time before anyone dies. Some people are thirty years old and have never seen a dead body, especially of someone they know who is close to them, because in the house there is just the parents and children. By the time the parents die they're ninety. By that time the children are sixty years old or more.

There was one lady, forty years old, who was a director of TV commercials. One day she went to visit a friend who was a nurse in a country hospital. Her friend led her to the room where she was staying. While her friend was taking her to her room, they passed a building that the hospital used to store bodies before they were sent back to their hometowns. While they were passing, the hospital workers happened to be moving a body out of the building. That lady, seeing this, was startled and asked her friend, "What's that?" Her friend the nurse replied, "That's a dead body. The relatives have come to take it home." That lady exclaimed, "Wow, are there really dead people?" It was the first time she had ever seen a dead body. Before, when she had made her movies, when someone died or was shot, they got up again—because it was just a movie, just acting. The only death she had experienced was the kind where after you died you got up again. This was the first time she had ever seen a real dead person. She was over forty, and it was the first time she had ever seen a dead person.

In fact, we all know that one day we will die, but it's just a thought. When this lady saw a real dead person, she was shocked. Her life was probably no different from city people nowadays. Death is taken away, hidden away from life. We live like someone who has forgotten death, even though we know it must happen one day. This kind of life makes death seem remote. When death is seen as remote, then when death does happen we are shocked. We haven't prepared our minds, because we've never realized that death is a normal thing for life. Because we're afraid of death, we push it away from us; we don't want to know about it.

Seeing death as remote and fear of death are related. Eventually we all must die. If you're afraid of death, just thinking about it is scary. As death approaches, then you really suffer. If you don't want to be like that, you must train. Train your mind to be less afraid of death. How do you make your mind less afraid of death? See that death is a part of nature. Accept that our death is something that is inevitable. And importantly, we must train the mind to reduce wanting and attachment. The more you attach, the more afraid of dying you will be. If you attach less, you will be less afraid of dying. Be it attachment to possessions, or attachment to your body, as being me and mine, these are all attachments that lead to fear—fear of loss and ultimately fear of death.

GLOSSARY

This glossary contains words that occur frequently throughout the text. Definitions are indicative only and are strictly designed for quick reference purposes.

AKUSALA: unskillful, unwholesome
ANATTĀ: not-self; one of the three characteristics
ANICCA: impermanence; one of the three characteristics
ARAHANT: a fully enlightened being
ĀRAMMAṆA: mental object
AVIJJĀ: fundamental ignorance
BHAVA: becoming, the state ripe for birth
BHĀVANĀ: (mental) cultivation, meditation
BHIKKHU: a male Buddhist monk
BHIKKHUNĪ: a female Buddhist monk
BRAHMA: a divine being, existing on a more refined level than the devas
CITTA: the mind
DĀNA: the act of giving, generosity
DEVA: a celestial being
DHAMMA: the Truth, the Buddha's teaching, as in "practicing the Dhamma," "listening to the Dhamma," "this is the Dhamma"
DHAMMA(S): things, phenomena, qualities, as in "all dhammas are not self," "unskillful dhammas and skillful dhammas"
DHUTAṄGA: any one of the thirteen austere practices allowed by the Buddha, such as eating only from the alms bowl
DIṬṬHI: views, opinions
DOSA: anger, aversion
DUKKHA: suffering, stress, stressfulness; one of the three characteristics and one of the four noble truths

JHĀNA: absorption; a profound meditation state

KHANDHAS: the five groups of conditions that make up a human life: form, feeling, perception, mental activities, and consciousness

KILESA: mental stains, defilements; e.g., greed, hatred, anger

KUSALA: skillful, wholesome

LOBHA: greed

LOKUTTARA: that which is beyond the world, transcendent

MOHA: delusion

NĀMADHAMMA: mentality, immateriality, the metaphysical world, the mind

PAÑÑĀ: wisdom

PAṬICCASAMUPPĀDA: the principle of dependent origination

PUTHUJJANA: an unenlightened being, an ordinary person

RŪPADHAMMA: materiality, physicality, the physical world, the body

SABHĀVADHAMMA: natural realities, things as they are in nature

SAKIDĀGĀMI: a once returner; one who has experienced the second level of transcendent insight

SAMĀDHI: concentration, meditation

SAMATHA: calm, calmness meditation

SAṀSĀRA: the realm of rebirth and delusion

SAṄKHĀRĀ (general): formations

SAṄKHĀRĀ (in the five khandhas): volitional activities or kamma formations

SAṄKHĀRĀ (in the paṭiccasamuppāda): volition

SĪLA: morality

SOTĀPANNA: a "stream enterer;" one who has experienced transcendent insight and has entered the true path to liberation

TAṆHĀ: craving, desire

TATHĀGATA: the "Thus-Gone One;" an epithet of the Buddha

UPĀDĀNA: attachment, clinging

VIPASSANĀ: insight, insight meditation

NOTES

INTRODUCTION

1. A bhikkhu is a fully ordained Buddhist monk. The female equivalent is bhikkhunī.

2. The Buddha's answer is noteworthy in that, unlike his bhikkhu disciples, he was not answering in accordance with his personality (his work was, after all, already done), but more in the capacity of teacher: his answer was more an injunction for future practitioners.

LIVING WITH AJAHN CHAH

1. In the fifty years since then, the temple has undergone major developments, and the description given here no longer matches the reality.

2. This is what we called them in the temple, but in Central Thai they are called *mot tanoi*. It's possible my loose translation is incorrect, as I have not been able to find any official reference online. Given the vagaries of Northeastern Thai pronunciation, it could also have been *mot lin* or *mot rin*.

3. The three-month rains retreat is timed according to the lunar calendar, and so varies from year to year, but it usually falls between July and October.

4. A white-robed postulant, keeping eight precepts.

5. For the *samaṇera* and bhikkhu ordinations, I was accompanied by two and three other candidates respectively, one of whom, on both occasions, was the bhikkhu who is now Venerable Ajahn Munindo, abbot of Aruna Ratanagiri Monastery in Harnham, United Kingdom.

6. *Bruce* proved hard for most Thais to pronounce, so I quickly became known as Burut, the Thai word for "man" or "gentleman." This theme continued when I obtained my official bhikkhu name—Puriso—which means the same.

7. The meaning of the Thai word *tudong* has strayed from its Pali root *dhutaṅga*. *Dhutaṅga* refers to the thirteen official practices (such as eating one meal a day and eating only from the alms bowl) allowed by the Buddha for bhikkhus who wish to practice a more austere lifestyle. *Tudong*

has come to mean traveling around on pilgrimage or looking for remote places to practice, possibly based on two of the *dhutaṅga* practices: living in a forest and staying at the foot of a tree. Coincidentally, the word *dong* in Thai means "forest." Luang Por used to quip that these days monks don't practice tudong, they practice *talu-dong* (meaning to "cut through the forest") on their ways hither and thither.

8. "Luang Ta" (Venerable Grandfather) is a Thai term used for a monk who ordains later in life. The famous Thai forest teacher Ajahn Maha Bua also adopted the title.

9. A chapter of which is translated in this collection.

10. As a testimony to the impermanence of memory, I am actually not clear whether it was the novice who was reading *Advice on Looking Inwards* or myself, but if the latter, that is certainly embarrassing, since I was reading from it for the better part of three months! Still, regardless of who was reading what, I cannot remember the third title from that rains retreat.

11. In Thailand, *mae chee* refers to the white-robed, eight-precept Buddhist nuns.

GIRIMĀNANDA SUTTA

1. *Pārājika* offenses are the four offenses of "defeat" (sexual intercourse, stealing, killing a human being, and bragging about superhuman attainments that one does not have), the committing of which automatically disqualifies a bhikkhu from the monkhood and from ever reentering the monkhood in that lifetime.

2. Tathāgata: "Thus-Gone One," an epithet of the Buddha.

3. To "go forth" (*pabajjā*) is to go forth into homelessness, i.e., to take ordination as a bhikkhu or bhikkhunī.

4. One of the realms of existence of the ancient system of Indian and Buddhist cosmology. In Buddhism it is regarded as the highest level of the celestial abodes.

5. A yojana is a unit of measure used in the Buddha's time. Its precise length is uncertain, with estimates varying between 2.5 and 9 miles.

6. *Ananta cakkavāḷa*: literally, "infinite universe."

7. The Pāṭimokkha precepts are the 227 rules making up the main body of precepts for a bhikkhu.

8. *Jhāna*: absorption meditation, a profound state of concentration.

9. *Māra*: The Buddhist personification of evil, or that which obstructs the development of virtue and enlightenment.

Chao Khun Upāli

1. The harsh rural conditions of Ubon Ratchathani proved to be a fertile field for famous Buddhist monks, being the birthplace of Ajahn Mun, Ajahn Sao, Ajahn Khao, and Ajahn Chah.

2. Somdet Wanarat (1806–1892) was one of the ten senior bhikkhus who established the Dhammayuttika sect of the Thai saṅgha in the early 1820s. Venerable Hasapañño of Vimokkharama Forest Hermitage in Melbourne has produced an English translation of the *Saṅkhittovāda*, published for free distribution.

3. A "rains retreat" (*vassa*) is the traditional time each year when bhikkhus will stop wandering and stay in one place for the rainy season—a period of about three months. Traditionally, bhikkhus will also count their seniority in terms of "rains" or "rains retreats," so a bhikkhu of five rains has been ordained for five years.

4. Dhammapada, verse 40.

5. The nine doorways are two eyes, two ears, two nostrils, mouth, genital organ, and anus.

6. Written as Phra Debmoli, c. 1917.

7. The proper translation of this Pali title eludes me. The English title is a bit of "poetic license" on the part of the translator.

8. This and the following section are in reference to the three knowledges in regard to the four noble truths, which are *saccañāṇa* (knowledge of the truth), *kiccañāṇa* (knowledge of what needs to be done in regard to that truth), and *katañāṇa* (knowledge that what needed to be done has been done). The subject is dealt with in detail in chapter 3.

9. I.e., as a bhikkhunī.

10. Such references to physical or mental disabilities being obstacles to Dhamma practice are not uncommon in Thai Dhamma teachings. It should be understood that the aim is to alert people to take full advantage of their physical and mental capacities rather than to make a judgment on disabilities. I am not aware of any records of the Buddha stating that certain disabilities would be obstacles to enlightenment, and indeed, it is recorded that there were those who attained enlightenment who were blind or of low intelligence.

11. A mind that is imperfect as a result of past kamma.

12. The *duhetukapaṭisandhi citta* and the *tihetukapaṭisandhi citta* are rebirth consciousness endowed with either two (nongreed and nonhatred) or three (nongreed, nonhatred, and wisdom) causal factors respectively.

13. A sense of urgency.

14 รู้ตัวดี—This could also be translated as to "know oneself well."

15. รู้ตัวชั่ว—This could also be translated as "to know oneself badly."

AJAHN BUDDHADĀSA

1. From a talk given on July 4, 1974.

2. The Pali *sammā saṅkappa* is often translated as right thought, but here the translation is per the Thai, ความปรารถนาถูกต้อง.

3. The *Kesamutti Sutta*, popularly known as the *Kālāma Sutta*, is widely regarded as one of the most important teachings given by the Buddha. In it he advises the people of Kālāma village not to blindly believe following external factors such as tradition, guesswork, what they've read, or even out of reverence for a teacher, but to examine and see the truth for themselves. Ajahn Buddhadāsa refers to it often in his teachings.

4. This is a reference to the fact that among Thai Buddhists, Māra is the name of the tempter who tried to distract the Buddha from his enlightenment. The term *māra* is therefore not commonly associated with a deva-like being.

BHIKKHU P. A. PAYUTTO

1. The five *khandhas* (aggregates or groups) are the groups of conditions that make up human life: body, feeling, perception, volitional activities, and consciousness.

2. The three characteristics: impermanence (*anicca*), suffering or stress (*dukkha*), and not-self (*anattā*).

3. This unknowing is called *avijjā* (ignorance).

4. One who has experienced a first glimpse of transcendental insight, thus entering the "stream" to nibbāna.

UPĀSIKĀ KEE NANAYON

1. The traditional pathway in Thailand for women interested in leaving the household life to practice the Dhamma is that of the *mae chee*, an eight-precept "nun" who shaves her head and wears white robes.

2. An *upāsikā* is a female lay follower who does not necessarily leave the homelife but may keep the five or eight precepts and does not shave her head.

3 . From a talk given on December 4, 1964.

4. Part of the traditional morning chanting.

5. That is, at Buddhist funerals.

6. Direct knowledge and vision.

AJAHN PRAMOTE

1. Talk given on May 22, 2022.

2. King Bhumibol Adulyadej, Rama IX.

3. Ta Khai, or Ai Khai, is a statue of a child at a temple in Nakhon Si Thammarat Province that had become famous and revered as having mystical powers.

4. Stream enterer, the first level of attainment of transcendent insight.

5. Once returner, the second level of attainment of transcendent insight.

6. The khandha (group) of volitional activities, one of the five khandhas.

7. The mindfulness of the mind, the third of the four foundations of mindfulness.

8. Jhana = "absorption," an advanced concentration state of undivided attention.

9. Ajahn Sucheep Punyanuphap was a well-known and highly respected lay Buddhist writer and thinker.

10. "Sideways posture" (Thai *phap-phiap*) is the traditional polite sitting posture, with the legs tucked behind to one side.

11. A Dhamma talk given on September 12, 2020.

12. A character in the Vessantara Jataka known for his excessive greed.

13. Dhamma talk given on May 12, 2019.

14. This is a reference to the source teaching on the four foundations of mindfulness, the *Mahasatipaṭṭhāna Sutta*, where the instructions are given to "see the body in the body, the feelings in feelings, the mind in the mind, and dhammas in dhammas." The teaching is interpreted in many different ways.

AJAHN PAISAL

1. Prime minister of Thailand, 1963–1973. He was one of a number of military prime ministers who gained and held power through force, and his return to the country in 1976 triggered massive student protests that were violently suppressed.

2. Dhamma talk given at Wat Pa Sukato on May 7, 2020.

3. This is in reference to the meditation technique taught by Luang Por Thien and practiced by Ajahn Paisal, which incorporates stylized movements of the arms.

4. Dhamma talk given at Wat Pa Sukato on June 26, 2022.

5. Dhamma talk given at Wat Pa Sukato on December 14, 2021.

6. The Thai political scene following WWII was dominated by military dictatorships interspersed with failed attempts at democracy. Field Marshal Sarit staged a coup to take power from strongman Phibun Songkhram in 1957 and was in power until his death in 1963.

7. A Buddha image in a temple in Phitsanulok, Northern Thailand, widely regarded as the country's most beautiful.

CREDITS

TEXT

"Dhammacakkappavattana Sutta" by Ajahn Buddhadāsa, translated with permission of the Buddhadāsa Indapañño Archives.

"Helping Yourself to Help Others" by P. A. Payutto, translated with permission of the author.

"Sweeping Away the Dirt" by Upāsikā Kee Nanayon, translated with permission of the Khao Suan Luang Dhamma Community.

"Introduction to Dhamma Practice," "Separating the Khandas," and "The Task in Relation to Suffering" by Ajahn Pramote, translated with permission of the Luang Pu Pramote Pamojjo Teaching Media Foundation.

"Managing Expectations," "Readying the Mind for Turmoil," and "Reflections on Death" by Ajahn Paisal, translated with permission of the author.

PHOTOS

"Living with Ajahn Chah," page 6. Photographer unknown.

Girimānanda Sutta, page 26. Credit: National Library of Laos, Vientiane. Digital Library of Lao Manuscripts 01012902009_00. Digital reproduction of an image made available by the State Library of Berlin. Public Domain Mark 1.0.

Chao Khun Upāli, page 74. Photographer unknown.

Ajahn Buddhadāsa, page 100. Credit: Buddhadāsa Indapañño Archives.

Bhikkhu P. A. Payutto, page 120. Credit: Venerable Phra Khru Pan Ketuñano.

Upāsikā Kee Nanayon, page 142. Credit: Buddhadāsa Indapañño Archives.

Ajahn Pramote, page 160. Credit: Luang Pu Pramote Pamojjo Teaching Media Foundation.

Ajahn Paisal, page 202. Credit: Sudarat Kaewthae.

ABOUT THE TRANSLATOR

BRUCE EVANS WAS BORN IN 1952 in Melbourne, Australia. He is a translator, editor, and Theravada Buddhist practitioner. He took bhikkhu ordination under Ajahn Chah in the 1970s and lived for seventeen years as a monk in Thailand, during which time he translated three volumes of Ajahn Chah's teachings for free distribution: *A Taste of Freedom*, *Food for the Heart*, and *Living Dhamma*. From 1985 to 1992, he served as abbot of a remote monastery on the Thailand-Laos border. In the mid-1990s he developed an interest in translating the works of Venerable P. A. Payutto, impressed by his clear and authoritative explanations of the Buddha's teachings. He left the monkhood in 1997 and took up residence with his partner in Bangkok, where he worked for the Buddhadhamma Foundation translating and editing Buddhist texts. For many years he worked on an abridged translation of Ven. Payutto's magnum opus, *Buddhadhamma*, that was published in 2024 as *The Essential Buddhadhamma: The Teachings and Practice of Theravada Buddhism*. He currently lives in Melbourne.

01 14

"Former longtime monk Bruce Evans presents a sampling of the leading lights in Thailand's vast firmament of meditation masters, learned scholar-meditators, and realized adepts. These teachers are part of a tradition of making Buddhist teaching and practice accessible—a tradition that has long permeated and shaped Thai society in ways that can't be overstated. There is something here for everybody, from clear expositions of classical Buddhist doctrine to practical advice on working with the neuroses specific to our age of rampant consumerism and technological frenzy. This volume opens a window onto a way to peace and happiness that has proven its worth and effectiveness for over 2,500 years."

—PAUL BREITER, translator of Ajahn Chah's *Being Dharma* and *Everything Arises, Everything Falls Away*

"From Bruce Evans's engagingly vivid account of his experiences as a young monk with Ajahn Chah, to a new translation of a Thai version of the *Girimānanda Sutta*, to contributions from Ajahn Buddhadāsa, Bhikkhu Payutto, and, unusually, a laywoman, Upāsikā Kee Nanayon, this anthology opens windows on Thai Buddhist traditions, their meditative life, and their practices. It introduces the interpretative wisdom and surprising humor that often characterize Thai Dhamma teachers. As Evans points out, the different 'flavors' of the different teachers represented show us how different they all are in character and tone. All, however, bear the unmistakable stamp of a simple and direct approach to Buddhist practice. This accessible book offers a richly humane introduction to Thai Buddhism and its meditative understandings."

—SARAH SHAW, author of *Breathing Mindfulness* and *The Art of Listening*